Drowning in the Sea of Love

Books by Al Young

Dancing (poems)
Snakes (novel)
The Song Turning Back into Itself (poems)
Who Is Angelina? (novel)
Geography of the Near Past (poems)
Sitting Pretty (novel)
Ask Me Now (novel)
Bodies & Soul (musical memoirs)
The Blues Don't Change: New and Selected Poems
Kinds of Blue (musical memoirs)
Things Ain't What They Used to Be (musical memoirs)
Seduction by Light (novel)
Mingus Mingus: Two Memoirs (with Janet Coleman)
Heaven: Collected Poems 1956–1990
Straight No Chaser (poems)
Drowning in the Sea of Love (musical memoirs)

Drowning in the Sea of Love

MUSICAL MEMOIRS

Al Young

The Ecco Press

Portions of this work originally appeared in
different form under the following titles:
Bodies & Soul; *Kinds of Blue*; *Things Ain't What They Used to Be.*

THE ECCO PRESS
100 West Broad Street
Hopewell, New Jersey 08525
Published simultaneously in Canada by
Penguin Books Canada Ltd., Ontario
Printed in the United States of America
Designed by Debby Jay
FIRST EDITION

Library of Congress Cataloging-in-Publication Data

Young, Al, 1939-
    Drowning in the sea of love : musical memoirs / Al Young. — 1st
ed.
        p.   cm.
    1. Jazz—History and criticism. 2. Jazz musicians—United States.
I. Title.
ML3507.Y686   1995
781.65—dc20   94-33861
    ISBN 0-88001-388-5

The text of this book is set in Adobe Garamond

Contents

Set 2

Set 3

Encore

Introduction: Something Old, Something New, Something Borrowed Out of the Blue

I've been down one time;
I've been down two times—
And now I'm drowning,
Drowning in the sea of love.
                    —Joe Simon

O N MY ACTOR brother Richard Young's bedroom boombox at the time of his death by suicide back in 1984 was a cassette tape cued to Tony Bennett's recording of Antonio Carlos Jobim's "Wave," long a favorite of mine too:

"The fundamental loneliness goes
When two can dream a dream together."

Word of Richard's death reached me by phone that Fourth of July night, right after police telephoned a cousin, who telephoned me. I flew at once from San Francisco to Los Angeles. In L.A., where Richard had moved and settled right after high school in Detroit, I joined our cousin Pierre and other consoling family members, who helped make funeral arrangements. Pierre and I went to Richard's longtime apartment in a late 1950s-style building directly across the street from Hollywood High, where we spent the better part of a week clearing and cleaning and doing our best to set his affairs in order.

"Wave" kept rippling, floating, fluttering, and surging through my head as I worked. Seemingly, it was the bittersweet bb and flow of the melody—to say nothing of the song's exquisite lyric, poetic yet singable—that was swelling the sorrow I felt. But, looking back, I see now that it was probably no more the song that had done this to me than the bend and sway of smog-soaked palm trees whose branches I could see from practically every window in Richard's apartment those deaf afternoons crammed with cruel sunshine; traffic and transfiguration in perfectly sad California clarity.

"The music of a sad room," one of poet-novelist Clarence Major's early pet licks—it occurred in his poems and again in his fiction—caught my ear. It nailed down and identified the moment for me the way music of any kind can pinpoint the intimate past with giddying exactness.

And because Richard (who dreamed of starring in commercials—*commercials!*) had bought the Hollywood glamour package—heartbreak and all—I couldn't help but think again of Nathaniel West's early twentieth century novel about Hollywood, *Day of the Locust.* Even though I was by then already at work on *Seduction By Light,* my own Hollywood metaphor of a novel, West's book, as far as I was concerned, had scripted this primal North American myth for all time's sake. And the beautiful thing about myths, you know, even Hollywood's, is that they're like lovingly crafted baskets or jugs you carry in your arms or on your head or on your back. What you actually put in those vessels, how you fill them—well, that's quite up to you. Not surprisingly, Richard, by then an Angeleno to the core, had staged or, in any case, contrived his own death by carbon monoxide poisoning.

Up to my knees in Richard's belongings and unfinished business, I thought of a line I had memorized as a teenager from William Saroyan's *The Bicycle Rider of Beverly Hills,* a midlife autobiographical memoir penned at a time when everybody seemed—as Saroyan might have put it—was counting nine on him. He was determined, whatever it took, to get back on his feet and go the distance. "It is the dirt of the world with the sun shining on it," Saroyan had written, "that astonishes a poet when he is a boy."

When I was a boy, a pre-school kid, I used to like to sit in front of the family's coal-burning heater with my brothers, Richard, Billy and Franchot, and listen to our father's 78 rpm records. The little heater's opaque door-screen allowed us to glimpse patterns the flames shaped as they smoldered and raged. And while we listened and stared into that fire-screen, the pioneer rhythm & blues quartet known as the Ravens jazzed "Ol' Man River," Louis Jordan and His Tympani Five asked "Is You Is or Is You Ain't My Baby?" The Mills Brothers—who even then had been around a little bit of forever—cut up on "Paper Doll," and the Nat King Cole Trio, all-time greats, took it on out with "It's Only a Paper Moon." Johnny Mercer, genius lyricist and songster founder of Capitol Records, advised us to "Ac-cen-tchu-ate the Positive." (We thought the song was called "Don't Mess with Mr. In-Between," just as Duke Ellington's "Don't Get Around Much Anymore," thanks to our mishearing, was "Mr. Saturday Night.")

Decades before the bossa nova craze, Xavier Cugat samba'd us with "Brazil"; Artie Shaw's sophisticated Gramercy Five drove us home to "Summit Ridge Drive," wherever that was; and numbers like pianist Eddie Heywood's "Begin the Beguine" transported us, in our ignorance, to some blissful, inner place we could feel, even if we couldn't always talk about it.

While we sat or stood in front of that active heater, it was no big deal to picture in the screen-framed flames anything musical our innocent ears picked up from the phonograph or radio. And this was especially so of *wordless* song, popular or classical. We would project our pictures of *Scheherezade,* or Tommy Dorsey's "Song of India" right out there in front of ourselves, trembling at arm's length—the way we always project our thoughts, our feelings, when there's a fireplace or an ocean in front of us. And, had it been necessary, we could have stepped right up to that screen and pointed out or traced the shapes of our mind-pictures, for there they danced and shimmered, illumined before our very eyes in firelight and shadow.

And—like the tap dance and shuffle of rain on the roof; the choo-choo of trains blowing in from Memphis, chugging past our front-yard window, or fading like a record into the Pascagoula-Alabama-Louisiana distance; the steady, giddy crickets; the way wind sounds traveling through treetops—these images never played the same way twice. Kids spend more time than grown folks can imagine thinking about what they sing and, worse, even singing what they think. "You see," Ray Charles told me years and years ago, "you can say so many things through music. You can make people cry, you can make them think through music, and it's not distasteful."

"Thinking the world into existence," anthropologist Gary Witherspoon wrote in *Language and Art in the Navajo Universe*, "attributes a definite kind of power to thought and song." For the late bassist and composer Charles Mingus, the blues weren't a color but a feeling. And now physicists say we appear to be co-creating the universe at the same time that we're participating in it. But that's the beauty of music and every other art and science that springs from human imagination by way of intuitive intelligence: The truths they express are so simple as to seem childlike and airy to the window-less grown-up mind.

The law of entropy tells us the same thing we get from reading just the title, borrowed from a Samuel Butler Yeats poem, of Nigerian-born storyteller Chinua Achebe's most famous novel, *Things Fall Apart.* This third law of thermodynamics states that "the amount of disorder in any isolated system cannot decrease with time." In other words, unless fresh energy in the way of maintenance is introduced, old-fashioned vinyl records get shackly and messy, roofs start leaking, weeds take over, topsoil erodes, farms bottom out, cities grow crowded, economics and international relations grow shaky, and galaxies explode.

When my father was getting ready to leave this world, I was fortunate to have been on hand, by his bedside mostly, to share the intense pleasure he derived from listening to tape recordings I brought to him of the very music on which he had weaned me.

"This brings it all back," he said, beaming and positively clear of eye, shrunken though he was from cancer. "Those were the happiest days of my life. I can hear everything. I can see it. I try to keep up, you know, but the stuff they play now—with all that fancy equipment and electricity they got—somehow it just don't sound like music to me."

I was only too happy to be giving back to my father—if only for a fraction of a moment in eternity—some of the lasting magic he lavished on me while I was still a child in Mississippi and Michigan in no hurry whatever to become an adult. Because of Dad, I grew up in a house filled with records and with living music. Music was always there with me—at home, on the streets, in church, at school, on the radio, at movies, social gatherings, dances; in concert halls, nightclubs, restaurants, lofts, shacks, mansions, kitchens, backrooms, warehouses, labs, hotel rooms, tents, alleys, elevators, shops, automobiles, on boats; in love, at war, in peace, and even in my sleep. I can still remember, as clearly as if it were today, early songs I sang, the first notes I ever sounded on a piano, spacious cricket and locust concertos on summer nights, the tinkle of spoons against cups and water glasses, birdcalls, blues, spirituals, and actual hollers in Mississippi fields, where I picked my early share of cotton and cut far less cane than I raised.

And I won't forget the sound of my grandmother's voice; her constant humming as she went about her everyday tasks; the melodious rises and falls in the voices of Afro-Christian preachers in little tumble-down country churches; the rapid rat-a-tat of country western peckerwood percussion, slow biscuit-and-molasses laments; heavy-duty juke joint fried fish and barbecue funk; jazz in all its endless guises and disguises; the crisp swish of leaves; the gritty, gut-washed chitlin stench and rush of cities; the sudden hush of streams; and the soulful flow of rivers, older than silver or gold, rolling and pulling along time itself in their wet and shining voyages and journeys back to sea.

Whether Jobim titled his song "Wave" to mean an actual ocean wave—an undulation, an oscillation, a fluctuation, a nutation, a pendulation, or a vibration or pulsation—he alone knows. For all we know, he could've been musically describing the kind of wave we signal with our hands when we say hello or say goodbye, on our way into or out of some world.

And we could get even more particular than that, and chant or scat of particles and waves. We could sit on good old Albert Einstein's lap and have him look into our oceanic souls with his avuncular St. Bernard eyes. He would explain—as he did to the world way back in 1905—the "wave-particle duality." He'd break it clean on down: Electrons don't elect to be either/or, or even neither/nor, but our own infinity-clogged minds keep causing problems and solving them, making stuff up as we go along. "Light's path in math," I imagine Einstein might say, or words to that effect, just as Louis Armstrong is supposed to have said, "And there you has jazz." I have no trouble imagining this. Be careful, though; you're listening to the same man who has trouble imagining how Einstein would've sounded playing second fiddle to Armstrong's acoustical sailings.

Everything you are about to read is made up out of real stuff. Since beginning this series, it has taken some time for me to realize how flexible and unpredictable a so-called "musical memoir" can be. There's no defining it, just as there is no way to define poetry or the blues, which are, by nature of the indomitable life-force that feeds them, unruly and wild.

The minute the academy thinks it has poetry or the blues theoretically mapped out, wrapped up, or coldly codified, along comes some ignorant or unassuming genius—someone who either does or doesn't know any better—to make a poem do something it has never done before, or make a blues line uncoil and snake its way into places where other blues haven't gone.

All readers need to know is that it's crucial to recall, as you read along or skip around in these tender pages, that music can become a powerful way of remembering. Sometimes the remembering takes the form of a story or personal myth. At other times, the interplay between the author and the reader and the song shapes itself as reverie, prose poem, essay, solo, a take, a break, a fantasy, soliloquy, a solo.

Little did I know when I began this book that I would be opening up within myself a region so vast that it could never be fully explored or even charted.

If I stray a bit from the melody at times and vary the beat, it's because I'm learning what you already know so well about the meaning and sense of it all. Lean in and listen: "The Nearness of You" touched poet Carolyn Kizer so deeply that she lifted it whole right out of Hoagy Carmichael's song to name a powerful book of her own. The idea that there should even be such concepts as nearness, distance, here-and-nowness first began to strike me as strange when I listened to music in childhood. The song, indeed, has always been you, and it will forever be turning back into itself; drowning, as it were, in itself. "No wave can exist," Paramahansa Yogananda reminds us in *The Divine Romance,* "Without the ocean behind it."

May you sooner or later find yourself adrift in an open sea of sound, or, as singer Joe Simon put it so lastingly in his soulful 1972 gospel-washed rhythm and blues hit: "Drowning in the Sea of Love."

AL YOUNG

Set One

Body and Soul

Coleman Hawkins, 1939

MY FATHER, who used to bicycle thirty miles one way to court my mother, had this record among his dust-needled 78s. He'd already worn out several copies before I learned to love it from memory, never knowing until much later what a cause it had stirred.

Imagine it's 1939. You talk about a hellraising year, that one had to take the cake with Hitler taking Czechoslovakia, Bohemia, Moravia and Poland; with Stalin taking Finland and Poland (poor Poland); Franco taking Spain; Great Britain and France declaring war on Germany; Mussolini taking Albania; Stalin and Hitler signing their infamous non-aggression pact that would splinter and split all the left-leaning parents of kids I would later meet at college and beyond. My own folks, peasants and proles, knew next to nothing about the left wing or right wing of anything but chickens, but they did know right from wrong. Politics to them had something to do with money and power, which in white Mississippi were one and the same.

History and truth are so easily misconstrued. Even dates, names, facts and figures can lie—"Aught's an aught / Figger's a figger / All for the white man / None for the nigger"—depending on who's doing the dating, doing the naming, doing the figuring. The telling of truth is the poet's proper domain, and in the head-whipping nations of this darkening, fact-ridden world, people still look to poets and the music they make for light, sweet light illumining everything everywhere.

If it's true that in this alleged 1939 the New York World's Fair "World of Tomorrow" ran for five straight months and that TVA got the Supreme Court go-ahead and that TV in the U.S. was first broadcast publicly from the Empire State Building (covering the opening of that same World's Fair), then it's equally fair to imagine Coleman Hawkins in that crowded year. In October, the Golden Gate Bridge closed down for repairs, while on the eleventh day of that same month, Hawkins, just back from a rewarding stay in war-hungry Europe, repaired to the RCA Victor New York studios with some musical friends and cut "Body and Soul"—just like that, in the shadow of the Empire State Building.

You can even picture him slouched in front of one of those weighty old condenser boom mikes, surrounded by smoke, suspended and hatted, thinking something like: "Well, let's see how what I'm feeling's gonna come out sounding this time, so we can get this session wrapped up and get back to the gig and really do some blowing." After the take he probably remembered how he'd performed this wee hours ballad better a hundred times before. "I'll get it down yet," he told himself, "but this'll have to do for now." And, children, that was that.

When the record came out, saxophonists all over the world, hearing it and sensing that things would never be the same, started woodshedding Hawkins's impassioned licks in their closets and on the stand. Why'd he have to go and do that? Of course, everybody fell in love with it. My father would play, it, take it off, play something else, then put it back on. This went on for years. What was he listening for? What were we listening to? What did it mean? What were all those funny, throaty squawks and sighs and cries all about? I knew what a body was, but what was a soul? You kept hearing people say, "Well, bless his soul!" You thought you knew what they meant, but really, you could only imagine as you must now. You knew what they meant when they said "Bless her heart!" because you could put your hand to your heart and feel the beat, and your Aunt Ethel sometimes fried up chicken hearts along with gizzards, livers and feet. But a soul was unseeable. Did animals have souls too? Did birds, dogs, cows, mules, pigs, snakes, bees? And what about other stuff, like corn, okra, creeks, rivers, moonlight, sunshine, trees, the ground, the rain, the sky? Did white folks have souls?

Was a soul something like a breeze: something you couldn't picture or grab but could only feel, like you could the wind off the Gulf when the day cooled down, or the way the ground would tremble when the train roared past across the street from where we lived?

Thirty-nine, forty, fifty, a hundred, thousands—who's to say how many rosy-chilled Octobers have befallen us, each one engraved in micro-moments of this innocent utterance, electrically notated but, like light in a photograph, never quite captured in detail, only in essence. Essence in this instance is private song, is you hearing your secret sorrow and joy blown back through Coleman Hawkins, invisibly connected to you and played back through countless bodies, each one an embodiment of the same soul force.

All poetry is about silent music, invisible art and the clothing of time for the ages.

Cocktails
for Two

Spike Jones & his
City Slickers, 1946

"**I**T'S A FACT," Bookus told me that night as he stared through the windshield at the foggy highway ahead and sucked on the butt of a Camel. "When I was a kid I was crazy about bullshit—Fatty Arbuckle, Andy Gump, Bob Steele, Butterbeans and Suzie, Stepin Fetchit, Tarzan, Krazy Kat and all like that. You too young to know about it, but we couldn't get enough of that stuff, the same as you can't get enough of this Spike Jones."

Our destination: Chicago. That's right—Chicago Ella Noise, as Bookus called it. My mother, for some forgotten reason, had packed my toothbrush, a sweater, some underwear, pajamas, fresh britches and funnybooks and turned me loose with Bookus McGee. With his razorline mustache, Army issue slacks, scuffed brown zip-up leather jacket and greasy broadbrimmed hat, Bookus looked pretty much like the colored version of every second-string villain you've ever beheld in a 1940s B movie, except we didn't rate them that way then; to us they were all just pictures.

Picture us hunched up in that all-but-rusted-out humpback V-8 Ford with the radio playing more static than fade. What Bookus was doing was hauling a load of bootleg whiskey he had distilled and bottled himself, hauling it across southern Michigan to northern Illinois. If any cop had stopped us, it would've been curtains for Bookus, and no telling what might've happened to me. Naturally, I didn't know that then. All I knew was we were on a weekend trip to visit an old buddy of his who owned a gas station way out in the Land of California, Sweet Home Chicago. Chicago. As in boom-chicka / boom-chicka / Chi /Ca / Go.

And go we did. Chugging us along, cargo and all, was Bookus with his Camels, Bookus with his spearmint gum, Bookus with his toothpicks, Bookus with his facial scars from a car crash of years ago that had gotten him off hooch (his own and anybody else's) except to sell. There was also Bookus who used to sing blues and play the guitar, Bookus with his Army stories, and Bookus with his dreams.

"Yeah," he kept saying, "all kids love bullshit."

And it was true, for I loved Bookus with his scary tales of what had gone on before I was born, and his way of selling futures tickled me.

"We git to my buddy's gas station," he winked, "and you can drink all the sodapop your belly can hold and don't even have to pay."

And that was true too. All next day I soaked up Pepsis, Nehis and 7-Ups while they did their grown folks' talk and leaned on cars and crawled under them. That night I peed the bed something awful and got up wanting to hide on Mars.

"Well," said Bookus, "look like we gon' have to tie a little milk bottle around your weenie when you get put to bed."

We laughed at that, but I was looking at it literally and thinking about how I might have to sleep sitting up all night.

The moment I hear "Cocktails for Two" with all those razzes and clinks and horns going "Ooooga-Ooooga!" I fall back into the back seat of that car to grab a nap and look at how it all started out for me, a curious little sub-American boy recalling with perfect clarity the sound of Bookus' Mississippi voice saying, "That's right, it use to be all kids loved bullshit. Now, commence to find out, grown people like it too. That's all you git nowdays is more and more bullshit. You mark my words, the day's comin when bullshit will rule this very world."

Fingertips (Part 2)

Stevie Wonder, 1963

THAT WAS A YEAR I'm still working with. My days and nights ran all the way from prehistoric times to right now, backward and forward, with God's eyes shining out of skies while I stayed up and up for days on joy. I zipped around cities and towns, flew to the sun, shivered and shouted, dragged beer cartons and shopping bags full of hot papered ideas from coast to coast, and peed love.

Sometimes when Tom Heineman would be upstairs practicing Mozart sonatas on his mellowing cello, I'd be right there under him in my student-style digs, plucking out handwoven nitwit music on a borrowed guitar. That was the same spring that (Little) Stevie Wonder started spreading his happiness all over the place.

The first time I caught it was on bassist Tom Glass' car radio. What a jolt that was! It followed us all the way to Sierra Sound studios in South Berkeley where we were headed to make a record produced by Chris "Arhoolie" Strachwitz, the man who gave the world so many beautiful Mance Lipscombs. At the time Chris was seriously toying with the idea of putting out a 45 rpm single of me, by then the most reluctant of folksingers. For two Saturdays in a row, we sweated miking, technical problems and intrusions by an engineer who didn't seem to like people. We worked our butts off on renditions of "San Francisco Bay Blues," Jesse Fuller's tune, and the classic "Baby, Please Don't Go." Bluesman K. C. Douglas, who's dead now, even turned up at the session in his city worker overalls and San Francisco Giants baseball cap to lend support, white-haired and encouraging as he loomed in the background. Still, it just didn't work out. The record never happened. Luck, as it turned out, was with us.

But Stevie's hit took off and followed me all across the country. In Motown that same year I witnessed a crumbling Detroit noisily poised at the beginning of its end: a preview of the condition that would later turn malignant. When he sang, *"Clap your hands / just a little bit louder / Clap your hands / just a little bit louder!"* Stevie could just as easily have been talking about the fall of the Arsenal of Democracy (Detroit's old nickname from the War) as he was the heated performance at hand.

New York after that was more than just a permissible dream: It was proof that pets, cockroaches and pigeons have New Yorks, just as chopped chicken liver lovers have their New Yorks, and derelicts and Fifth Avenuers, and even a visiting Californian such as my old flaming self, infected with Stevie and wanderlust, could still pony up a stack of shining New Yorks.

"Fingertips" trailed me everywhere that year, right onto the boat bound for Portugal, which disembarked toward the end of that summer from Brooklyn, with its proud Jews, Italians and Negroes (soon to become known again as Blacks), where poet Matt Kahn's grandmother, warm of eye and crusty of voice, said to me: "Europe? Why in the world would you want to go there? It's nothing. I know. I came from there."

Stevie's music comforted me all across the ocean. Somehow it seems to have always been waiting in the offing, blind and crouched, like its creator, to sniff and sound us all out. *"Just a little bit of sooo-uuu-woull-woulll!"*

Sweet Lorraine

Nat King Cole, 1943

WHEN NAT SANG that line about how each night he prayed that no one would steal her heart away, my brothers' ears and mine picked the line up as "Each night I pray / that no one will steal / her hot away."

Her hot away. Now that meant something to three Southern-nurtured tots suddenly brought north where, for that first frozen winter, we were forbidden to venture outside. Can you imagine how frightened our mother must have been for us?

It was a normal situation. Dad had just come back from Navy duty and this was heaven on the second floor of our aunt's and uncle-in-law's phony-bricked home. It was Aunt Ethel who finally told us one warm late March afternoon, when our mother wasn't around, that we could go outside and play in the backyard. And what a spring we stepped out into! There were ants, sowbugs, cocoons—*kacoombs* to us—under logs. And you should've seen the butterflies! We headed directly for the cherry tree to do some climbing. We've been climbing ever since, although not so much straight up as out and around and down into the world.

Nat Cole's world was the sound of warmth. His heated whisper melted hearts. We'd fooled around up there in the house long enough to love his voice, which, like the voices of most hit singers, sounded instantly familiar. It was as if it had always been there, nibbling at the edges of our earlobes.

We didn't know who Lorraine was and we didn't care. The fact that she was sweet was good enough. Hot was all we wanted to be. Sure, we understood that part of the lyric that dealt with when it was raining and the sunshine being there in her eyes. But the feeling of the record, as we grew to kind of love it, was so smooth that it was a little like being dunked into a warm bath of inexplicable sound.

"Choo-choo-choy," he sang, meaning *choo-choo-toy.*

Hey, we were right there, digging on Nat King Cole who, as far as we were concerned, was as much a part of our lives as the faithful baloney sandwiches Mother Dear fixed for Daddy to take to work at the Chevy plant, or the times they would get into physical, knife-brandishing fights, or the very way that things, when you're a kid, go crazy and fester inside your impressionable head for years on end.

Eventually we each dispersed to find our own special joy in a cold and hateful, gold-plated world where happiness is becoming a corny concept tolerated mostly in comic strips and greeting cards.

Only the Lonely

Frank Sinatra, 1958

O LET ME TELL YOU, you could get dangerously sentimental and deep down into that dark mushiness that saturates the soul past one in the morning when the party isn't over but should be. It was Irish-born poet James McAuley who first sprang that phrase "dark mushiness" on me, over beers at country singer Faron Young's Nashville nightclub years ago. McAuley used it to describe the feeling that comes over gatherers back home in Dublin pubs when the hour is late and singing begins. Eggplant mushiness might be more suitable for my purpose, perhaps to better evoke the color of severely dimmed off-hour party light, or perhaps to best indicate the tipsy capacity that frolicking, late-staying party guests have for absorbing foolishness and self-pity, just as an eggplant can almost endlessly absorb oils and fats.

Looking back, I can easily see how *Only the Lonely* was, in its quiet way, a kind of torchy pop erotica. Emotionally, the album was also equivalent to the mood induced by Fred Astaire in a bar scene from the 1943 movie musical, *The Sky's the Limit,* where he's the only drunk left at the bar. Decked out tastefully, as always, Astaire closes the joint spectacularly by turning to the straight-man bar-tender and addressing him in song as he moodily intones "One For My Baby (And One More for the Road)."

You may not know it either, but I too am a kind of poet, one who's got a lot of things to say about how someone would inevitably drag out this evergreen LP at the butt end of a party. The album it-self, with its *hotel moderne* jacket illustration, depicted Sinatra as a Laugh-Sad-Clown Pagliacci with reddened bittersweet teardrops slipping from his Modigliani greasepaint eyes. And the rightness of his crooning against a mutely fiddled background, cutting through the smoke of a room that had begun to fill on Saturday night and in which you'd languished until Sunday before dawn—well, that sound was all you needed to hear to know that this might very well be your last chance to do some woozy, slow-motion stumbling and fumbling around the dance floor.

It was at such a Berkeley party in the very early sixties that I heard longshoreman intellectual Jimmy Lynn tell some boogie-happy guest of his: "Hey, man, be quiet and let the paddy boy sing! White folks got a right to sing too, you know."

Thus was the mutually solitary mood contained and maintained. Responding to inner alarms, we all slid slowly down that well-greased pole of self-pity and raced with muffled sirens directly to where the fire was.

Fire, schmire! Desire was what it was all about, or, more properly, longing—a longing so vague and at the same time so vast and un-quenchable that it still would've been pointless for either you or your momentary partner to shed your clothes and offer your quiv-ering bodies, wet or erect, to one another right there on the spot in the middle of "Willow Weep for Me."

Backwater Blues

Bessie Smith, 1927

BESSIE'S GOT HER FLOOD and I've got mine. Mine was 1947, the year I lived with my Aunt Doris and Uncle Cleve and their kids, my cousins Mary, Martha and Ray in Laurel, Mississippi.

It rained and rained for days and days. In that Southern Baptist household, we took the Old Testament—and the New Testament, for that matter—literally. "God getting ready to claim His own," Aunt Lou kept telling us—Aunt Lou, my uncle's strangely sanctified sister who went around habitually in a blueberry-colored nun's outfit of her own design.

Finally it looked as if her words were coming true when the creek water rose so high that my cousin Ray and I came out one morning to see the front steps submerged. Aw, it was something! We kids, of course, were all pulling for the flood since it meant we wouldn't have to go to school. "Just stay home and play and have fun and stuff," I told Cousin Ray. He had to admit it was great all right, "but what if we all get drownded?" Somehow I knew that wasn't going to happen.

Schedules collapsed. A local state of emergency was declared. Just like in the song, my Uncle Cleve, wearing hip boots and a raincoat, rowed a little boat up to the front door late one dark afternoon and, hallelujah, lowered us down into it one by one. Were we overjoyed? Is water wet? Do boats float? What do kids know or care about furniture and rugs getting ruined or building foundations getting waterlogged? Our ace was adventure.

We rowed up and docked on dry land at the house of some family friends who had plenty of kids for us to play with. In no time we became acquainted with their brand of family nonsense and their outlandish ways.

That was just the point. We were all in the world in our own particular ways, and the world was a play place the size of any universe. The world just then was Mississippi with its chinaberry trees and mud, with old rusty roller skates and medicine bottles bubbling up out of what we hoped wasn't polio water. We didn't pay any more attention to grown folks than they paid to us.

Birds still flew. Flies landed. We bit into pomegranates (*pumma-granites,* we called 'em) right off trees. We played ball, rolled tires, acted out dreams and wrestled. I gave my cousin Ray, the household bully, a fair and square whipping he never forgot. Uncle Cleve kept playing that record he loved called "Little Joe from Chicago" that had a Louis Jordan bounce to it. My aunt and the other women sighed in kitchens where they made fires, washed greens, snapped beans, and fixed neckbones and rice while telling their stories in verbal jam sessions that stopped but never ended.

There we all were, heroes in a story about a flood that few people knew about, in a place that few people cared about or even knew existed.

Pennies from Heaven

Frank Rosolino, 1959

LONG BEFORE he joined the Stan Kenton band and became famous worldwide, trombonist Frank Rosolino was a flashy, ebullient Motor City Italian born with bebop in his soul. His old boss Stan Kenton once publicly described Rosolino as "a man of few if any quiet moody moments," and that was just how it seemed and sounded when he'd take to the bandstand and heft that tailgate horn of his. The music he made was happy and uplifting, and whenever he opened his mouth to speak or sing, the mood he created was inevitably upbeat and joyful.

Like any good jazz singer worthy of the name, Rosolino took casual liberties with the melody or words of any piece he thought enough of to perform. Without seriously altering the shape or beauty of a song, he was able to make it his own, emotionally and idiomatically, often by slyly personalizing its lyrics. "Everytime it rains, it rains," he used to proclaim, "matzohs and meatballs!" Or, "Everytime it rains, it rains—pretty little white girls!"

That last one used to break them up when he was working Klein's Show Bar, later to become Club 12, at the corner of Pingree and 12th Street in Detroit, right up the street from 1632 Pingree where I lived just before the family moved further north, a mile away, to Edison and 12th. This was the early 1950s, which would put me in Hutchins Junior High, barely into my teens, and so godawful hip and spoiling to be sainted that it must have been all my parents and teachers could do to stand being in the same room with me. There was very little that got past me and my pals. I mean, we knew we'd been dealt a cruel fate by not having been brought up in New York. That kept us from being The Cat's Meow. But at least, considering the sphere we moved in (a kind of pre-pubescent, highly charged stratosphere, really), nobody could say we weren't the Mosquito's Knees, and did we ever buzz! When we heard Charlie Parker and Miles Davis doing "Buzzy," we just took it for granted that they must've been speaking directly to us.

And Frank Rosolino wasn't really talking to nobody but me, poised out there on the nighttime sidewalk in front of Klein's where the aroma of barbecued ribs, fried shrimp and corned beef blended, stalemated, in a neighborhood that was shifting full tilt from Jewish to Black. Most of the Jewish kids were retreating to Dexter or further northwest, eventually to end up in places like Oak Park. My Uncle James—ever the nimble-tongued operator, who loved the Jews—said, "After the white folks get tired of a neighborhood, they start moving out and sell it to the Jews, then when the Jews get through running it into the ground, they let the Negroes move in, and after that, looks like, it's only the real poor Negroes left to take over."

Frank Rosolino was one of those Black Bottom Sicilians from the Far Eastside who, if I remember correctly, came out of Miller High, as notorious a public school as they allowed in that day. You always heard about students packing guns and switchblades and giving teachers hell at Miller long before *Blackboard Jungle* (with a sound-track by Bill Haley and the Comets) came out and made all that into a poisonous cliché. Culturally, Rosolino seemed to owe more to Black urban heritage than to his Sicilian ancestors—not that the two traditions were ever mutually exclusive. Jazz impresario

Norman Granz, for one, always maintained that the basic audience for his jazz at the Philharmonic concerts were young Blacks, young Jews and young Italians. Let the sociologists and ethno-musicologists quibble and quarrel over that one.

My point is that Frank Rosolino, from my Detroit on down through my California days, had always struck me as being one of the happiest, most even-tempered men I'd ever seen. A sharp dresser and ever the raffish, bebop Pagliacci, he cut an attractive figure.

In the early 1960s in Oakland, California, Rosolino turned up at a curious little club called the Gold Nugget which appears to have been owned by a Stan Kenton acolyte who regularly brought first-rate former Kenton sidemen up from L.A. to work for a weekend in a small combo setting, or to work as featured soloist with Johnny Coppola's big band. The Sunday night that Rosolino was guesting, I dropped by the Nugget, feeling highly conspicuous as the only Black person in the crowd. Between sets, I got to speak with Rosolino, who insisted that I call him Frank. I told him about the old days when I used to hang around outside Klein's as a kid to catch him.

Frank rolled his big brown eyes, plucked at his dark operatic mustache and, leaning forward, told me in a low voice. "Hey, Blood, I hope you ain't been runnin around tellin everybody about that, 'cause, see, back here over the last few years I been tryin my damndest to pass!"

He did all right for himself too, passing through this world, making people feel good, getting steady work as a much sought-after recording and TV studio musician. In recent years he had worked with Benny Carter and Maria Muldaur, toured Europe and Japan, was featured soloist on the Merv Griffin Show and had cut any number of memorable albums.

In the summer of 1979 word reached me that Frank Rosolino had shot his wife dead in their Southern California home, then shot both of their sons before turning the gun on himself and blowing his own brains out.

What went wrong? What was the matter? I've since heard explanations, and yet, given the self-portrait the man painted in sound, none of them truly make sense.

You never quite know what kind of pain anyone is suffering from when they pass through your life, smiling and wishing you well, yet leaving entire fields of themselves closed to you as if they sensed the explosive kinds of mines that might lie hidden there. What can I say? Frank won the war most artists must wage against time and the times to go on creating and growing. He'd won the war but lost some battle we'll never know about. Somewhere along the way, that very rain he played in so dauntlessly must have given way to a raging, private storm that demolished his umbrella and blew his whole house away.

Cucurrucucu Paloma

El Trio los Panchos, 1962

EVERYTHING was all rainbowed up. Even the Orange Crush I was sipping didn't seem quite real. The pastel light of Mexico can strike you that way.

A fly floated right down to my damp nose before changing its mind about making a buzz landing.

So this was Los Mochis, a tiny town in northern Mexico; a rest stop on the bus run from Tijuana to Guadalajara. Guidebooks had taught me that Los Mochis meant The Flies. Still curious, I had gotten it into my sweating head to check out the regional history and mythology of this place the very next time I visited a library.

It was steamy August in Los Mochis. The antique jukebox glowed and flashed as it sagged in one corner under the heaviness of *guitarras, guitarrones,* Spanishy sighs and Mexican *ayyys* and that singular languor that lingers between the lines of Mexican ballads and *huapangos.* F. Scott Fitzgerald had been right on the track when he wrote, "The train slowed with midsummer languor."

It was the twilight hour when all the noisy men were heatedly cooling themselves over beers, tequilas and rotgut pulques in the swinging-doored cantinas. Women and children and quieter men languished in the zócalo beneath Pepsi legends, speaking Spanish so drowsily that even I, a vacationing fool in his moneyless youth, could understand most of their talk without straining too hard.

While waiting for my *pollo* and *frijoles* (chicken and beans) at the bus station snack counter, I pressed the iced sodapop bottle to my forehead and slid it down around my lowered eyes and cheeks, savoring the cool, momentary contact. I had been dead asleep when the bus pulled into town. Now, ritually aroused, I began to look around and listen closely to where I was.

That's when I became aware of the Trio Los Panchos on the jukebox. *"Cucurrucucu, cantaba,"* they crooned, and *"Cucurrucucu, no llores."* As the music grew on me, I realized how much the words dealt with love in the here and now. That was, after all, where love lived, wasn't it? At the same time I was noticing how I had constantly been fanning flies from the moment I'd set foot in Los Mochis. The pesky things were everywhere! Glancing around, I observed that everyone else was too busy shooing their own flies to pay much attention to mine.

When a flat-faced Indian—El Chato, they might call him—with a Cantinflas mustache walked in workshirted, trailed by what had to be a hefty percentage of the town's fly population, I could no longer contain myself. I doubled over, rested my head on the counter and began to laugh out loud, too loudly.

The whole joint grew silent as everybody turned to stare. It just so happened that I'd also knocked my drink over. One side of my face was soon resting in a bubbly pool of *Oranch Croosh.*

Even as the paunchy counterman was shrugging and winking at the gawking crowd and shaping tiny circles at his graying temples with his index finger, I found myself enjoying every moment of the spectacle I was making.

Watching him drag out his counter-wiping rag, I sat up wondering if I would ever be able to describe the satisfaction it gave me to never have to look up the history of Los Mochis.

The Barber of Seville

Gioachino Antonio Rossini, composer

POSSIBLY BECAUSE of the Lone Ranger, who, as any seasoned Detroiter will tell you, originated from the local studios of radio station WXYZ, I got on a Rossini kick one summer and devoured his work, even though I wasn't naturally drawn to opera. But I was playing tuba and sometimes baritone horn, instruments my father had played professionally in his youth, in the Central High School Band. I was also studying trumpet on the side. In addition to the usual marches, light classics and cutesy-poo pop, the band was playing modified arrangements of Schubert's *Unfinished,* Tchaikovsky's *Nutcracker Suite* and Ravel's *Bolero.*

Every time Mr. Kurtez, the band conductor, stepped out of the room, we would rag and jazz whatever score we happened to be rehearsing with the kind of sneering irreverence that adolescents the world over savor. It was the same spirit that, sheltered in large auditorium groups, prompted us to sing "Walking in My Winter

Underwear" instead of "Walking in a Winter Wonderland." Or, on the sly, to open "The Star Spangled Banner" with the words: "O say can you see / Any bedbugs on me? If you do / Pick a few / And I'll fry them for you." The chorus of singer Lloyd Price's winning rhythm & blues tune, "Personality," had to do with someone having personality and great big heart to boot. Inevitably, gathered in freewheeling locker-room chorales, we sang: "'Cause you got / Personality / Personality / Plus you got a great big ha-aarrrrd!" When Jack "Dragnet" Webb's former wife Julie London came out with "Cry Me a River," we faithfully transformed it into "Fry Me a Liver." There was even one tiresomely clever, if not brilliant, lad who had nothing better to do than change the entire score of the Broadway musical *Guys and Dolls* into an off-color, pubescent parody by substituting his own dumb, smutty lyrics for Frank Loesser's. It seems that no matter how busy they're kept, teenagers somehow find plenty of time to cut up and be silly.

In the middle of my teens, during my summertime Rossini Period, and probably crazed by my determination to get at the essence of *The Barber of Seville,* which I was listening to repeatedly, I decided to give myself a haircut. Undetected by the rest of the family, I stood in front of the bathroom mirror shaving my head with an electric razor that once belonged to an uncle who used to cut the family hair. There I shaved and shaved away, trying to create a proper design. Gradually I succeeded in shearing myself bald: so bald, in fact, that I could see the ridges and humps on my own scalp. They resembled little plow rows of the skull. I screamed in terror and, delighted at the same time, rushed out to either buy or find a hat. In all likelihood, I dug up the hat in our attic where all the throwaway clothes that hadn't or couldn't be passed on were stored.

Painfully vain, I wore that old slouch hat for most of the summer, only taking it off to sleep. Girls and even my friends laughed at me. Shaved heads were in fashion in a modest way, even in the distant, dark fifties, but mine looked ridiculous. My mother thought it so funny that she snickered at me continuously and defiantly. I didn't have to get another haircut for months, and when I finally did, it wasn't because I wanted to but, rather, because my stepfather mashed the money into my hand and said, "For Chrissake, please go get some of that mess cut offa your head!"

I might've been dumb, but I never pulled that number again. About the closest I've ever come since has been the time or two that I've compulsively shaved off my mustache without truly meaning to, and on each occasion it was almost as though some mischievous tramp spirit had stepped into my body to take possession.

Rossini himself, more than likely, knew a little something about the value of impulsive acts. Early in his lucrative career he settled for a spell in Bologna where he struck up a deal with the theater and gambling casino impresario, Barbaja. As it turned out, Rossini had to knock out one opera a year for the Teatro San Carlo and the Teatro del Fondo at Naples. For good measure, he was also cut in on a piece of the action at Barbaja's gaming tables. Besides producing a string of hits, Signor Rossini hit it off beautifully with his courtly and aristocratic groupies both in Italy and abroad. His first wife was a successful singer; his last, a cultured French studio model. Retiring to France, he still had plenty of time to disengage himself and look back on it all with witty indifference, detachment and humility.

Looking back on my ephemeral involvement with *The Barber of Seville,* I can't help but dwell on my old hair and that floppy old hat. Both are like dreams to me now. I also can't help wondering whatever happened to the hat once it got out of my hands. Did it curiously find its way to Detroit's old Skid Row, then on perhaps to Boston's Scollay Square, the Bowery in Manhattan, Denver's Larimer Street, or the Mission in San Francisco? How did its smell change? Maybe some little boy once donned it comically with a flower plucked out of someone's yard to amuse a little girl.

What's become of that garment and all the old shirts, shoes, trousers and sweaters, all the apparel of the passing flow? Where does it all end up—old dreams, old music, old songs, fleeting enthusiasms and, of course, all that shorn hair that was once alive? Where, pray tell, have I gone since? For fun, I could wear that slouch hat tonight for a few minutes and think about all my ungainly transformations. I'd stand in front of the bathroom mirror and laugh at myself, at how utterly foolish I was then and still am, and I'd laugh at how I, just like that crumply headpiece, remain completely silly, beside the point and unconcernedly beautiful.

Just think about it.

Today, there are still more people around who remember the Lone Ranger, his horse Silver, his faithful Indian companion Tonto and his archenemy Butch Cavendish when they hear the *William Tell Overture* than there are faithful listeners to Rossini's grand and rigidly formal opera.

You never know. Satchel Paige was right again: "Don't look back; something might be gaining on you."

In a Mist

Bix Beiderbecke, 1927

PLAY IT ONE MORE TIME, Bix, so I can cascade down your waterfall of tears and up again all on my own.

I can tell by the silence of the notes you aren't hitting that your head's getting funny again from sitting up all night, every night, night after night, banking on bad speak booze to navigate you through seas of sound on boats that leave but never dock, at least never long enough to unload your steamy cargo—a love affair with sound itself, and what it can and cannot do.

Tell me, Bix, jazz darling, legendary refugee from Iowa and Cincinnati Oom-Pah-Pah, is there really any difference (besides time, that is) between your 1920s twenties and the twenties of Nineteen Now? All that appetizing ear food, those saucy, futuristic chords you cook up on piano to go, and heat back up on cornet—where, if anywhere, will it end up? Better than any physicist, you already know that time, space, motion, stillness, distance and nearness are one. What you're deep into now is the whirling of planets as notated by Gustav Holst, your favorite composer after Louis Armstrong: the sibilant motion of heavenly bodies, and the whispering of the hours going by and by and by.

Tell me, doesn't that same lonesome-looking moon still pull, bringing women around in a cycle as different from man-made lunacy as bathwater from gin? And isn't what you've always loved and dreamed still as American as aspirin or atomic secrets; as American as apple pie frozen in color on a television screen?

That's the part of music's mystery they're going to have to get a law out against: your secret ingredient, your mystical spray capable of shattering whole cities and countrysides while—unlike a neutron bomb—it leaves listeners intact, craving infinity. Your spirit need only be there, contained inside the mystery.

I, they, you, we—we all need your mistiness, Bix. Play it again please, won't you? Again and again and again—life is so long, and always too short.

What Now My Love

Herb Alpert & The Tijuana Brass, 1965

IMAGINE ME, not exactly one of our favorite sons, pulling up as usual on the San Diego bus via San Ysidro to that little wire fence where a brown-shirted cop on the U.S. side once told me that he had never, in fifteen years of working that post, been across the border to Mexico—which to him was one big Tijuana—and never would. That was in the very early sixties. He made me and Bob Mates, my travel companion at the time, produce what Bob called "I.D. up the kazoo" to prove we hadn't been in jail and weren't secret gangsters, part of the kiddy underworld.

Now it's three years later, 1965. Haight Ashbury is going on: lysergic acid, the ubiquitous Beatles, Timothy Leary, Richie Havens, The Lovin' Spoonful, Ravi Shankar, gurus, the Black Panthers, Ornette Coleman, the Sexual Freedom League, witchcraft, communes, riots, copulation in the streets, the Rolling Stones, Bob Dylan, macrobiotics, dashikis, enormous Afros, Otis Redding, bell-bottoms, fat belts with big buckles, apocalyptic chitchat, secret home arsenals and Vietnam.

This time I get off the bus just when it's turning dark. There isn't anyone guarding anything at the border, so I'm free to walk across like the proverbial human being. A fat customs official checks the tourist papers that've been typed up so nicely for me at the Mexican Consulate on Market Street in San Francisco only days before. Everything's in order. The show is on. From here on out, I'm thinking, it's going to be Mexico and How It Got That Way—for a little while anyway, for a few dreams at least.

Then the oddest things begin to happen—odd enough to make me think to examine my own lopsided karma, or what I believe to be just that, being newly curious about the realness of God's laws. I behold the smoking taxi driver that a little boy leads me to in the drizzling night. This driver, he don't say nothing when I climb into his cab, not until we shoot out from customs and down the block toward the bus station; then suddenly he breaks into that local lingo, the Tijuanese, yakking all about how things've been, cha-cha-cha, and *quien sabe?* and *po siiii* and *gringuistas* and who knows what all. Having at first taken me to be a true Latino of some kind, he's made to realize by my muffled replies in Spanish that either (a) I've been out of practice speaking the language for some time now, or (b)—and more probably—that I must be that occasional *gringo negro* who slips across the border, usually from the San Diego Naval Yard to either get high or get laid, and this cabbie's determined to get all he can out of the deal.

"How much?" I ask when we're safely in front of the Three Gold Star bus station *(Tres Estrellas de Oro).*

Still rapping, as talk was hiply called then, in Baja Californian, he breaks out into an attitude that's plainly North American. He says, *"Tres dólares."*

"Three dollars! For what? You must mean three pesos!"

Nope, he don't mean that at all. He means three dollars—*tres dólares.* "Want me to write it out, *señor?"*

Now, to be honest, I've been counting on that three dollars, which was all I had in sheer cash in my pocket, to get me through one or two days on the road at those upcoming bus-ride meal stops, but no—now it's going to be poured down that hole in the hand that everybody's holding out for the *yanqui* dollah. I stutter and sputter, but the cabbie will have none of it. "Can't you take a dollar? That's really all I've got."

"Lo siento, señor, pero no lo pue'o!" (Nope, sorry, I can't!)

We retreat into quietude while I realize that huge clops of rain are bombarding the taxi top. "Can you at least wait till I go inside and cash a traveler's check?"

"They won't cash a traveler's check in there."

"Then where?"

"Nowhere, *señor.*"

How come he's got to lie like that for a rudimentary three bucks? But then again, I had lied by claiming not to have that much money. We each wait it out until finally I can't stand it. I want to be out of this dreaded Tijuana and back into what to me is the real Mexico, so I hand him the three U.S. dollars, my last. This leaves me with close to fifty or sixty cents to blow as I wish.

My thoughts of the moment go something like this:

This middle-aged gent with the pudgy form and gray mustachios probably has eight kids at home and they all want new leather coats, transistor radios and racing bikes for presents, constantly and on a rotating basis. Besides, there's that familiar menacing stare I've come to recognize down here as meaning: "You fatuous person, *oye!* We know you've got all the money in the world, don't care what you say. Otherwise, how come it is you're able to be vacationing down South of the Border when the only way we get up there on the up and up's when your Secretary of Labor signs a bill with ours saying it's OK to ship, to sheep like peegs, *señor*, like cattle, so many thousands of *braceros* to pick your stupid sun-kissed oranges, your grapes, your beans, onions, tomatoes, asparagus, lettuce, your harvests that go into cans and deep freezes for shiny supermarket shelves and displays so that Joe Dog and Nancy Bitch can pull up in new cars to run inside and grab a can of Libby's or Del Monte's on special as advertised in order to heat that queek meal for deener for the family to smack its lips upon and then go *burp*, Bromo Seltzer, and fade out in front of the news flashing over the TV that's in everybody's brand new house. We know all about it. We have to look at your

TV and movies too and read *Time* and *Newsweek.* So you see, *señor,* you must cough up, like you say, the *dinero,* in order that I might nourish my own thin family."

The cabbie's attitude doesn't change one drop as I hand over the loot, resolving in my head to tell everyone I run across who's headed this way in the future not to take a taxi but to *walk* the three blocks from the border to the bus station.

I strain to picture myself as this ruthless taxi driver, and what's amazing is that I actually can, whereupon from my lips cometh the words, *"Vaya con Diós, señor."* Of course, I'm aware that I've by-passed the pop sentimental meaning of this phrase of parting (popularized in Les Paul and Mary Ford's hit record of the early 1950s) and penetrated its gut spiritual origin. I say it with just the slightest hint of an undertone, perhaps an overtone that translates: "See, you treat me as if I were a murderous, fat, capitalist lackey, and yet I think enough of you to express my humble blessings for your well-being."

As for the cabbie, well, he smiles. He smiles, folding the dirty, pitiful dollars away, making them disappear sleight-of-hand style. And what does he tell me? Smiling, he twists in his seat and says, "And may God be with you too, *amigo.*"

Zapped now, I collect my bags and go blow my last few coins on milk and a tunafish roll, a *torta,* at the station snack counter. The man in the ticket cage listens to my story, then explains my predicament to the young bus driver personally. Fortunately for me, this driver's a gentleman.

"Pues," he saith unto me, "you're gonna have trouble cashing any traveler's checks before we get into the south—to Mazatlán anyway, maybe even as far as Guadalajara. You see, the counterfeiting of such documents has become so commonplace that nobody'll take them any more up this way. So why don't you just get on the bus and ride anyway? By and by we'll get your checks cashed for you, yes? Also, my friend, you'll be needing a little money for eating along the way, will you not? Here you have fifty pesos I'm lending you. You pay me back when you cash your check, OK?"

This is what's known as goodness, and it is all that holds Creation together.

# Black Pearls

John Coltrane, 1958

IN THE SPRING of 1957, half crazy with hunger for the whole sad world, I hitched a ride from Detroit to New York to wander the streets of that fabled city, probably to prove to myself that it actually existed but also to see where much of the music I loved was coming from. Music to me, then as now, represented a higher reality, a luminous touchstone, my polar connection, one of the only real reasons for staying alive.

Checking in at the Sloane House Y on West 34th Street, I walked and subwayed everywhere, keeping a nightly diary of my doings and sightings, wolfing down my daily meal in lonely automats or at hotdog/papaya drink stands. I even had the nerve to ring up famous musicians such as Horace Silver and Thelonious Monk whose numbers I was shocked to find listed in the Manhattan directory. What a romantic time I thought I was having as rain poured down and my ten-day stash of quarters and dimes trickled down to nickels.

I actually faked my way into jazz clubs, Birdland mostly, which wasn't all that hard to do since I was seventeen but seemed older and the local drinking age was eighteen. Seated in Birdland's gallery one drizzly off-night, a Monday, I got into a beery conversation with a portly, talkative, older jazz fiend who thought he knew everything about the music by dint of being a New Yorker. He was really what they called in those days a hippie, although the term didn't yet carry its later, more complicated, connotation.

We were listening, Mr. Talk and I, to a quartet led by tenor saxophonist Teo Macero, who would later become Miles Davis' producer at Columbia. I was fond of a little ten-inch album Macero had cut on bassist/composer Charles Mingus' Debut label. Between sets the subject of tenor players came up as it usually did in those jazz-as-contest days.

It just so happened that a splendid young horn man named Sonny Rollins was carving a solid reputation for himself as the champion tenorist of the day, the man most likely to inherit the silver cup that had been passed around among such legendary forerunners as Coleman Hawkins, Ben Webster and Lester Young. Mr. Talk, to hear him tell it, had personally known and dug them all and could elaborate at length on the fine points of their respective careers right on down to the catalog numbers of labels they'd recorded for. I was impressed and intimidated.

"What do you think of this man Trane?" he asked finally.

"John Coltrane? I like him very much—at least from what little I've heard of him on record with Miles. He's got a strong, soulful sound. There's a lot of the blues in there. You don't forget it."

Cookin', the first of four unforgettably brilliant Miles Davis Quintet LPs—all of them taped, as I later learned, in two all-day sessions the year before—had just been released. Practically everyone I knew back around Detroit had been turned around by the band's sound and by Coltrane in particular. Paul Chambers, the quintet's bassist, was from Detroit, a highly jazz-conscious city at the time.

"Let me tell you something," Mr. Talk went on. "Keep an eye on this dude Coltrane. The man is definitely into something. I don't think he's really got himself completely together yet, but look out! I've been watching him for a couple of years now, ever since he hooked up with Miles. He keeps getting stronger and stranger by the minute."

"How do you mean?"

"How do I mean?" Mr. Talk laughed and took a very long sip from his latest drink. "Ha! You haven't caught that band in person yet?"

True, I hadn't. Back in Michigan you still had to be twenty-one to get into a club.

"Well, when you finally do catch Trane live on the set, you'll hear exactly what I mean. He plays that horn of his to death! He's all up under it and all on top of it. He takes long runs that wear me out just listening. Sometimes it's almost like he's woodshedding right up there on the stand, practicing scales and exercises and stuff. He's after something. I don't know what it is, but I sure am glad to be in on the search. One of these days he'll find what he's looking for and then, watch out! Sonny and them just might have to get their hats. Check him up close first chance you get!"

I must have left New York around the same time Coltrane was leaving Miles temporarily to spend the summer working with Thelonious Monk at the Five Spot Cafe downtown. Back in the midwest, I spent the summer washing dishes and busing tables, following the music scene through the trade press and through first- and second-hand accounts provided by musicians who were fellow devotees. The grapevine was quivering with excitement.

I can only speculate that Monk and Trane must have loved one another musically. Listen to the way the pianist shouts his name— "Coltrane! Coltrane!"—on that old out-of-print Riverside LP *Monk's Music*. Monk, at the end of his solo on "Well You Needn't," pages Trane, who takes up where his leader trails off, with an exhilarating statement that electrifies.

Certainly, Coltrane regarded the older musician with great admiration. "I would talk to Monk about musical problems," he later said, "and he would sit at the piano and show me the answers just by playing them." Among other things, Monk taught him the technique of sounding two to three notes on his horn simultaneously, a device which he subsequently put to delightful use in many of his exploratory solos.

Soon, however, Coltrane was back blowing and groping more

daringly than ever with the re-formed Davis quintet, which, with some personnel changes and additions, was transformed into the remarkable sextet that brought him together with the alto saxophonist Cannonball Adderley and pianist Bill Evans to produce the classic *Kind of Blue* album that will doubtless sound as timeless and meaningful in a century as it does now and as it did in the late 1950s when it first made history.

Nineteen fifty-eight was the year Coltrane began to be widely talked about. He had by then become the most controversial new instrumentalist on the scene.

Time is funny. Coltrane was born in 1926 in Hamlet, North Carolina, son of a tailor who played music for fun, right around the time Louis Armstrong had come over to New York from Chicago and New Orleans and upset everybody once and for all. In his early twenties, following a hitch with the Navy band in Hawaii, he'd worked with such rhythm and blues stalwarts as Eddie "Clean Head" Vinson and Earl Bostic. Before joining Miles, he had toured with Dizzy Gillespie and Johnny Hodges. Now in his thirties, Coltrane was new. It's important, I think, to mention here that, besides being ardent romantics, jazz enthusiasts are not unlike sports fans, journalists, academicians and theologians in their enduring love of controversy and the passionate discourse it generates.

Was Coltrane the new messiah or just another flashy, promising charlatan? Fifteen years previously, Charlie Parker had caught so many dutiful jazz eavesdroppers napping that fans, critics and active musicians alike were going out of their way almost comically to remain wakeful lest another elusive musical prophet sneak up on them unawares and unannounced.

"All you really gotta do," a trumpet-playing friend told me, "is to look at Tranes's initials. J.C. That oughtta tell you *something*."

But there were those people who were simply baffled or even irritated by what the man was playing. Many were outright hostile. All those showerings of sixteenth and thirty-second notes, those weird scales and modes, that polytonality—what the hell was it all supposed to mean?

"They can't dig Trane," my friend commented, "because he's too fast for them. They listen to him sounding all gentle on some ballad and think they've got him down. Then he'll turn around and double-time and triple-time 'em outta their minds. He's got too many things going on at the same time. He's too peculiar-sounding and unpredictable. You never know what kinda entrance he's gonna make. People get upset behind that. They wanna know is he for real or is he jiving? Now you don't mean to tell me Dizzy and Miles and Monk and them can't tell a good musician from a jive one?"

The jazz press of the day was hotly divided in its appraisal of his talent and significance. "Sheets of sound" was the term created by writer Ira Gitler to describe the overall effect that Coltrane's playing of that period achieved for him personally. The phrase, for better or worse, caught on. *Sheets of sound,* hmmm, that had an imaginative, perceptive ring to it. Maybe the man should be given the benefit of a doubt, and listened to more closely.

Comparisons between Coltrane's and Rollins' approaches to the tenor saxophone continued to be drawn until 1960, when Rollins went into self-imposed retirement for two years. It never seemed to matter that the two men were active contemporaries, each one respectful of the other's sound, style and capacity for inventiveness.

I found myself mistrustful of the assessments, pronouncements and exhortations of all the jazz commentators, professional and amateur, whose aim at core appears to have been to put this upstart newcomer in his place. And just where, if anywhere, was Coltrane's rightful place in the scheme of things? Obviously this was a matter that could only be settled in the hearts and aural imagination of individual listeners.

The overwhelming emotional and lyrical appeal of Coltrane's playing was clear to me from the moment he first invaded my world. I've never recovered from its strength, beauty and yea-saying exuberance, the same way I've never gotten over Coleman Hawkins.

Conveniently perhaps, the history of the music that's still called jazz is also a history of recorded performances. What a luxury it is to be able to fly around through time preserved as sound on record or tape. Re-entering such captured moments, it becomes increasingly difficult, if not impossible, to discern how much time itself transforms what I may actually hear. What was once shocking or disturbing to the ear might soon enough become acceptable, cherished or even hackneyed.

Recorded jazz is also the history of a process whereby individual musicians, following the dictates of some secret ear, are forever casting their ideas upon winds that, all too often, blow those same creations back to them without benefit of copyright or royalties.

Coltrane was more fortunate than most in this respect. He didn't die penniless or washed up in anybody's poignant gutter. What's more, before he slipped out of the world he lived to see a lot of people change their ideas about his earlier performances, while he went on developing himself, extending and supplanting his own ideas about music at such a rapid rate that it was taxing for sympathetic fellow musicians (much less the public at large) to keep up with him.

I finally caught the Davis sextet live at Birdland in the summer of 1959. Two century-long years had passed in my life. Sure enough, there stood Coltrane, sounding totally different from the way he did on the latest recordings I'd gathered. It was the very night Miles Davis stepped outside between sets and got into an altercation with some cops about loitering. He had to be hospitalized. The band, winding up the evening without its leader, went on smoking and burning until the very air crackled with flames scorching enough to warm the heart of even a plainclothes policeman. It was truly a Coltrane night. Mr. Talk hadn't been just talking.

I followed his music from then on until his sudden death in 1967, catching him live at every opportunity on both coasts.

I watched him pick up a whole new audience, a very broad-based one, when he picked up soprano saxophone and came out with "My Favorite Things" in 1960. I also watched him lose a few of those same puzzled fans when he showed up at the Jazz Workshop in San Francisco with altoist Eric Dolphy about a season later.

The Coltrane controversy resumed and never really subsided.

"Oh, that was terrible," he told Frank Kofsky in his last interview, published in *Jazz & Pop*. "I couldn't believe it, you know, it just seemed so preposterous. It was so ridiculous, man . . . because they made it appear that we didn't even know the first thing about music. . . . And there we were really trying to push things off."

John Coltrane made no distinction between music, philosophy, religion and life. In his vision, they were all aspects of the same search for spiritual wholeness, as his later recordings and comments attest. "I'm sure others will be a part of the music," he said in that final interview. "I know that there are bad forces put here that bring suffering to others and misery in the world, but I want to be the force which is truly for good."

Much has been said and written about the Coltrane of the mid-1960s—a good deal of it reverential—but there were many Coltranes, just as there are many musics that go to make up what is universally called jazz, better described as Afro-American classical music. A lifetime of listening has led me to believe that spirituals, blues, ragtime, New Orleans jazz, boogie-woogie, rhythm & blues, swing, bop and their derivatives are all indeed aspects of an enduring and self-regenerative musical tradition (or continuum, if you will) to which John William Coltrane has made lasting contributions.

He was glowing each time I met him, beginning with Berkeley in 1962 when he was visiting Wes Montgomery at the late Elton Mills' home (which was really a musicians' commune), and again the following year in a very wintry San Francisco. When I shook his hand and told him how reassuring it was for me and a great many others to know that he was still here in the world, he simply smiled and looked beyond me shyly.

Feels
So Good

Chuck Mangione, 1978

IT WAS ONE of those unscheduled deals where I found myself with a whole day left over after working at a poetry festival on Long Island. Exhausted from having expended all of the physical, emotional and psychic energy that literary bashes require, I decided to drive into Manhattan with a poet friend and spend twenty-four hours doing as little as possible before flying back West.

"Well," said my friend, "if you're only staying overnight, I've got the key to an apartment upstairs from mine that this Columbia architecture student's vacated for the summer. It's quiet up there and you can rest up and sleep well."

It was quiet all right, by big city standards, but I barely got any of the sleep I needed. Like so many destinations in my New York world, this place was at the very top of a long, narrow, airless flight of stairs. Once I'd gotten past the inevitable web of key locks, fox locks, chain locks and *whew!*—the first sound to greet me as I stepped inside poured from a table radio that was all aglow with the pop/disco hit of that feverish season: Chuck Mangione's "Feels So

Good." By leaving the radio on and the lights hooked up to an automatic timer, the regular tenant sought to give the impression that the apartment was occupied. All the same, I kept thinking that if I were a sophisticated burglar scoping this joint—and there's no other kind of burglar in New York City—I would've known right away from the curtainless windows that somebody was running some kind of elaborate scam. But since it was anything but easy to get inside the building and the unit itself was up several tough flights, maybe my ghostly, absentee host had known what he was doing after all.

I wasn't feeling so good. Cruising into town across the George Washington Bridge had been almost as big a shock for me as the first time I'd subjected myself to a steambath when I'd been a teenager working the locker room and shoe-shine parlor at the Sidney Hill Health Club in downtown Detroit. This midsummer heat was like a solvent that, combined with the overpowering odor of uncollected garbage, turned me into compost long before I dragged my bags out of my friend's car to mount that brutal staircase.

In spite of the windows that were painted shut, and in spite of the sweat and grit pouring out of me, it still felt good in a queasy sort of way to be at liberty in a town that has always run me ragged. Not only didn't I have to call or call on anyone; there was no threat of being interrupted, since only one person in town even knew where I was. The most pressing chore that lay before me was to pry open a couple of windows to get what I, a naive Californian, believed would be a breath of air.

"The strangest things always happen to you in New York," my old friend Ann McIntosh used to say whenever I hit town. "Stuff that couldn't possibly happen to anybody else!"

I was thinking about this when I went for a late afternoon stroll along Duke Ellington Avenue. But what strange experience could possibly befall me this time? There was absolutely nothing doing, and I loved it. Deciding not to dine in a fancy Chinese-Cuban restaurant, I chowed down instead on pizza by the slice at some hole-in-the-wall where Barry Manilow's thumping "Copacabana," just released, kept the Puerto Rican counterman cranking up the volume on his radio, one of those big, booming, twin-speakered, proletarian specials specifically designed to induce apoplexy on buses and subways. No, this time in Manhattan I was determined to simply walk right in, sit right down and let my quiet mind roll on. Privately delighted at the prospect of having an absolutely un-eventful time, I treated myself to some fresh fruit at a curbside pro-duce stand, picked up the *Times,* and strolled back home in a relatively hushed twilight that falsely promised a touch of breezy relief from the heat.

The minute I was back and settled at a desk in front of the tall, bare front windows—equipped with pen and plenty of paper to begin doing what a writer does—my attention was drawn across the street at once to a window shade that was suddenly being yanked all the way up. In the window stood a man in nothing but briefs who then fell back upon an unmade double bed across which a young woman reclined. They appeared to be in their late twenties, perhaps early thirties, and both had mousey brown hair. The woman was wearing tennis shorts and a T-shirt.

In no time at all, while I tried to work, this couple had gotten the preliminary necking out of the way and were now about to get down, as the saying goes. Off came the clothes. I couldn't believe it. I also can't believe that I sat there in the full light of a glossy, hi-tech desk lamp and watched. Four stories down, kids were still playing in the street while people dawdled and chattered on crowded stoops, and thugs came and went. From where I sat, there were per-haps fifteen to twenty window scenes lit up before me, but in almost all of them, people were busy either watching or not watching their illuminated television screens. This one window alone had its own show going on, and it was undeniably x-rated. At first I felt embar-rassed watching their performance, but as the evening wore on it gradually struck me that what this rabbity pair craved, possibly even more than sensual delight, was an audience.

Between couplings, the man would casually come to the window, still butt naked, and poke his tousled head outside to survey the siren world and catch his breath. Then he'd sit on the floor, remove papers from a briefcase, and begin to study them. He never got very far because the woman, ardently aroused—that is, hot to trot—would crawl to where he was plopped, and, serpent-like, she'd begin tempting him again with nibbles and bites from her well-fruited garden. They must've carried on for hours on end, because at one point I doused my own light, took to bed, woke up to get a glass of water in the depths of night, looked across the way, and saw that they were still at it.

As strange as it was to observe first-hand two human beings making passionate love, it was also unarousing and surprisingly, if not ridiculously, clinical. The experience made me realize how enormous a role personal involvement, emotion, anticipation and imagination play in giving the sex act its almost irrepressible power and titillating appeal. On that muggy night it became clear to me that sexual communion, however closely it might resemble a physical tournament, is anything but a spectator sport.

But the strangest leg of that incidental episode took place the following morning, in broad daylight, when I descended to the street with my luggage to flag a taxi. Who should be emerging from the building across the street at that very moment but my uninhibited exhibitionists: he in his business suit with tortured briefcase in tow, and she in a crisp, proper summer office dress with her long hair pinned up. I might only have imagined this, but I could swear she glanced across the street at me with a lingering simper. And that's not all. The minute I settled in the cab and slammed the door, the cheerful driver snapped on his AM radio and there was Chuck Mangione and his brother Gap again, sending me off to the Eastside Airlines Terminal and back to California with "Feels So Good."

Like the pleasantly inoffensive breakfast aroma of steaming decaffeinated coffee with non-dairy creamer, Tang, scrambly powdered eggs, simulated bacon and two slices of hot-margarined Wonder Bread toast, the warm, polyunsaturated sound of Chuck Mangione's bronze record transported me through the rest of that morning, hatless and beardless, and on out into what remained of that American summer. Oh, the Bee Gees were "Staying Alive" and Bonnie Tyler was belting out "It's a Heartache," but somehow Chuck stuck. And everywhere I caught him grinning and hugging on that horn of his in a TV spot promoting the record, I couldn't help wondering what it must feel like to make love to the world with all the lights turned on and the windows hoisted high.

Gifts and Messages

Rahsaan Roland Kirk, 1965

RAHSAAN'S MUSIC is about as predictable as the rhythms of thunder breaking on a warm August night, or the evanescent shapes of falling snowflakes. It is solidly rooted in what he called Black Classical American tradition, and yet it is always attractively new.

Consider the evening, years ago, when his quartet opened a set at San Francisco's defunct Jazz Workshop with what was then a fresh, bossa-nova-flavored ballad called "The Shadow of Your Smile."

Soloing, Rahsaan descended from the stand and ambled through the audience, pausing at tables to permit one patron after another, just for the fun of it, to press a key on his tenor saxophone while he continued to blow. Working his way back toward the bar situated near the club's entrance, he lingered to slap hands with some latecomer and then—to the slow turning of heads—disappeared out the door. It didn't take long for most of us to realize that Rahsaan, with all of those exotic-looking instruments slung round his neck, had stepped out to stroll along Broadway, the avenue outside.

The rhythm section continued to cook and smoulder, taking, by turns, some memorable solos before Rahsaan re-entered the Workshop, still playing beautifully and trailed by a queue of strung-out listeners picked up during his brief Pied Piper excursion. Head bobbing, horn cocked at the jauntiest of angles, he meandered right back up to the bandstand, never missing a beat, and topped things off with an unforgettable finale sounded simultaneously on manzello, strich and tenor sax.

The crowd went berserk.

Light My Fire

The Doors, 1967
José Feliciano, 1968

THEY WERE LIGHTING FIRES like nobody's business then, and it wasn't all exactly what insurance investigators used to call Jewish Lightning. Early in the decade author James Baldwin, a resident of France, struck it big in America with a book that matched all his previous collections of essays for sheer intensity. Seemingly prophetic in the Biblical sense, Baldwin's perceptive volume, *The Fire Next Time,* hit home in its thoughtful and articulate assessment and indictment of American society at that urgent hour. Not long afterwards, television bombarded us with images of Watts on fire, Detroit on fire, Asian children being napalmed to a crisp in vivid, color footage that had nothing to do with the fancy footwork of James Brown and the Fabulous Flames.

And what a time that was! I used to get up mornings and pack, along with lunch, a very moist washcloth that I was careful to bag in plastic. I was enrolled at U.C. Berkeley where class attendance was increasingly becoming the last concern of students and profes-

46

sors. I should've been packing a hard hat as well, or, in any case, a helmet, but I seem to have been harried by other, more pressing concerns. You needed all this, that juicy rag and head protection. It was an everyday occurrence to be strolling across campus, not bothering anybody, passing through one of those jerry-rigged, scaffolded construction passages when, all of a sudden, I might look up and see as many as a hundred people bolting toward me with policemen, sheriff's deputies or the National Guard in wicked pursuit, and— pshht!—I'd hear the pop of a tear gas cannister. This usually meant that there was just time enough to reach down into my brown-bag lunch and retrieve that dripping washcloth, press it to my eyes, my nose, my mouth, then turn tail and haul ass all the way back to where I'd just come from.

It was Third World Strike, it was People's Park, it was Free So-and-So, it was Vietnam blazing in the foreground, and it was one hell of a time to be going back to school! Dante assigned no circle in his Inferno to hypocrite revolutionaries, but I have no doubt that he would've done so had he run into some of the power-starved tricksters and buzzards who posed as radicals during that sadly trivialized epoch. It hurt, for example, to see so many minority-labeled freshmen flunk out under the dubious and thoughtless leadership of graduate students who organized the so-called Third World Strike at Cal. Most of these new undergraduates were on very special scholarships at this overwhelmingly white state university. What would you do if you picked up the phone one night to hear someone say: "Never mind who this is. This is a warning. You go to class tomorrow and it's all over for your ass! Got that?" And as if that weren't cruelty enough, there were nights I'd run into some of those mastermind rascals in the campus library where they would be diligently cramming and preparing for their own exams, papers or theses.

One particularly eager and bloodthirsty self-styled campus militant let me know in no uncertain terms where aspiring artists such as myself stood in his particular political cult's scheme of justice: "Well, Al Young," he said. "You go on and keep writing your novels and poems and stories and shit. But after the revolution comes down, we intend to deal severely with niggers like you."

Who, I kept asking myself, was the Enemy? It wasn't until I had an important talk with Luis Monguió, an endearing Professor of Spanish and Latin American Literature at the University, and quite a compassionate man with a wry sense of humor, that I was made to understand where writers, artists and intellectuals stood with regard to belligerent politics and abrupt social change. Sr. Monguió, a Spaniard who had fought on the side that met with defeat in his troubled country's Civil War, explained how he had jettisoned a law career and come to America, where he took up literature. I had come to his office to discuss some translations I'd done of work by Nicolás Guillén, the great Cuban poet. After making some important and (to me) embarrassing minor corrections, Monguió encouraged me to continue translating and, more importantly, writing. Then he happened to glance out his office window at the campus scene below where scruffy students were preparing to do battle with the Blue Meanies, as those tear gas- and mace-wielding Alameda County Sheriff's Deputies were called because of the color of their uniforms. From my chair I too could see both sides psyching themselves up for what had become a daily scenario, complete with television news cameras to get it all down for posterity and the Six O'Clock News zombies.

"The Spanish Civil War," Monguió said, "taught me that, when it comes to bloody coups and revolts, artists and writers always have a choice. They can either choose to be lined up and shot by their enemies or by their friends. That's the way it always is. What you are doing and the degree you are working for will ultimately prove to be more important than all of this rhetoric about radicalism, revolution and the ghetto. And let us not forget to call these so-called ghettoes by their true name. You know as well as I do that they are slums. Slums! Those poor people, your people—they need what you have to offer."

Ever since Jack Kennedy got bumped in Dallas, the heat's been moving in. Now you can feel it coming from every direction in this corporate republic. People mean nothing; profits, everything. Even the time-honored precept of benign self-interest, like the proverbial baby with the bathwater, has been thrown out. The curtains have all but been drawn on an American era that once offered hope and promise to millions, to all but the miscolored anyway.

Back in those very sizzling sixties, the sensational interplanetary musician Sun Ra was saying: "The Man used to just be at a few people's door; now he's at everybody's door." Masses of middle-class Americans either don't know this yet, or don't care. Since the debacle and embarrassment of the Vietnam War, the country has been hiding its head in sands that continue to shift and blow out to uncertain seas ruled—crest, wave and bottom line—by unimaginably powerful, multinational pirates who salute no flag and answer to no electorate except their own Boards of Directors, whose members, as I once pointed out in a long poem, "do not operate under the influence of music." Like the erect male member in the popular saying, they have no conscience either.

Jim Morrison, singing leader of The Doors, was known as much for exposing himself on stage as for the music his group performed and the poetry he wrote. "Light My Fire." I can hear it now: the vaguely baroque-sounding intro on organ, the pounding drums, the banshee-squeal of electronic guitar, the steamy, bumptiously erected anapestic climax. Unngh!—there was, indeed, no time to hesitate or wallow in the mire. In those days, when everything had to happen now and all at once, and you weren't allowed to hold more than one opinion at a time. Later, José Feliciano—a blind, Puerto Rican-born marvel—covered that same hit with a mellow, leisurely version of his own, one that didn't so much burn as warm. The Doors were finally slammed shut. Feliciano, now sadly neglected, seems to have gotten locked into hard times, but he still jangles his musical keys.

Fire, of course, has always served as an incandescent metaphor for passion in poetry and song. That its image triumphed as the title of one of the hottest pop records in the declining years of the American Century seems to indicate something. I think it might have something to do with just how explosive and destructive the Empire has become.

I Did It My Way

Frank Sinatra, 1975

WHEN THE STOUT CHAPEL organist sang this Paul Anka song over the public address system at my stepbrother Walter's funeral in Detroit, my beautiful Aunt Mae, whom I've loved since I was three, leaned over with tears in her eyes and whispered, "Well, they got that part right about Walter Junior, didn't they? The child really did do it his way."

Walter Simmons, Jr. was fair-skinned, butterscotch-colored, what people of color used to call light-complected. He had woolly brown hair and light brown eyes, and he was also light-hearted, big-hearted and thin-skinned. Juju, as he'd been nicknamed from childhood by his slightly older sister Aveda, was so naturally generous that he would give you the hair off his head. All you had to do was ask. His father, my stepfather, died in his middle fifties when Juju was just entering his teens. My stepsister Aveda—whom I feel funny calling my stepsister since we were raised to accept one another full-bloodedly—had a knack for renaming people. She was the one who came up with Mr. Toasty as an affectionate tag for Walter Simmons, Sr. Mr. Toasty had very little formal schooling, but he was a superbly talented and enterprising gambler and businessman who had holdings in a restaurant known as The Green Hornet, several hotels, a fleet of delivery trucks and a couple of racehorses, all of which he managed masterfully. Anyway, my sister's nicknames took. They took the way Lester Young's handles for his musician friends endured, for it was Lester—the President of the Tenor Saxophone, Prez—who put the monicker of Sweets on trumpeter Harry Edison, affixed the titular Sir to pianist Charles Thompson's name, and who personally pinned, like a flower, the fragrant sobriquet of Lady Day on Billie Holiday.

Walter Junior, Juju, by any other name you called him, was brilliant. I tend to remember him most as a kid because by the time he'd turned seven I was packing all the books and records in my attic room to leave for college. The kid was able to recall anything that he'd seen, heard or read in distinct detail. He was blessed with the kind of photographic memory that I intuitively attributed to a character named Shakes in my first novel, *Snakes*. Even after he became addicted to heroin, Juju maintained a high grade average as a business major at Wayne State University before he dropped out. He took an accounting job in a bank. Goodly sums of cash began to disappear and even though the bank was never able to determine exactly how money was being siphoned from its computer-controlled supply, my mother and others put two and two together. Juju was fired.

The house began to be burglarized. My mother didn't care to press charges. Long, distressing phone conversations between California and Michigan darken my memories of those intervening years. Finally, Juju was banned from the house. He drifted into a hand-to-mouth—or ought I say hand-to-vein—existence. Like all of his addict friends, if you could call them friends, he lived only to get high. Aveda, whom he loved and in whom he confided to the end, told me that there were times when he would find himself resurrected from a near overdose and say, "Sis, I almost got away from here that time! Oh well, maybe next time."

What must be mentioned is that Detroit was probably the key

heroin capital of the continental United States in those days. The stuff was everywhere: in the streets, in the schools, on the playground, in the auto plants, in the suburbs, at universities—everywhere! The one-time head of Detroit's Narcotics Squad allegedly resigned from the Police Department to work for the other side. He then went on to become one of the richest dope dealers in the Middle West. In a sense, I suppose you could say that Juju was simply following out the normal peer patterns of his times.

But what was wrong? Years later I'm still trying to piece it all together, and it remains too painful a subject to range over at length. During rare visits home I would try to talk to Juju, but he would either be too stoned or cleverly evasive. He was proud of his oldest brother who was writing books, even to the point of introducing me to some of his pals who had all read *Snakes* and loved the way it seemed to speak directly to them and their immediate, everyday problems. There's a character in the book named Champ who gets strung out on skag, but who is careful to warn his younger buddies not to follow along in his dumb footsteps. "You really got the whole thing down, man," one of them told me. "We passed that book around until the pages got raggedy and started falling out!" But these young men seemed helpless to help themselves.

Juju gradually enlisted in a methadone maintenance program. I've always had mixed feelings about this alternative since it seems to prolong and foster a dependence on drugs. Heroin itself was developed as a cure for opium and morphine addiction, which was practically epidemic in America in the early 1900s, the heyday of patent medicines and elixirs. So here we were, doomed again. Besides, Henry Ford had long ago dismissed history as "bunk." Methadone went on the black market. To hear Juju and Aveda tell it, even the social workers who were supposed to be administrating these so-called maintenance programs, even *they* were sampling their own cure and nodding out over desks right there on the job.

Just when Juju seemed to be making some delicate semblance of progress, he got it into his head somewhere in 1974 to take an unloaded pistol into a Big Boy burger joint and pull a stickup. Within minutes, squadrons of Detroit's Finest were on their way to haul him off. A first-time offender, he got six months to a year at Jackson

State Penitentiary. To no one's surprise, he was a model prisoner and was paroled after serving six months. Out on good behavior, he fell back into his old habits, violated parole and in no time at all was back in the slam. Like Jimmy Reed sings in one of his jump blues, Juju told Mother, "You better take out some insurance on me." She never did.

He was found dead in his cell one morning during a routine wake-up call. From what I've been able to piece together, Juju must have been surreptitiously injecting himself in the joint. Aveda remembers the last visit he'd paid to her, shortly before he was locked up again, when he was rheumy of eye and jaundiced-looking. The autopsy report cited serum hepatitis as the cause of death. Again, I can only speculate, but it seems reasonable to presume that Juju, probably knowing that he was infected, possibly through the use of unclean needles, deliberately avoided revealing his condition to prison health authorities. And the question circles my mind again and again: How badly did he truly want to slip out of this vulnerable cocoon of flesh?

At the funeral service, I spoke briefly about how Walter Junior had never felt loved. What I couldn't say and can only halfway say now is that something happened to Juju after his father died. He felt betrayed and, in many ways, blamed the world, for which he saw no hope, certainly not for Black people; and he blamed our mother. The year before, I had flown home to help bury my father, a victim of cancer, and now I was back to bury my brother, barely 25, a victim of another kind of unbenign growth, and of his own persistent and self-destructive brilliance. For him the body must have seemed like a painful and troublesome encumbrance, like bandaging, like a shroud, like a burden the mind thinks it no longer needs in its clumsy, insatiable hunger for nothing less than total, ineffable bliss.

Goodbye Porkpie Hat

Charles Mingus, 1959
Jeff Beck, 1975
Joni Mitchell, 1979

YES, THAT WAS SADNESS you saw shining out of Lester's lidded eyes upturned beneath that porkpie hat; but what manner of sadness?

Was it the sadness of New Orleans trumpet legend King Oliver in his December years where we find him selling fruit and vegetables from a roadside truck for a living? Could it be anything like the bittersweet sadness of the overlooked bop arranger and pianist Tadd Dameron dialing "B for Beauty" on an old French telephone at Fontainbleu, who early abandoned a medical career because he thought the world was sorely in need of beauty? And what about the sumptuous sadness of Coleman Hawkins, inventor of jazz saxophone, and colorist and shaper of horn poems?

No, the sadness you heard was Lester's alone. Charles Mingus captured it in "Goodbye Porkpie Hat," Jeff Beck picked up on it, and Joni Mitchell recites and recounts it as best she can in mere words. But Lester, of course, is himself the source: a musical force that gave the world so much loving sound that it still hurts to play his final recordings or to remember how pitifully wasted he was during those declining Jazz At The Philharmonic concert years when much of his exuberance and genius had fled him, when everything that he had to say on his horn sounded like variations on sighs of resignation. Whatever became of all that wondrous discourse that used to pour and trickle and skeet out of him like light from some heavenly reservoir? New Orleans? Kansas City? New York? The world? Like youthful fame and stamina, the past must have seemed a dream to him as he willfully let himself go.

Prez, the President, who never campaigned for any office, was resigned by then as only genius can be resigned. Weary of telling his story this way and that, night after night, flight upon flight; climbing, descending, he was ready to step aside and do his brooding in private.

His eyes were sad with gin and what it drowns. We fish who swam his ocean keep him young. I used to lie and say he was a distant cousin, but it was true.

If I Had Wings Like Noah's Dove

Al Young *Live,* 1964

IT WAS MY GRANDMOTHER—Mrs. Lillian Campbell of Pachuta, Mississippi—who passed down to me the first folk songs I ever learned, and they were mostly old Negro spirituals along the order of "Steal Away," "Meetin' at the Buildin'," "Didn't My Lord Deliver Daniel," and "Pharoah's Army." There seemed to be hundreds of them that she would half-sing and half-hum in the classic fashion that musicologists have learned to call "moaning." Morning, noon and nighttime, from dawn to dark, one song would turn into another or back into itself as Mama drew water from the well, washed, milked, cooked, swept, scrubbed, gardened, quilted, sewed, doctored, scolded and wrung the necks of chickens. Often I would study her at the kitchen woodstove, getting up a big iron pot of something for early-afternoon dinner and moaning to herself while she smiled out the window at fig trees or at a particular red bird. Music was merely one of her ways of getting through days.

We didn't have electricity, running water, gas or a car; nor did we have any idea that what we sang or listened to was American folk music.

At the age of seven, I made up my own folk song in the manner of Hank Williams, who was knocking everybody down out there by then with his "Hey, Goodlookin'," and "Move It Over." Mama would crack up when I sat out in the porch swing with my little cigar box guitar and whined:

O Hopalong Cass'dy
You treated me nasty
when I was in Texas, Tennessee. . . .

I wanted to grow up and be a cowboy. Like all the other boys my age, I wanted to go galloping across plains giving crooks the upper-cut, the same as Tex Ritter, Gene Autry, Roy Rogers and all the others; hammering out a tune by the campfire nights; and just generally being It. It was Mama who put the facts to me one rainy afternoon when Cousin Jesse and I were lollygagging around the woodpile by the fireplace, polishing up our cap pistols, tickled that it was too wet to be out in the field picking cotton.

"Boys, y'all ever heard tell of a colored cowboy? You ever seen one at the picture show or in a funnybook?"

Of course, we hadn't. There was nothing out on the Negro cowboys at that time, although I was later to learn how many of them there had actually been. That was one dream I had to gradually let go.

But I hung onto the music as it went charging through my blood in the form of gospel, folk song, blues, country & western, rhythm & blues, pop, bebop, cool, modern, classical, international—and then came the first fun chord I learned to strum on a real guitar. Suddenly I was back into folk.

By then, I'd become a freshman at the University of Michigan, Ann Arbor, and the Cold War was massacring hearts and minds. A few days after I moved into South Quad, the resident House

Mother had me to lunch, along with the roommate they'd placed me with. His name was Bill McAdoo, and he was older; a working-class political firebrand from Detroit. Bill's mother was Jewish and his father Black. At one point during our simple repast of mash potatoes, shiny gravy, tinned peas and something called City Chicken, our blue-haired Dorm Mother squinted across the table. "I'll have you boys know," she glowered and announced, "that we believe in taking regular showers and baths around here."

At the end of that first semester, I flew the coop. I moved out of all dormitories into the world at large where the living was never easy, but where at least there was room to breathe. Not having been raised white, Republican or middle class, I had no recourse but to go my own way, and I've been going my own way ever since. If you were different in those days, you were automatically slap-sticker-labeled Communist, or Red or Pinko at worst, and beatnik at best. I was never even either. I'd done a lot and read a lot—or so I thought—but, leery of schools, I was starving for lasting knowl-edge, spiritual growth and stimulating friendship. Classes weren't enough somehow. Fraternities seemed both fatuous and stifling. And all the beautiful girls of the colored aristocracy were busy plan-ning their coming-out parties or sensibly stalking their own kind—boys from good backgrounds with good hair and lucrative futures. Not much had changed since earlier days at Hutchins Intermediate in Detroit when I sat backstage with Mary Jean Tomlin, later to be-come Lily, at some school show in which we were both performing, speculating about what became of talented kids who didn't come from privileged families.

In college I gravitated toward activities germane to my natural in-terests, and toward people who, like myself, remained open to ex-perience. So it wasn't surprising to find myself taking up with budding writers, poets, playwrights, dreamers, journalists, intellec-tual mavericks, politicos, painters, sculptors, photographers, actors, hipsters, renegades, math visionaries, townies, composers, all man-ner of self-invented misfits, including, of course, musicians.

Music soothed. Music helped. Music helped soothe the loneli-ness and my sense of uncertainty, just as it eased the sting and nag-ging strain of color prejudice, social awkwardness, McCarthy Era paranoia and the all-around savagery of blooming adolescence it-self—a beastly climbing rosebush with thorns no more imaginary than the wounds they open. Red with passion and hopelessly ro-mantic, it eventually took a witty professor of Spanish to thought-fully point out that the writers who were *románticos* by and large lived very short lives (1803–1836), whereas the classicists tended to have gravestones that read 1795–1889. As it had done for my grandmother, music still got me through days.

Occasionally I would sit up all night by myself, grave, deter-mined not to turn in before I had mastered some difficult Leadbelly lick or learned the changes to something Sonny Terry and Brownie McGhee had recorded. I was learning stuff from everybody: Blind Willie Johnson, Snooks Eaglin, Reverend Gary Davis, chain-gang prisoners taped by Alan Lomax at Mississippi State Penitentiary (Parchman Farm), Odetta, Blind Blake, Woody Guthrie, Missis-sippi John Hurt, Lonnie Johnson, Elizabeth Cotten, John Lee Hooker, Robert Johnson, Bascom Lunsford, Jean Ritchie, Pete Seeger, The Weavers, Josh White, Big Bill Broonzy, Muddy Waters, Howlin' Wolf, Bo Diddley, Harry Belafonte, Len Chandler, Cynthia Gooding, Jesse Fuller, Theodore Bikel, Sister Rosetta Tharpe, The Staple Singers, Lightin' Hopkins, Charles Mingus, Ray Charles, and from sources all around me.

All of it was "ethnic" as far as I was concerned. I mean, I took the late Billy Broonzy's word for it when he made that remark of his that went: "Anything a man can play is folk music; you don't hear no dogs or cats or horses singing it, do you?" At the time I wasn't aware that Louis Armstrong had said something similar long before that. I was hung up for a spell on quite a few backwoodsmen and citybillies, to say nothing of all those meditative foreigners with their thumb pianos, bouzoukis, balalaikas and sitars.

As I came upon other amateurs given to similar habits, we would work out songs, tunes and pieces and get together regularly to swap material and techniques as well as show off our fragile accomplish-ments. These get-togethers, when they weren't strictly for fun, were called hoots, and hoots were serious and very big at college.

If a hootenanny was jubilant enough, you were apt to hear English majors doing field hollers; pre-meds having a go at lumberjack songs; students of library science singing about robbing banks and hopping freight trains; business administration people getting all wrapped up in "Hallelujah, I'm a Bum"; eighth-generation Yanks armed with banjos, fiddles and mandolins, sounding more like Confederates than Flatt & Scruggs and the Foggy Mountain Boys; future ballistics missile experts working up a sweat on "Ain't Gonna Study War No More"; kids reared in traffic jams reminiscing about "The Old Cotton Fields Back Home."

There were doctrinaire folkniks who took themselves and their image quite seriously. I can see now how, in many ways, they helped usher in the great costume phenomenon that would overtake the Western World by the time the sixties ended. Personally, I had grown weary of workshirts, neckerchiefs, buckskin coats, clunky boots, railroad caps, peasant dresses and blouses, cowboy hats, Levi suits, leather vests, Paul Bunyan shirts and thrift shop resurrections long before that overly studied mode of dress gave way to Jesus gowns, capes, plumage, Shakespearian garb, Salvation Army bandleader coats, paratrooper gear, dashikis, Cossack uniforms, Mao jackets, coolie togs, aviator helmetry, sharecropper bibs and sundry Me-Tarzan-You-Jane getups.

At length, I came to perform; sometimes around town as a single and other times with well-rehearsed string combos such as those formed variously with the likes of Marc Silber, Perry Lederman, Bernie Krause, Joe Dassin and Felix Pappalardi. Marc became a guitar maker and opened—first in New York and then in Berkeley—a shop called Fretted Instruments. Perry hooked up with Indian sarodist Ali Akhbar Khan and became immersed in ragas and a personal mysticism. Bernie went on to replace Eric Darling in the Weavers and later teamed with fellow synthesist Fred Beaver from Beaver and Krause, a pioneering fusion repertory unit. Joe Dassin, son of film director Jules Dassin, returned to France, where he became a pop music idol before suffering a fatal heart attack in Tahiti in 1980. As for Felix Pappalardi, the only bona fide conservatory trainee among us—who was equally at home on guitar, bass, fiddle and trumpet—he launched the rock band Cream, became an international success, and remained highly visible and respected as a player, arranger and producer on the New York music scene.

Show business was something I could never hack, not on any sustained basis. It got to the point where it felt too much like jail. It also didn't seem to matter where I worked—the Midwest, the East, the West Coast. I took care of business on the gig; I always delivered. The money, especially at college, paid for rent, food, clothing, free time, and also kept my digs overrun with staples such as books, records, tapes and beer. But then I would catch glimpses of myself, a captive on the stand or on stage all those professional nights when I would've been happier writing or reading or—rather than merely singing about it—actually out walking with my baby down by the San Francisco Bay.

Perhaps I did become, after all, that singing cowboy my grandmother lovingly discouraged. Then again, for all I know, I might very well still be in show biz. But I've changed my axe and I've changed my act, and the changes never seem to stop coming.

One Hundred Years from Today

Sarah Vaughan, 1950

BROUGHT UP on Sarah and on every other form of music that was available to me—just as surely as I was raised on grits, greens and beans—I can never forget the impact that this hushed, workaday ballad had on our rambling household. There was always something musical going on, and the wonder was that we didn't drive the neighbors crazy.

I started picking out tunes, rather accurately, on other people's pianos. I must have been halfway through my first decade. Perceiving this talent, my mother had an old upright hauled into our sparse digs in the projects on Beaubien Street in Detroit. That's when my brother Franchot, whom we now call Frank, got interested in piano and took the thing over. He was remarkable. He was so good, in fact, that my mother enrolled him for lessons with Dean Robert Nolan, a local conservatory-trained teacher who, in almost no time, it seems, had Frank tossing off vibrant renditions of Debussy's "Clair de Lune," Beethoven's "Moonlight Sonata," Bach's

"Gavotte" and Rimsky-Korsakov's "Flight of the Bumblebee." Frank was a prodigy who went on television, won himself a four-year scholarship to the University of Michigan's School of Music, performed with prestigious symphony orchestras, and toured the world a couple of times. At length, he was invited by President and Mrs. Johnson to perform at the White House, an honor that he and the family still cherish. Frank, however, was shy, practically reclusive, and intensely sensitive, so that the strain and vicissitudes of pursuing a concertizing career weighed heavily on him. Following a long-term stint as a professor of music at Talladega College in Alabama, he has devoted himself entirely to freelance teaching and composing.

Franchot Young's formidable command of piano was intimidating, to say the least. My younger sister Michele and I used to sneak upstairs to the attic when Frank wasn't around and practice our little homemade stuff that was unrespectable by classical standards. Michele was taking up the violin rather halfheartedly and I was doling out precious paper route money to take trumpet lessons at the Teal Studios downtown while holding down the first tuba chair in the school band and sacrificing my Saturday mornings to rehearse with the grandiose All-City Orchestra.

My mother was a Sarah Vaughan fan in the worst way. She loved to sing and her not so secret ambition was to sing just like Sarah; so much so that she learned by heart every song, every tone, every nuance of everything Sarah recorded that came within grazing range of her ear. And she didn't just mouth the sound of those tunes; she absorbed them the way the digestive system assimilates food. Whenever Sassy or the Divine Miss Vaughan—as Sarah was variously billed—hit town, Mother would be there in a front row seat, and often she took me along with her. In fact, as a consequence of her pursuit of Sarah, I was exposed at an early age to such incomparable musical legends as Nat King Cole, Billy Eckstine, Duke Ellington (whose featured saxophone soloist Johnny Hodges once invited Mom to accompany him to Paris), Jimmy Rushing, Count Basie, Dizzy Gillespie, Charlie Parker, George Shearing, Roy Haynes, Lester Young, Stan Getz, Stan Kenton, The Five Step Brothers and untold others who came rolling through the Motor

City in packaged shows that played, inevitably it seems, to packed and rip-roaring crowds. Detroit was one working-class town that loved its music, and we were Detroiters then too, weren't we?—crazy Detroiters perhaps but Detroiters all the same.

When Sarah came out with "Perdido," the Juan Tizol tune that was long a staple in the associated Ellington book, the lyric had a line about someone losing their heart at a fiesta in Toledo, referring of course to the town in Spain. My mother and I figured Sarah was talking about nearby Toledo, Ohio. What's more, Sarah did little to dispel that misinterpretation when she performed in that area of the Midwest. I'm reminded of the Ray Charles rendering of "Making Whoopee," recorded live in California, where Ray pauses ever so slightly at the word "funny," as in "some judge who thinks he's *funny*," to elicit shrieks of delight from what I imagine to be the bi-sexual element in the crowd. Great performers always take command of their material, put their own unmistakable stamp on it and then deliver it in such a way as to make each individual in the audience feel like a creative collaborator.

And could Sarah Vaughan ever do that! She did it so beautifully and so movingly that I've never forgotten the tears in my mother's eyes the first time she listened to Sarah do "Street of Dreams."

She looked up at me, clutching a Kleenex, and said, "You know, she's right. 'Kings don't mean a thing.' Now, that's poetry, pure poetry—whatever poetry is or is supposed to be about. That's the genuine article."

Consider my mother: lovely and eccentric, a product of the Deep American South, seated by the household piano, the home tape recorder rolling, signaling either Frank, Michele or me to provide a little back-up while she tries out her singing voice; longing to touch upon that magic something that'll carry her out of this nasty, sassy world to the portals of the divine, to a billowy, barely tangible realm of the soul where kings don't mean a thing.

"Now, just listen at that, will you," I can still hear her saying as she settles back on the sofa or into a hard kitchen chair, wherever the music happened to be stationed. "It's true, you know. What difference is any of this going to make one hundred years from today?"

Set Two

Java Jive

The Ink Spots, 1943

FOR SEVERAL MORNINGS at the age of three, I stood quietly by the living-room window in our little one-story house in Ocean Springs and studied the way a spider trapped a fly in his web and carefully devoured her. Why I thought the fly was a she and the spider a he would be tough to explain, but that was the way it played in my literal head of dream pictures whose images, now that I think about it, were clearly made up of tiny quivering dots the way magazine or newspaper photos look when you subject them to intensive magnification.

Words didn't come easily for what I was seeing, yet somehow I knew deep beneath or beyond what little mind I must've had by then that I was glimpsing a mystery of some kind; some important, worldly essence was being vividly played out before my unblinking eyes.

Then, finally, it all fell into place. The sun—like a hot, luminous magnet—happened to be shining powerfully that antique afternoon. My father was busy being his auto mechanic self and I could see him through the dusty window screen out there in the grass and dirt and clay of the sideyard driveway, fixing on our dark blue Chevy coupe, grease all over his face and forearms: black on black. Pious as a minister or metaphysician, he was bent on fixing that car.

My mother was in the next room, the kitchen, fixing red beans and rice. My very intestines were tingling with gladness, for red beans and rice, as far as I was concerned, had no parallel; there simply wasn't anything like it anywhere in the world, whatever the world was. To dine every day on red beans and rice—or to breakfast, lunch or snack on them—would've suited me just fine. Lifetimes from my spider-and-fly-moment, just before nightfall, I knew we children would be gobbling our portions of dinner—complete with chopped onions and oleo-margarined slices of white Bond bread—on the linoleum down under the kitchen table with newspaper for placemats. And I'd be spoiling to tell everybody about the spider and how he'd stuck it to the fly with his web, even though it was going to be years—and I seem to have glimpsed this too—before I'd be able to make heads or tails of any of it, in words anyway.

From the big Zenith radio console, its wood case shining with furniture oil, probably lemon, the Ink Spots were singing "Java Jive." Except for "I like coffee/I like tea," the words made no sense to me, but I liked the way the tune kept winding around and around to make its point, and I loved the way they came out of it all with: "A cup/a cup/a cup/a cup/a cup, ahhhhhhh!" That sigh at the tag meant everything, said it all: it signalled my Aunt Ethel, the big coffee addict in the family who, even then, always came to mind with her lips cradling the edge of some hot cup, breathing and exhaling steam and steaminess, big fogs of warmth in which sugar and sweetmilk or Pet Milk played some part. Watching her I could not fail to get the idea that something glad was going on between Aunt Ethel and that coffee of hers. If you or anyone else had taken time out to explain that the coffee bean and its narcotizing effect on people everywhere was an industry that involved colored peoples doing the picking all over the world, I wouldn't have connected with what you were saying anymore than I would've understood the meaning of the Man in the Moon, but I might've had a notion. Around the same time, you see, the Andrews Sisters were drawing checks off something called "They've Got an Awful Lot of Coffee in Brazil."

Being three, you see, isn't that much different from being a hundred and three, particularly when you begin to understand it's all a matter of putting two and two together.

July seeped into the room, quiescent with harmony and heat, the beat; the beating of the fly's wings as the spider ingested her from head to toe; boodie and sole. I stood there. I stood still. Time stood still and the whole of Mississippi, maybe the whole world, stood there soaking up this three-year-old's vision of how the world really works whether you realize it or not. It was as if, for me at least at that moment, my father had pried open the engine of life itself and motioned me over to have a look at how it worked and then, without so much as a 7th grade shop class explanation, snapped the lid back on, leaving me with the idea that there was something, some mechanism or cause that lay behind any and everything I could ever experience in this ever-shifting, not-to-be-believed existence that mystics—when you boil what they say down to a simmering, low gravy—say is only a movie, the acting out of something vaster than ourselves; the cosmic drama, if you will.

I wanted to taste this java, sample this coffee, this tea they were rhythmizing so invitingly. Feeling my insides beginning to gladden, I rushed out into the yard to hear my father say, "Hey, Skippy! C'mere, boy, and gimme some sugar!"—meaning: *Let me kiss you smack on the jaw.* I liked that. I liked it so much, I got confused. I wanted to race over and blurt out to him everything I'd just figured out about the spider and the world and the mystery and the tingling I felt inside, even though I didn't feel ready yet to pull the words together. There were no words, really; there was only this soundless understanding puffing up with feeling like a rainbow-colored balloon filling up all too fast with smooth summer air.

Just then, just as I was about to make my move toward Daddy, I saw a bright aquaplane zoom in close overhead, low enough for me to see the pilot, a white man, making me think at once of a crisp, airborne Nabisco saltine. He was wearing one of those old-time aviator helmets with earflaps and goggles. He waved at me. He waved and smiled and now, millions of mind-hours later, I can draw a wayward cloud of a comic strip balloon over his head that shows him thinking: "Long as I'm up here foolin around, lemme just wave at that lil ole colored boy on the ground down there and give him a thrill!"

This bubbling moment and all that led up to it—like the family's first tentative move to Detroit and the unbelievable coldness of ice and snow and the tight light of what my folks kept calling "movin up north to the city"—is etched into me like the lines of some play; a kind of play that's had to settle for being sliced up over the years into what I eventually learned to call poetry or prose.

We lived close enough to the Gulf of Mexico for low-flying aquaplanes to be a commonplace, but that had been the very first time I'd ever seen a pilot up close. It was entirely different from those black-out nights when coastal air raid alerts were up, When Ella Mae Morse would be on the Zenith singing "The House of Blue Lights" and there we'd be, me and my brothers sprawled on the floor or blanketed down in bed, listening and remembering, with those blue emergency lightbulbs screwed into the lamp and ceiling sockets, their cooling glow softening the edge that was forever cutting a line between the seeable and the hearable worlds.

I rushed into my father's arms, gave him that sugar, wondering why we called those people crackers and why kids weren't supposed to fool with coffee.

As for the spider and the fly and my insights into the mystery of that spectacle, all I can say is that the craziness of my excitement has thickened over the years. Now I'm given to believing that the web is only the world, the spider desire, and the fly the fickle, innocent and positively neutral nature of existence. Beyond that stands some youthful presence, more consciousness than thing, taking it all in with astonishment and, as a matter of fact, aiding and abetting and allowing it all to happen as if—like the web—it was either staged or created by design.

G̶reen Onions

Booker T. & the MG's, 1962

"**D**RESS THE PART," American humorist and realist George Ade used to say, "and the role plays itself." The dress was laboratory garb, which mostly meant a clean, crisply starched white lab coat. Whether you chose to wear a dress shirt or tie beneath it was strictly a personal matter, but everybody on the job, intentionally or not, eventually developed some kind of relationship with this uniform.

As for me, I was a lab aide, one of two at the Laboratory for Comparative Biology out in Richmond, California. Our job was to wash chemical glassware and other apparatus such as test tubes, beakers, flasks, pipettes, crucibles, weighing bottles and so forth. We were also responsible for the sterilization of certain articles and solutions, and this usually involved subjecting them to high temperatures in the autoclave. Washing was done in an acid bath solution and for this you wore heavy rubber gloves and a hooded mask. That acid solution was something else; the fumes alone slowly ate away your clothing and you had to be extra careful about rinsing all traces of it from your skin. I used to have nightmares about the stuff.

Lab aides were flunkies: the maintenance crew of the scientific world. You were the one they pulled over to assist in the preparation or analysis of experiments of any kind. One day you might find yourself running organic substances or samples through the centrifuge machine; another day you might be sitting at a table or bench, stringing or snapping green beans or chopping up the stems of green onions. It was a gig that was anything but dull, and I must say I never worked around so many lab-coated eccentrics as I did the year I spent at LCB, which was housed in the lab wing of Kaiser Hospital in working-class Richmond. Anything was likely to happen and usually did.

Booker T. and the MG's came out with "Green Onions" the year I started work there, and it was always playing on the jukebox either at the A&W Root Beer franchise across the street or at Gray's Club a little further down on Cutting Boulevard or at the Slick Chick, a cryptic greasy spoon, along the same strip. There was also a chili joint whose name I've forgotten where I'd go for lunch with Ethel Holmes, the older black woman who was the other full-time lab aide in this operation. We'd sit there—a Louisianan and a Mississippian—munching on our chili beans and rice, talking that drowsy lingo Southerners and ex-Southerners slip into whenever they get together, listening to Booker T. Jones, Steve Cropper and the rest of the MG's laying down that jumping, bluesy Memphis sound in the background.

"Green Onions" was on the radio, on the jukeboxes and, subliminally it seems, on everybody's mind. If you paid close attention—as I did at the time, for I was also gigging weekends in coffee houses and cabarets, singing and playing guitar—you could hear how this particular tune with its mesmerizing vamp was influencing pop music. You couldn't get away from "Green Onions," and the fact that it was an instrumental probably lengthened its life considerably. An elderly gentleman at a neighborhood house party told me, "How come it look like everything else seem to come and go, but people still crazy bout 'Green Onions'? You in the music business, so explain that to me if you can."

I couldn't explain it, but I did know it was infectious. The Gray's Club I speak of was about as elemental as they came. The sign out front was hand-lettered and semi-literate. The "S" in Gray's had been brushed on in such a way that it looked bigger than the rest of the name, and the letterer hadn't bothered painting in an apostrophe. Wes Jacobs, who was one of two black lab assistants at LCB, used to call it the Gray S Club, and that name stuck. Wes was a Buffaloan who, like me, had done time in Detroit and Ann Arbor. "Hey,' he'd say, "they're throwin another one of those Blue Monday parties over at the Gray S Club. What say we jump in there and pick up on some of those free turnip greens and cornbread and black-eyed peas and fried chicken?" And that's what we'd do after work some Mondays. They'd be advertising blues singer Jimmy McCracklin, scheduled for Friday and Saturday night, but guess what they'd be playing on the jukebox?

Whenever I'd show up anyplace in my lab coat, and expecially if I wore a tie, which I did sometimes just to bolster the old ego or give my low status a momentary, arbitrary facelift, people behind the counters would often—usually after making change—say something like, "You know, Doctor, I been feelin this funny pain right up under my ribs for bout a week now. Like, when I breathe, that's when I feel it sharpest. What you reckon I oughtta do?"

At first, I'd trip all over myself trying to explain how I really wasn't a doctor and, look, you better have that checked out because it sounds serious to me. But after awhile, I came to realize it was the look of me, and only the look of me, they were responding to. That white lab coat was what rounded out the effect. Soon I'd change my tune, and when they'd hit me with their medical problems, I'd finger the pencil in my lab coat chest pocket, look away thoughtfully, and say, "Take two aspirin, get a few good nights sleep, get some exercise, and then tell me how you feel."

And, by Godfrey, it worked!

There was a fellow we'll call Janocz who'd come to the States from Hungary after the 1956 uprising by way of Brazil. Somewhere along the line, probably some moon-drenched night on a Rio beach, he'd got it in his head he was going to be a doctor of something. By the time he'd begun becoming an American citizen, he was working with one of the top biologists at LCB. One afternoon I happened to be present when the boss—a chunky woman, thoroughly lovable, with a round, Germanic face framed by a severe, short, bowl-cut hairdo—asked Janocz to rattle off the valence of some chemical element. He, uh, he, uh, wasn't sure what she meant or, rather, what the valence should've been, uh— That's when Janocz got busted down to the level of rat keeper for the resident toxicologist, an Austrian who, because he didn't hold a degree in medicine from an American school, had to travel the backroads and byways of the profession he'd been trained for. I remember he'd spent a lot of time on Tahiti and, at some point, had actually met the English novelist Somerset Maugham, or, rather—depending on which version of the story he was dishing out of a particular morning or afternoon—he had spent some time with the real-life woman who had served as the model for the prostitute-become-religious-convert in Maugham's famous short story, "Rain." Joan Crawford portrayed her in *Rain*, the 1932 movie based on that story. Either way, the good doctor was a voracious reader and lover of literature who was enamoured of the fact that Maugham, like himself, had been trained as a physician. He too had literary ambitions and planned some day to knock out a few short stories or maybe a novel or two about his own adventures and travels. For the time being, he was the LCB toxicologist—the Rat Man, we called him—and the one Dr. Mary Bell Allen farmed you out to assist when you started messing up and your lab future was growing uncertain.

I myself grew rather fast and loose in my handling of lab protocol as the months wore on, so that one reckless mid-morning Dr. Allen, brandishing her steely, businesslike grin, asked me to submit my schedule. That was the tip-off. When she asked you to submit a schedule—which was what she'd asked of Janocz—you could be certain you were skating on thin ice, indeed. Discipline around LCB, for lower-level workers anyway, was anything but tight. With your hands pushed down into the pockets of your lab coat and wearing the proper expression of authority, you could mingle leisurely and roam at large. Such roaming, if you didn't look out, was apt to get you in trouble.

I should perhaps explain that the facilities of the Laboratory for Comparative Biology were spread around the immediate neighborhood. The main facility, for example, was where my work was headquartered, but I had occasion—sometimes dozens of times a day—to walk across the street and make use of the autoclave, or to deliver specimens to the Rat Man or to pick up equipment that needed cleaning from any of several associates who ran mini-labs on that side of Cutting Boulevard. Further down the block was a storage and warehouse building. Another lab aide named Ken—one of two so named; both of them hired after Ethel and I had gotten on—used to go with me down there on one errand or another, and sometimes we'd linger and joke around for the fun of it. Or else Wes Jacobs and I would make a run over to Cutter Labs or some other scientific firm along the Bay, on business, of course, and always with the blessings and under the unquestionable protection of our official uniforms.

It was Janocz, though, who took the cake when it came to abusing lab coat privileges. He actually had the nerve to wear his lab coat to work mornings, and he was fond of carrying a little black leather bag. Whenever Janocz got stopped for speeding by some highway patrolman, all he had to do was blush or look flustered, then point to his black bag on the car seat beside him and say, "Oh, officer, I must have gotten carried away in the face of this emergency." And the patrolman would inevitably presume him to be an M.D. of some kind and wave the little imposter on. Janocz was almost unstoppable. It took me a long time to catch on to his clever gambit of arriving late to the job, loosening his tie, then disappearing with a clipboard into one of the back rooms where he and his boss had some manner of experiment set up. That way, should Dr. Allen come looking for him, he could always emerge from his hideaway, breathless and tousled, and give her the impression that he'd been on the scene all along, taking care of business.

At the time, I was in my early twenties. Everything was serious, but not too serious. A college dropout and would-be writer, I was busiest of all with life itself and the process of getting it lived. The idea here was to hold down enough of a day job to eat and meet the rent of $75 a month and to drop into a cookie jar the earnings I picked up from music gigs on the weekends and part-time disk-jockeying at a local radio station nights.

Along the way I gathered enough mental notes to paper a book on that lab experience, which will always be punctuated with blasts from Booker T. & the MG's "Green Onions." Now I'm forced to realize that I was the one who was green at one end and sprouting at the other. And while shedding one layer after another, I was getting to know the world in ways that never paid off so much materially as they did experientially. It never occurred to me then, for instance, that there would have to be no fewer than a thousand chapters in this imagined volume devoted to that year, for the Laboratory for Comparative Biology—whose personnel came from the States, Europe, Japan, India, China, Canada, Australia and the Middle East—was nothing but a complex crew of biological space cadets. Once their ship was off the ground, they had proceeded to cajole, color, rank, play off against, condemn, investigate, experiment, consort and fall in love with one another like any other random batch of humans being human.

Sometimes, even now, years later, I like to get together with Wes Jacobs, a staunch survivor of that era, and talk about the time Dr. Allen—who used to get juiced at lab parties—did a striptease, or the time when ethanol theft grew to such proportions that she had to send down an order that its use be strictly regulated. I've never forgotten that it was chemist and former winemaker Jack Murchio who introduced me to the work of novelist George P. Elliot and the writings of Alfred Döblin, the German Expressionist novelist who wrote *Berlin Alexanderplatz*. It was also around that time that I heard Ken Fishler play piano—the other of those lab aides named Ken—long before he joined with his singing wife to form the duo known as Bobbi & I, and also before he went on the road with singer Anita O'Day.

Betcha you never played "Green Onions," Kenny. But I did. I stole and stuck it—vamp chords, that is—directly into a song arrangement. That was around the time in my life when things started falling into place, when being around systematic processes of analysis infiltrated some mindless part of me to the point where I'd get flashes now and then, usually when showering to go to work, that we were all formed of earth and spirit and had as our goal the realization that, like a rainbow of flames in a Bunsen burner, we were emanating from the same ignited pilot.

Ruby My Dear

Thelonious Monk, 1959

YOU ARE BACK AGAIN, re-entering the central train of trails: the quintessential U.S.A. of drowsy fields and sleepy fast-food chains; the U.S.A. of nipped buds and layaways negotiated in harsh, flatland cracker accents. Surrounded by them, hemmed in, you sometimes feel a little like one of those brainy slicksters over at the Federal Penitentiary in Milan, Michigan, for, like them, you're locked up and keyed down.

"Ruby My Dear" comes drifting down Lake Huron in the saline marshlands of an eternal summer. The midwestern night is steamy hot with mosquitoes, the air knotted and thick with gnats like Monk's gracefully gnarled chordal clusters; notes and spiraling nodes, encoded, glistening like Milky Way-encrusted swirls and specks of darkness.

You know what you're hearing is human yearning and rushes of the Divine calling you home to all the Africanized galaxies in this shimmering island universe.

Cold Sweat

James Brown, 1967

"**E**XCUSE ME while I do the boogaloo!"

Outrageous!

I couldn't believe it!

I sat riveted behind the wheel, realizing at last why those panty-hose packagers had the insight and audacity to name their product Sheer Energy.

Sheer energy was what James Brown was pushing; pushing and pulling and radiating in ultra-violet concentric circles of thermo-radiant funk. It was sheer energy with a whole lot of soul and blues slipped in—or, rather, *thrown* in, the way you might sell somebody a 45 rpm disk or a .45 pistol—in this case, it doesn't matter—and throw in a shiny new Peterbilt truck for good measure, for the hell of it.

I was so carried away by the blues-grounded yet floating, gritty glide of it that I pulled the car I was driving off to some side-street curb, cut the engine, cranked up the radio volume, and just sat there, steaming in the warmth of that afternoon to let myself be swayed and lilted and swooshed away by the James Brown sound.

James Brown and the Famous Flames. He had that right too: the band was on fire. I sat in the car, my limbs going limp, sweat popping out of my forehead. I rolled the windows down in time to catch a lazy, passing breeze. That's when it hit me.

Right then and there the whole arrangement was etched into my burning brain; I soaked it all up—blowzy blue lines, vine-like rhythm, the works. It happened so fast and took so completely that when I found myself out on a dance floor at a party a few nights later, all I had to do when "Cold Sweat" came on was combine what I'd absorbed with the feeling of the moment, and the movements and motions took care of themselves. The trance was complete. I and my partner, we must've been glowing out there with the lights down low.

What it was was hypnosis; hypnosis by osmosis. The hips gyrate; the nose opens. There was nothing subtle about it. I can even remember sitting there in the car, thinking: "They oughtn't be broadcasting this thing to drivers of cars. In fact, they need to slap one of those warning blurbs on the record itself that says, 'Under no circumstances is this music to be listened to while driving or operating dangerous machinery!'" And even while we were dancing, working ourselves up into a fever, I kept flashing on those festive occasions in the Caribbean where, when funk grew too thick or the body heat too scalding, all you had to do was dash outside, race down to the seashore, peel off your duds, and rush into the water to cool down.

"Cold Sweat," the first time I heard it, had me swaying so far out there in musical space I was ready to either melt into the upholstery or get out and dance all over the top of the car. And by the time James Brown and the brothers broke into their cries of "Give the drummer some!" my sticky, hot hands were already playing the dashboard as though it were a three-piece conga set.

"Funky as you wanna be!"

"Keep it right there!"

"Excuse me while I do the boogaloo!"

The Sidewinder

Lee Morgan, 1965

AFTER A HARD DAY, a work day, a bad day, a sad day or a Saturday, he'd come home, pop open two ice-cold cans of beer, empty them into a schooner-sized glass with a giant olive, sip a little of it, unbutton his shirt, kick off his shoes, and put "The Sidewinder" on the turntable.

By the time the beer was half finished the record would be almost over and he'd be feeling like himself again—private and powerful.

Sometimes he wondered about it. Was it the music or the beer that refreshed him? Or was it just being on his own turf again, that landscape inside of him surrounded by seas as vast as life itself, all of it longing to be voyaged forever?

All he could really pin down was the pegleg rhythm of it: the way the beat mixed in with the horns and the web-like piano to produce something he was so in need of hearing that he'd actually cancelled dates and excused himself from social engagements to lie on the rug in the middle of his miniscule apartment and listen to Lee Morgan on all those Blue Note albums.

To him it was amazing, the flashes of say-so, the swagger,

Morgan's sun-washed nerve, his urban innocence on ballads, the beat melting, pliant to the spirit he breathed into it. And all he really knew about the man was that Lee Morgan, like Clifford Brown, was another of those musical prodigies from the City of Brotherly Love. Along the grapevine word had traveled of his marriage to a Tokyo woman, someone he'd fallen in love with while touring Japan with Buhania, with Art Blakey's indefatigable Jazz Messengers. Morgan and his love came back to America and got married. He was happier than he'd ever been in his slender life, but his wife grew unhappy; she didn't speak much English and felt alienated. She missed her Land of the Rising Sun and soon flew out of his life to go back there.

Morgan was devastated and for well over a year wandered around New York feeling forlorn and uprooted. Then he married a Caribbean woman, someone older than himself. It didn't work out; tempers soared; there was misunderstanding, sorrow, a row—some kind of Frankie and Johnnie commotion. Then one night while he was on the stand at some club in New York, Morgan's new wife rushed in in mid-performance, stood off to the side in the crowd, pulled a revolver, took dead aim, and squeezed the trigger.

Blam!

She didn't miss.

Another jazz great was nipped in the bud; wiped out cold in the heated bloom of life.

He missed Lee Morgan but went on listening to "The Sidewinder" for years. The loping melody with its slowed-down Charleston accents kept going on in his world, relaxing him regularly by degrees. As far as he was concerned, Morgan could have titled it "The Unwinder." He loved it when jazz people got themselves a hit, and this one had to be a hit because it was moving in the stores and he heard it on the radio all the time.

After years of hosting the song in his bloodstream, he became curious about it and wanted to know what it meant. Late one afternoon, following a grueling day of work, he pulled out his *American Heritage Dictionary of the English Language* and turned to the word *sidewinder* and found that it was "(1) A small rattlesnake, *croatalus cerastes,* of the Southwestern United States and Mexico, that moves by a distinctive lateral looping motion of its body; (2) A powerful blow delivered from the side; (3) *Military.* A short-range supersonic air-to-air missile."

He was shaken. All this time he had never given the term much thought, although, somewhere along the upper reaches of his over-worded poet's mind, he'd given it the meaning of a sideways punch, or, sillier yet, he'd vaguely and privately associated it with the kind of electric emotionality that made one side of a record wind around and around. He really hadn't been ready to deal with the violent overtones of its triple meaning as they connected to Morgan's troubled lovelife and his sudden dismissal from this earth.

He stopped listening to "The Sidewinder" altogether and, for a long time, focused increasingly on the slow, flowing ballad side of his music-listening life.

Then the evening came when, easing his radio dial past an easy listening FM station—like a seasoned safecracker—he was slipped into the middle of a schmaltzy, mellow string orchestra performing "The Sidewinder." It surprised him to hear the snappy, syncopated strains of Lee Morgan's melody being played straight and literally in quasi-Muzak fashion. He couldn't believe that the piped-in elevator music community had picked up on the restful, energizing essences of Morgan's bluesy little popper.

He lay back, astonished, hands clasped behind his head, and wondered who was cashing the royalty checks.

aiden Voyage

Herbie Hancock, 1969

SHHH, LISTEN!

Can you hear it?

Listen. Listen. Shhh, it's like a soft, whispery, splashing sound. Symbolic. Cymbalic. It's a cymbal tap, the sound of wood barely touching a cymbal. The drummer's poised and ready to slip up on us. And the moment Herbie Hancock drops his fingers to the keyboard, real *pianissimo,* to sound that lovely, dark chord and four bass notes in tricky, off-accent time, we'll be off; we'll be on our way.

It's still astonishing, isn't it? What is time? I'm laying this down; you're picking it up. Everything happens at the same time. Ask any quantum physicist about the kind of dancing that goes on inside atoms, if you get my drift.

This time we'll be drifting over and across the Atlantic, sailing away from the Brooklyn Pier like an easy-going, recreational blimp in an amazing if not exactly good year. It just happens to be the very year they shot Medgar Evers in the back, the year they bombed that church in Birmingham and killed those little girls, the year the Russians put a woman in space, the year they marched 200,000 strong on Washington, D.C. and Martin Luther King and other black leaders met with the President, the year Defense Secretary Robert McNamara and South Vietnam's Ngo Dinh Diem started taking over the headlines, the year they were singing: "Aint gonna let nobody turn me round/turn me round/turn me round/Aint gonna let nobody turn me round/in Selma, Alabama!" while the governor was shouting: "Segregation forever!" It was the year they shot Kennedy down like a dog in Dallas. And when they started beating those little white kids, especially the girls, beating them with those billy clubs the way they've always done colored people, you knew the American Century was coming home to roost.

Shhh, Herbie's just mashed down on the go-forward pedal; George Coleman is sounding the ship whistle. The waves are churning all around us and if you look closely you'll see me, a little brown speck of a speck in eternity, standing on the deck of a freighter pushing off from the Brooklyn Pier. It's the 28th of August, sunny and hot. Standing on the deck, waving at the workers on a ship from India docked next to ours, I'm growing a little bit sad and joyous at the same time as I picture myself atop the timeless ocean, pondering the vastness of my animal-wrapped soul and vision, which I know I must cleanse of false learning before I can go the infinite way of Atlantics and Pacifics, Indian Oceans and Bering Seas. I stand there, watching the Statue of Liberty grow greener and tinier in the fog beginning to roll in now. "Roll with the boat," I'm remembering hearing somebody say. "Roll with the boat, don't fight it, and that way you won't get seasick."

We're rolling along right now with the beat, which isn't easy to pin down or measure, and all the ghosts outside our porthole ears seem to be carrying on in Portuguese. Timelessness, meanwhile, is enfolding and washing me clean on this maiden voyage.

Who am I?

What am I doing?

Where are we going?

All I am is daring. Absolutely. All I'm doing is drifting, but don't take that to mean I lack a sense of direction. And, now that you ask, we're headed for Lisbon in the off-season of a year surcharged with political meaning, spiritual greening and love everlastingly leaning in the only direction there is.

There's something we need to get straight before we get to trumpeter Freddie Hubbard, before we even reach the high seas. Herbie hasn't even recorded "Maiden Voyage" yet. For all we know, he's still inking and dotting the tabled version of "Watermelon Man," his jubilant blues-to-riches hit. But he's around like I'm around and I can sense the musical counterpart of what I'm going through on this Portuguese freighter, dancing in the air all around us like ocean air and spume, those half-thoughts, dreams, hunches and hints and radiant inspirations. It's the same shock of inspiration that put me suddenly out there with those picketers and hellraisers during an earlier version of the March on Washington, fully four years before the big one that made newspaper and TV history. We came close to getting stomped, remember? The time that mounted policeman was about to spur his horse into rearing up and crushing us underfoot on the Washington Memorial Monument Mall before that sidekick of his yelled: "Hey, hoss, calm down and let them kids live!" All we were doing was crowding around to wait for Harry Belafonte to come out and sing to us.

Remember too that, then as now, I was mostly thought, ideas, notions and drift. I even thought I had to grab hold of anything that went floating through my mind, either to act upon or pursue. I'm only slightly wiser than that now, but I can see quite clearly how I'd had it in my head for the longest to somehow beat my way to Europe. And magically there I was, finally doing it, equipped with nothing more than a steel-string guitar (a Gibson), a blue Navy surplus dufflebag crammed with clothing and books, and in my pockets there was something like $160 in Cook's Travelers Cheques to last for who knew how long? What in the world?—

But craziness craves company. The other passengers on that off-season freighter helped keep me sane. Listen to how Freddie Hubbard gets caught up in those surf-riding arpeggios of his on the "Maiden Voyage" he took with Herbie Hancock. The ocean'll change you; you'll go out a nut—roasted, salted and ready to be crunched in the hard-bop molars of restlessness—and, after days and nights of rocking in rhythm and smooth sailing, you'll reach another shore, land on the other side, softly throbbing, restored to your shell, ready to curl up, surrender and stalk back to the very vine that nurtured and spawned you.

Along the way, like a basket-tray of music being passed around and played, you'll find yourself changing when you realize you've gotten yourself into one of the most illuminating of situations. Without thinking, you've booked yourself on a scaled-down model of the planet itself. Suddenly the whole world's been reduced to everybody who happens to be on board. Surely that must have been what Texas-tetched storyteller Katherine Anne Porter had in mind when she spent close to twenty years writing that book she knowingly called *Ship of Fools*.

There was a chain-smoking old Portuguese-American married to someone who worked for the Portuguese Information Center in New York who used to sit on deck beside me and speak of nothing but how cheap leather and booze were in Spain. He even showed me his own painted belt. He called himself Charlie and he loved the States.

"We Americans," he once told me, "we are strong people, yes? The strongest next to West Germany—I dunno about the East. I am an American. My wife, no—she is Portuguese. 'Why be American?' she always say. I live in Bronx. You know where that is—uptown. In Portugal and in Spain you will see the *toros,* the best there is. In Spain they let you kill the bull. But not in Portugal. It's against the law. Me myself, I rather see the bull killed than the man because you can eat the bull. He make good meat, no? But not the man. You cannot eat the man, ha ha hahahahahaha!"

There was an aged woman, a columnist for the *Ladies Home Journal,* who plied me with Dramamine. "I'm one of the best-paid magazine writers in the business," she told me. At the time she was getting $500 a throw for her submissions. "They say it's read by seven million women all over the world." It seems she specialized in pieces on home and family life, short stories, anything she could come up with. "But now that my husband's dead," she went on, "and my family's grown up, I'm organizing my columns into a book, and I have to write another book on the life of my daughter who also died. It's for her children. I plan to spend the year in Lisbon." Then from out of nowhere she looked at me point-blank and said, "If you're a writer, where's your pad and pencil?"

"In my cabin," I shot back defensively.

"Then you may use my typewriter if you don't have one." And from then on during the course of that thoughtful exchange—between twitching attacks of obvious nausea—she carefully related the story of her publishing life, beginning with her college co-ed days when her father, a journalist, was something of a regional shaker and mover in midwestern Republican politics.

There was a bouncy, plump young woman who favored black— apparel, that is. She also liked to spruce her light-brown hair up with a pernicious bleached shock of blonde. She had a round, pink face and curious nostrils. When I told her Paris was my destination, she said she'd give me the name of a girlfriend who worked and lived there, who had a house.

"I met her," she explained, "when she worked for the Atomic Attaché in Washington. Did I see you bring an instrument aboard? —a guitar? Are you a folksinger? You must entertain us some night. My roommate used to date some famous folksingers. She was very interested in folk music. I happen to be going to Paris myself. Have you met the English lady aboard? She's from the British Consulate in Portugal. She's done so many things and travelled all over the world. She's gone on thirty-nine safaris with her husband in Africa. You must meet her."

It just so happened I *had* met the English woman. She spoke lovely, nasal Portuguese and reminded me of Miss Sample, a severe homeroom and Spanish teacher from Hutchins Intermediate School days in Detroit who, with her delicate features and robins-egg knit dress, went for blue-rinsing her white hair. From the way the English lady lifted her skirts whenever she was around the handsome first mate, I could tell that whatever she'd gone through with that husband of hers hadn't chilled the natural woman in her.

One afternoon following lunch, when a trio of us had climbed up to the first mate's quarters, he asked me if I knew how to play "Tequila" on guitar, that tired hit single by The Champs. I donned my fingerpicks and struck up the tune, which really wasn't much more than a Latin-accented rhythmic vamp broken up every few bars by the spirited interjection of the word *tequila!* The first mate, who had dragged the English lady up to dance in what tiny, cramped space there was, pronounced it *teh-kee-ya!* And when, in classic, uncool macho fashion, he removed his shirt to bare his sweaty, hairy chest, the lady from England, flushed with afternoon wine, giggled and cried: "I feel like taking something off too!"

Thus did we all take off, oddballs each of us, on a journey that now exists in mind alone. In no time—and largely because word got around the ship at once that I was something of an entertainer—I got to know everybody on board; everybody, that is, except the ship's captain and a pair of mousey nuns, two young missionary women who also happened to be sisters, siblings.

The captain, who looked as if he'd just stepped right off the Lipton's Tea package, never invited me to have dinner with him as he did all the other passengers. It hurt me at first, but gradually I concluded that he had funny feelings about people of color. As for the nuns, those pale-faced Americans who spent most of the trip in their cabin stricken with seasickness, they disapproved of drinking, smoking, music, dancing, bingo and liveliness in general. In short, they were down on all those activities that made the crossing so-cially workable. I had a hard time picturing how they were going to instill religion in the "savages" in the wilds of Angola to which they'd been dispatched by their dreary mission. Secretly I'd catch myself pulling for rough sailing that would keep them locked away in their quarters, protected, so to speak, from the rest of us.

I had some favorites, though, among the passengers and crew. There was a hearty gent named Slilvanho who always turned up at my table on the first call to breakfast, lunch or dinner. At every meal, the Portuguese, I found, ate like horses. I was known, in those days of skin and boniness, to put away some grub, but all that codfish *bacalao* and sautéed potatoes and vegetables and fruit and wine, lavishly drenched in olive oil, finally got to me. But Silvanho, all of sixty years of age, tall and solidly constructed, ate and ate and ate. He was the one who taught me how to peel fruit with a knife so that the skin got removed in one elegant, civilized spiral of a coil. He was a landscaper based in Massachusetts and this was his fourth crossing. Even the bald part of his head glistened tan and golden—I attributed it to liberal intakes of olive oil and garlic—in the midst of fluffy, gray locks. He told me he was married to the ex-wife of some ambassador. She had lost everything in the Second World War, so they were poor. Silvanho had children by a woman in Massachusetts, but none by his wife. He was anxious to get to Madeira, the capital of Funchal in the Azores Islands where we'd be stopping before continuing on to Lisbon.

"You married?" he asked me.

"No."

"Ah, that's wonderful. You do anything you want, go wherever you like. That's the way!"

"How long you planning to stay on Madiera?"

"Don't know. Maybe for good. I rather be buried there than in the United States."

I knew right away that he hoisted bright snifters of brandy all day long, but it took me a couple of days to find out he played harmonica.

"Hey," he said one night. "You and me. You play guitar, I play harmonica, and I teach you *fados*. Do you know what is *fado*?"

I told him I knew it was the Portuguese version of the Argentine tango, something like my people's folk music called blues.

"Exactly," he said, "and I teach you the *fado*, two or three *fados*, and in two or three nights we play them together in the *sala de fumar* before bingo. There is a lady, the one who is English, I wish to conquer with love songs."

We practiced, rehearsed and performed like champions, but he never got far with the English woman who, I'd learned by then, had married a man close to sixty when she was twenty. He was wealthy, which accounted for all those safaris they'd been on in Africa. According to her, the days were never long enough for them to say all they had to say to one another. He died at the age of eighty-nine, and she was still attending his grave once a week to "tell him everything." Born in Portugal, she had visited England several times—always on holiday—and the U.S. only once, and recently at that. She loved to drink and dance and talk trash to the men.

Finding out the nit and grit of what lay beneath everyone's skin prompted me to begin taking deep looks at the relationship of soul to fleshly entrapment, and what better situation than an ocean voyage to do it? "Desire binds man to earth," Gary Snyder had written in his book of poems, *Riprap,* packed in my dufflebag, and I was beginning to see how that Buddhistic truism worked.

The woman who wrote for the *Ladies Home Journal,* for instance, was given to showing me clippings of articles she'd penned, and she was singularly proud of an illustration Norman Rockwell had done to illustrate a story of hers. Most of her writing had been done long before my time. When I thought about her during sleepless, porthole-hungry hours, I found her sad, noting that writing was all she had to show for an otherwise colorless life. Then and there I determined I was never going to separate my writing life from myself, and that risks, whatever danger taking them entailed, were something I'd never rule out.

Among the crew, I grew fond of Marx, the man my own age who tended the cabins, who knew a great deal about passengers' personal habits and vices since he was the one who took orders for liquor and tobacco and also passed the stuff out. Marx—don't ask me how he came by his name—told me that he loved his job because it kept him out of Salazar's Portugal for long periods. He loved his country, but was profoundly saddened by the tyrannical regime that had been governing and milking it for all too long. He was also busy studying English on his own and read a lot. I've never forgotten the morning following breakfast when I ran into him coming out of my cabin, which he'd just finished tidying.

"Senhor," he said with his curly-headed, boyish face of a smile, "you drink too much brandy, much too much for a man so young in years."

"Do you really think so?" I said, startled.

"Yes, and I do not understand why. The old men, yes, I understand the sadness of why they drink, but you, no. Are you so unhappy?"

"No, no I don't really think I am."

"You play the guitarra and sing so happy, and you write, yes?"

"I write a lot, yes."

"What do you write?"

"Oh, poetry and stories and I keep a journal."

Marx's handsome face seemed to brighten with heightened comprehension when I told him this. "I must arrange that you meet the ship nurse. He too writes in a how-you-say journal. Very funny man, very funny. This, ah, journal of his, it is big, very big—twenty-five big notebooks."

"Oh," I said, delighted, "I must see it!"

Marx shrugged and shook his head indifferently. "I do not understand this journal business. It is crazy. When he is writing in his notebooks and he look up and see a satellite go by up in the sky, then he write on his page: 'While I write I look up and see a satellite in the sky.' Writers, they are funny. Do you read this prisoner, this man who write a book in California at prison, but who commit the murders?"

"What's the name of the book?"

All of this sea-going talk, mind you, was being carried on in Portuguese and Spanish with little bursts of English.

Marx screwed up his face in all seriousness and, in curious English, said, "It is called *The Kayeed Waz a Kailler.*"

I pondered this while Marx stared at me intently, waiting for his long-shot, homemade pronunciation to somehow hit home.

"Aha!" I shot back at last. "You mean, *The Kid Was a Killer.* Caryl Chessman, yes?"

"Sim, sim," he cried, "that is it, that is it! Now, how you say it in real English?

We laughed and then talked about Chessman in our babbling stew of a lingo. It struck me for the first time that people in different parts of the world could be in tune and care about one another on a highly accurate, static-free frequency without necessarily knowing how to put it in words.

But language helped and, as I hung over the railing morning after morning, inhaling the sea and sky and, in my lightened head, beholding the past as if it were a sharply experienced dream, I couldn't help but realize how all the interest I'd taken in getting to know bits and pieces of other languages seemed to foretell that I'd be taking this trip. Ah, there's nothing like all that wind and water to help you recall the root meaning of everything you've ever thought or done. I was up on deck, regaling in this one day when a portly old crewman with a beret pulled snugly across his head approached me with a smile as big as the universe and proceeded to flap his arms at his sides and squeal and grunt in imitation of a walrus. He even yelled out the Portuguese word for walrus—*morsa*—and pointed at himself to indicate that this was, in fact, him. One glance at his drooping, gray, thick mustache and hooded eyes was enough to confirm and corroborate the likeness.

It wasn't long after this that Walrus, who proudly showed me his many volumes of diaries—all penned in admirably neat Portuguese with pictures and clippings from magazines pasted in meaning-fully—decided it was high time I met the ship's cook. It was a Saturday afternoon. The Atlantic was very South Pacific-like; it was calm. That's all he said, that I should meet the cook.

Actually, the cook and I had been taking peeps at one another from the moment I'd climbed aboard, but, coming as I was from the States, I never suspected he was the one in charge of the kitchen. Cultural brainwashing runs deep. He was a thin-boned black man of slight build in soiled white apron and chef's cap who put me in mind of Texas folk songster Mance Lipscomb. Suddenly it became impossible to ignore that we were brothers of the skin greeting one another.

"You Americano?" he said.

"*Si*," I said, still Spanish-oriented. Right away he broke into Portuguese and I rushed to explain right off I could yak in Spanish far better than I could in Portuguese, slipping in a friendly *"Usted entiende el español?"*

"Ah, *sim!* You go Lisboa?"

"*Sim*," I said, *"entonces a Madrí."* (Yeah, then on to Madrid.)

He smiled and shook his head yes.

Then, because I'd run out of things to say, I told him, *"Las comidas por aquí son muy buenas."* (The chow around here's great.)

The little cook laughed, obviously understanding everything I wasn't able to say, so didn't try. He waved heartily, one traveler of African descent to the other.

There we stood, perceptible in memory alone, looking into one another as if we were mirrors; looking into one another with a careful gentleness that seemed to telepathically affirm our secret identities as ghostly figments, fragments, mere passing specks in a diaspora whose naturalizing influence and effect on the rest of mankind has been growing with the millenia, widening and deepening with every cymbal swish and each impassioned breath thrust into a vibratory mouthpiece or the flicker or flick of finger laid to rest against valve or key. Music, like thought or remembrance, was sloshing or rocking or frothing around and around us like the ocean itself, that watery tomb that reputedly spawned our species.

And on we sailed that way for days and days. Divisions between day and night gradually mattered less and less; waking consciousness began to merge with dream consciousness. Before long I was identifying with the ocean as neighborhood and eternal verity. All mankind, as far as I was concerned, resided right there on that boat which I began to vaguely view as Noah's Ark. We might not've been paired up two by two, yet the realness of the notion that everything has its opposite in this gnashing, splashing, miraculous environment, the ocean, drove me home. And where exactly was home? It certainly wasn't there in the Azores, nor was it in listless Lisbon. It was all crammed and situated right there in my own heart of hearts.

Listening to Hancock's "Maiden Voyage" washes it all ashore, that electrifying storehouse of memory, spoken and unspoken, whose kaleidoscopic message boiled down to this: We are only dribs and drabs and particles and waves in an infinite sea of possibilities. It's possible, for example, to step on a slow boat to China or any other distant destination and step off of it the epitome of newness; a whole other being.

I loved that.

I love the way Herbie Hancock took the sweet time to sit down and put it all in music, which is nothing if not a sisterly companion to its solemn brother mathematics.

By the time we reached Lisbon, where I was duly trailed and haunted by the Secret Police in Hollywood trenchcoats, I'd shaken myself loose from a lifetime of longing. Belonging to myself and to something vaster than I could ever possibly conceive, I felt like dancing the *fado* all over the Iberian Peninsula, and, although my

shipmates had grown strangely aloof and impersonal when we disembarked to traipse toward customs, I knew I'd always remember
my own first crossing. "Maiden Voyage" won't let me forget it.

The seeing sea can seed and seize you ceaselessly. And even when
its melody subsides, the harmony it lines out within our inner ear is
enough to make you want to sing along out loud and jump for joy.

And you don't even have to climb aboard a boat to feel it.

Shhh, listen!

Can you hear it?

Cup a simple seashell to your ear.

Now.

Can you hear it, can you hear it?

Mercedes-Benz

Janis Joplin, 1969

JANIS, YOUR SONG and my Sadies arrived the same year!

For $600 you couldn't beat it: a sparkling 220 Mercedes-Benz sedan in the darkest of midnight blue shades that the light would hit and make gleam just like one of those old British detective cars I used to admire in old J. Arthur Rank films of 1950s vintage; the kind of no-nonsense motor car Rita Tushingham seemed perfectly comfortable hopping in and out of between serio-comic episodes of a romantic story with a bittersweet twist.

I knew when I plunked my money down that I could've been buying a lemon. But when Adam and Lois Miller told me about that car one Saturday night at a sweltering dance party, I coolly made up my mind that very moment that they were right when they'd said: "This car's for you; it's you through and through. It's just the machine for a writer with a flare for simple elegance!"—or words to that special effect.

A few days later I boogie'd right up to the Oakland Hills and offered to buy the automobile from the owner, who had it parked in front of his house with one of those regulation red and white FOR

SALE signs displayed in one of the rear passenger windows. He was an uptight, prejudiced foothills resident who, I could tell right off, wasn't exactly ecstatic about the idea of selling his treasured, almost-classic vehicle to a mere Negro. Refusing to take my personal check, he insisted that I either bring cash or a certified bank draft to his place of business for the precise amount the following day. It just so happened he was an auto mechanic. Adam Miller, who had gone with me to check the car over, knew the score. I knew the score. Even though we were both black and professionally literate, we were still Americans. I wanted to call the whole thing off. Adam, who'd owned a Mercedes for years, said: "Just go and get the money and bring it to the bastard, then you'll have yourself a good car, OK?" I took his advice.

And what a car it was! It still had its original paint job from 1956, shiny chrome trimmings, white-wall tires (or ought I say *tyres?*), wood panel work along the dashboard and doors, attractively worn and partially cracked leather seats in a soft, dove gray upholstery; fog lights, scientific-looking meters and gauges, bucket seats, and thick floor carpeting. In short, it had all the right stuff to make you feel every bit as virtuous and glamorous as people treated you once you got behind that wheel, mashed down on the accelerator, and started tooling around town. I went right out too and invested in fancy car waxes to while away many a Saturday and Sunday afternoons working like a coolie to make my foreign car shine.

Snappy. That was the word. It was easily the snappiest-looking car I've ever owned. Remember, you're getting this from someone who didn't start driving until he was well into his twenties; someone who had previously owned a $50 Ford and a $200 American Motors Rambler Wagon. In that respect, I was anything but American; if anything, I was a thorough discredit to a nation of auto users and abusers.

Suddenly, though, I was something to be reckoned with. By dint of installing myself behind the wheel of what most people considered to be a luxury car, I was initiated at once into the grand scheme of things automotive according to which people do not ask, "Is this your car?" but, rather, "Is this you?"

Is this you? That was the key. No, it wasn't me; it could never be me. It was only an almost-antique auto I oughtn't have been fooling with in the first place, but the impression I gave off was that of a well-heeled, successful oddball who just happened to be driving one of Germany's finest industrial products in a country that measured human worth on the basis of an individual's material accumulations.

Was that Mercedes me? For awhile I thought it was; I wanted so for it to be me. How keenly I recall parking it in front of a San Francisco bookstore I've frequented for years and having one of the hip clerks rush out and shout: "Why, Al Young, you slick sonofabitch! So you finally sold out!" Or the afternoon I happened to be chatting on the street with another Mercedes owner who also happened to be my color. There we stood at curbside, leaning against our cars, when a derelict white man stumbled by across the street. He stood for a minute, staring at us, then cupped his hands to his mouth and screamed at the top of his ugly voice: "Hey! Hey! You niggers think you're takin over the world, don't you? You think you got everything sewed up! Well, you know what? Fuck you, you black assholes! Fuck every one of you black nigger bastards!"

Then there were the black people themselves who put me through changes. There was the hefty highway patrolman who pulled me over one summer evening, stomped around the sedan, checking every part of that car out, finally leaning over the hood and fingering the windshield wipers.

"I'm giving you a citation," he said at last.

"A citation for what?"

"Faulty windshield wipers!"

"May I ask what's wrong with the windshield wipers?"

"Sure, you can ask."

"Then, tell me, how are they faulty?"

"They're just faulty, that's all! You got that? Your windshield wipers are faulty! Now, you wanna get belligerent? I been pretty nice to you up till now."

And there were the dents and nicks and the stealing of the Mercedes chrome insignia that customarily graces the front of the hood. Sometimes you felt as if people went out of their way to do bodily harm to your car simply because it was supposed to be a luxury car. It wasn't unusual, for instance, to climb back inside of it at some parking garage to find that the car had been broken into and burglarized.

Mercedes-Benz repairmen—those immaculately garbed gentlemen in greaseless smocks—would take one look at me and sense intuitively that I had no business trying to maintain such a car. In fact, when the oil pump finally blew on the freeway one day and I had to have the car towed by Triple A to the nearest German auto garage, I was informed, forthrightly and bluntly, that the cost for repairing the frozen pistons was probably going to run higher than the value of the car. "And if you cannot afford to pay our fee," said the head mechanic, "then we want the thing towed from our premises within 48 hours. Do you understand?" I understood. Moreover, I was required to sign a prepared, written statement to that effect.

Oh, Janis, it was all too much! The next time you put in a request in your prayerful song for a Mercedes-Benz, be sure and ask the Lord to throw in some upkeep money to boot. And, while you're at it, you just might want to picture me leaving that alien garage on foot, walking two blocks to the closest bus stop, stepping aboard, plopping down in a window seat, and sighing while I thought to myself: "Ahhh, good riddance! That's one more possession that won't be possessing me no more!"

I got myself a brand-new Datsun 510 Wagon and drove back into the future.

The Years With Miles

ONE NIGHT, a wintry Sunday in the country of Seattle, I went for a walk and ended up bewitched in a record shop in the University District. To promote a "comeback concert" that never took place, the store was running a discount sale on all of Miles Davis's stuff. I'd been listening to his Columbia album, *The Man With the Horn,* on the radio, gone out to clear my head, seen the LP in the shop window, and—haunted by thoughts of incipient middle age—ducked right inside to shake the cold.

Positioned at the D's in the alphabetized jazz section, I flipped through dozens of Miles Davis LPs, finding it tough to believe I knew most of them by heart. Even more surprising was my instant realization that the music compressed in those vinyl grooves had played a strange and indefinable role in shaping me and the years I'd grown up in; years that saw me wobble down from the hills of adolescence toward the slippery banks of maturity.

Photos of Miles and inspired graphics gracing the albums were suddenly telling me stories. I couldn't tell if they were stories I'd originally spun around myself when I'd first listened to a given piece of Miles's music or whether I was now a character in the stories I'd told. The experience was, I suppose, a little like poring over a forgotten stash of family snapshots and portraits. When you do that, you aren't necessarily seeing or registering pictures and images. Often you're looking beyond to another vision altogether; an inner vision of feeling, emotional states or mini-dramas whose meanings can never truly be clear to anyone but you.

Such is the tricky, highly private process of memory, and such was my delight in rediscovering how much that eccentric man's musical communication had meant to me.

It isn't even easy to say when my deep affection for Miles's playing and the many groups he's led actually began to develop. I like to believe it's always been there, fully blown, like spring rain or summer storms. Hindsight, though, tells me differently. Increasingly, recall is mostly what I go by, and, since recall is as vulnerable and mercurial as emotion, I keep finding myself spread-legged beside an ocean, remembering how long the sea itself has been around and how it must have begun at some point or other. And you know what that means, don't you? Even the history of a sound in your mind, in your heart, in all parts of your powerful invisibility, and your aural imagination above all, must have begun somewhere, at a single point.

TEMPUS FUGIT, 1953

With Don and Al Wardlow, musical brothers and bebop buddies of mine, I skip school to go see Frank Sinatra as drummer Frankie Machine in the film version of Nelson Algren's *The Man with the Golden Arm*. Our mid-week truancy is propelled by the dark, brooding spiritedness of "Tempus Fugit," a tune devised by J.J. Johnson and recorded by Miles for Blue Note. We've been playing that little ten-inch LP until the grooves are white from needle wear.

It's hip and we know it, for in our amusement park minds we are hipness personified.

We've picked up on all the stories our heroes were telling on this album, even though words have nothing to do with it, and, as sly adolescents given to analyzing the world note by note and look by look, we're shot through with visions of the adult world as a hall of mirrors where nothing is as it appears to be.

In my own head, that world is dark, the color of a blood-red rose, a fragile flower that everybody seems to want to trample when they aren't busy stepping on one another's toes. Yet sunning itself in this garden of suspicion is the tender conviction that jazz, true jazz dedication and devotion, means being addicted to something. We're all on that wavelength, thinking that way; feeling so, anyway. Dumb and tender, we figure the addiction's got to be physical rather than mental or spiritual. We haven't yet learned that music is really all about ourselves.

And so off to the movies we rush to see how Sinatra portrays a junkie, the on-screen version of a heroin addict. We aren't so dumb as to not know that bebop and getting high went hand in hand somehow, even though we ourselves aren't addicted to anything yet, not even to the beer and whiskey and occasional reefer that comes our way from time to time.

The time we do our hardest listening is afternoon: two-story-flat, after-school afternoons spent in the dinning room, kitchen and living room of Don's and Al's parents' home on Gladstone Street. Sometimes we sneak shots of whiskey from their gym teacher father's Jim Beam or Seagram's Seven Crown bottles. Or, because I look older than my actual age, they'll paint a mustache on me and send me out to score jumbo quarts of Pfeiffer's or, better yet, Stroh's Bohemian beer. Then, with our senses systematically deranged for the moment, we kick back and get off into this swaggering, athletic, cultish music that speaks directly to the rebellious side of our delicate natures, the side that's determined to give the finger to the world and remain cool, be cool, be.

We jazzed June, and then some! Hey, man, just leave us be. Bebop? That's what they've named it but, strictly speaking, the music's got no name. At the time, bebop, to me anyway, is something else—cute and pat; the kind of sounds that cascaded in diminished and augmented chromatic runs along New York's 52nd Street with bee stings of heroin lubricating knuckles and embouchures and the snappy feet and wrists of skinny drummers just waiting for the chance to call themselves percussionists. No, this isn't bebop; not Miles's music with titles like "Kilo," "Lazy Susan," and "Tempus Fugit."

We've sought and have been granted asylum in the school band where—with other wearers of coal-black, horn-rimmed shades and Stetson shoes—we pour our tough little hearts and souls into our instruments, sneering at the bogus authority of home, parents, school and everything else familiar, established and therefore suspect. In darkest adolescence, we brood our way through corny marches and stock pop charts, waiting for a chance to slip our hip licks in and blow away the band instructor and the uninitiated among us.

In the poolroom when somebody says: "I ain't seen you since I don't know when," the proper, studied rejoinder is: "Well, you know how it is—*tempus* sure do *fugit*, don't it?"

And Don, who was truly comic back there in the heyday of Mack Man style, can stand in front of the poolroom across from the butcher's, fingering the brim of his stingybrim hat, puffing on a Chesterfield, going: "Uh, since I can't go to Birdland and hear me no sounds, I guess I'll walk over here to Meat Land and get me some meat."

It makes no more sense now than it did then, but the music still glues it all together like a vaudeville routine that's never been given the hook.

FOUR, 1955

Don't ask me how come, but suddenly it's high spring and the trees are all too much for me to take in their urban beauty and blossoming headiness. I'm sappy, I'm happy, I'm happening in a way that

makes me want to serve notice that I'm subject to fly clean out of
my body at any moment and stand still in the sky overlooking it all,
a crazy-faced hummingbird of spirit, drunk on sonic nectar.
Relaxed and ripening, I've got the perfect set of sounds to go with
what I'm feeling; got Blakey, got Percy, got Horace Silver, got Miles,
got Miles, got Miles to go.

"Four" is the name of the tune, all right, but four what? For now
it don't matter. For now I'm in love the way you're generically in
love when you're sixteen and gone. In love with what? A girl? Yes.
Which one? All girls.

But mainly it's this bubbling sense of late April ebullience that
floats me along the shores of the Detroit River, West Grand
Boulevard, Dexter Avenue, Palmer Park and 12th Street. Please
don't ask me to explain anything; it's all being said on the record by
Miles and them every time I put it on and take it off there's a different way they're saying the same thing which is what I remember
when I play it back in my head too and all it is is the only message
I've ever wanted to hear going way back into my deepest self that
sings and sails saying be happy love is all there is O can't you feel it
pulling you through the thaw of this frozen street the world into
melting warm waves of the fragrant heaven you've been reaching for
for so long?

Later, but not much later, along came singing poet Jon Hendricks with Dave Lambert and Annie Ross to sound it all out in crisp,
zigzag vocalese, citing truth, honor, happiness and love as the four
components essential to full living; putting words to all the solos. It
was a marvelous interpretation—true to Miles's and the other on-
the-spot composers' every note and nuance—only something got
lost.

Music's like that; it comes already translated, ready to be understood by anyone with ears. What I was hearing you already know,
but don't bank on it; there's too much beforeness and afterness
clouding our telepathy.

All you need to know is that the name of the song is "Four," and
no more.

Al Young

TUNE UP, 1955

The power of music is such that you'll find yourself wallowing on
the ground or floor of it on your way to eternity.

And what is eternity but a vibration; the same stuff we're made
of—vibrations—"I ain't got no body," being the musical truth of it.
The love, the kiss, the hug and sock and wham of it in doubles and
triples is sugar still; the I-love-you rushing through these hard
knocks and fists pounding in the sand of love; the soft let's do it
again and again of wet lips and eyes and muscles.

There are ways to say this in French, Tagalog, Japanese and
Maori, or in jazz. But I love you is all anybody can ever say by way
of commitment and surrender to Life, the Infinite, Divine
Intelligence, the only real Lover; the force to which the higher self
is always tuned whether you can hear it or not.

It's only the look of things that gets in the way; that is, until you
tune up and remember there's no such thing as "I Got Rhythm";
you are rhythm. And how could you ever let a song go out of your
heart, when you are already song?

O the beautiful changes!

BLUES FOR PABLO, 1957

And who was Pablo? What did it mean? Pablo Casals? Pablo
Picasso? Now, why would Miles Davis and Gil Evans be doing a
blues for Pablo Picasso? On the other hand, why not? Hadn't
Picasso come into his own, and somehow hadn't he—in spirit perhaps or by way of Matisse—gotten himself connected up with jazz?

Even I had grown up on those old fanciful, inky David Stone
Martin illustrations of musicians in their shoes and hats and instruments embellished with curlycue stitches all artsy and modern like
the packaging of jazz for the connoisseur you were for sure when
you kicked down two weeks of lunch money for one of Norman
Granz's glossy *Jazz at the Philharmonic* 33-1/3 long-playing mi-
crogroove recordings.

David Stone Martin was a disciple of the illustrious Ben Shahn, a painter whose political consciousness and leanings had grown dangerously unfashionable by then, the days of Pat Boone, Patti Page, Eddie Fisher and The Four Aces. It was black Detroit artist Harold Neal, one of my early mentors, who'd mentioned to me more than once how Shahn, a WPA survivor of the Great Depression, was said to have stayed up nights wielding a broken matchstick tip to achieve that jagged line and the intense effect that made his drawings and his imitators famous. Whether this is true or not no longer matters stylistically, but I've always associated Shahn with Pablo Picasso, that master of art-trend consciousness. And when the subject of Picasso comes up, I'm mindful that the world's foremost collector of Picasso's work for years and years was jazz producer Norman Granz, who, after abandoning the States to take up residence in Switzerland, even named his record label after the exiled Spaniard. Pablo Records has long been one of the most commercially successful of independent jazz labels.

But labels are one thing and substance another. I've imparted all this to indicate how eager I'd been at one time to pin down a title. Why that seemed important is now inexplicable. What matters is that *Miles Ahead* was the first long-playing album I'd ever heard with no silence separating its selections. One track gracefully segued into another. Later this kind of production came to be known in the industry as a "concept" album. It was Gil Evans's subtle yet intricate orchestral arrangements and Miles's cool-to-warm-to-torrid blowing that kept my blood simmering. It was the dressing up of the humble, old, irreducible blues form and the fresh-sounding modernity and paint job these artists had given it that startled. In fact, there was something so vital about this process of transformation, this blues-primed paint job, that "Blues for Pablo" still sounds as vivid and dewy today as it always did. Seductive—that's the word. "Blues for Pablo" sounds painted; sounds as if it's been painted right onto some invisible sound-conducting substance.

Ahead of myself, I'd walk around Ann Arbor when the season was nose-stiffening cold, then repair to my East William Street digs, the house with the bay window overlooking Maynard Street, slip on this record, and thaw out until my blue-brown nostrils were wide open. Sometimes I wonder who I thought I was then. What was all that craziness I seem to have made up about warming myself on January nights to mellowing sounds? What was it about those sounds—Miles's and Evans's versions of Brubeck's "The Duke" or Ahmad Jamal's "New Rhumba" or "Blues for Pablo"—that made me long to be walking around Central Park along the Manzanares River in Madrid or the Champs Elysées in early-blooming May?

BLUE IN GREEN, 1958

What you hear is what you are.

If rain is pouring out of Coltrane's horn and Cannonball Adderley and Bill Evans and Paul Chambers and Jimmy Cobb are floating beneath it bearing rainbowed umbrellas, that's because the melody you need loves a showered floor to move it along, the way ocean needs sand.

The beached house your mind occupies now is only just that; a dwelling place for now, for now. The pain you're feeling—played back to you as mischievous joy—is all you require to usher you out of this moment.

Put yourself on a boat going nowhere. Where does your journey end or begin?

Were you even born when this record first came out? Did you smooch to it like I did, clinging to behold the fundamental need and pleasure of physical affection and to be held? Did it make your scalp tingle the first time you heard it? Can you point out the lovers on this crossing in watery off-shore waltz time; the ones you knowingly sailed around or steered clear of, and which ones finally sneaked up and gotcha?

There are smooth or rocky transitions into or away from everything imaginable. Each gradation of approach has a color, and every color a name to be sounded—from prismatic blue to greasy green—and the distances we're talking about exist in mind, not time, and mind alone.

Consider fauna and flora and grit beneath water being pulled by beams of tightly packed light: a common kind of blue.

ALL BLUES, 1958

When, as a kid, I first heard the blues—heard them, that is, and paid attention to what I was hearing—I recognized their special quality at once. I understood exactly what they were. An instantaneous connection was made.

Perhaps if you'd come at me and asked me to explain, I wouldn've been tongue-tied, yet all the feelings were there, all the deep and scattered and complex emotions, even at the age of four. I can still conjure those feelings up today with all the intensity of sunlight directed through the lens of a magnifying glass; the magnifying glass me and my playmates used to roast ants to a crisp in the front and back yards of our ignorance.

Looking back, it's easy to see now how Mississippi wasn't a bad place to get initiated into the blues. It was all around us. I understood instantly what the blues meant, and that understanding had nothing to do with analysis or quantification; flatted thirds and fifth and sevenths or twelve or sixteen bars or tonal centers or the history of human oppression or class struggle. To paraphrase something the late Big Bill Broonzy once said off the cuff, you were simply living with the blues if you came up in the South around the time I was coming along.

The blues and I caught back up with each other in Jackson, Mississippi a few years ago when I was checking into the Hilton Hotel there as part of a gig Margaret Walker, author of the novel *Jubilee,* had put together at the University. It was one of those afternoons when the veritable shadow of Reconstruction, so to speak, was in effect. All the desk clerks and switchboard operators, just then anyway, were black, and all the bellboys white.

The gnarly lad who toted and carted my luggage up to the fifth floor was carrying on a flipflop conversation with me. His attention seemed to have perked up when I mentioned I was from Mississippi. He poked his doorkey in the lock of the room that was supposed to be mine, pushed until a chain lock blocked further entry, then started cussing. Then, while I waited, he descended by elevator to consult with the desk man. After that we went up to the seventh

floor, tried another door, and found that it too was already occupied.
Down he went again and came back up with yet another key. When
we finally got into a room that seemed free for me to move into, he
grimly performed his bellboy duties—hauling my bags in, snapping
on the lights, and so on—then waited patiently for his tip.

But once the buck had been snugly pocketed, he blinked at me
quizzically and, turning to leave, said, "How long you say you lived
in Mississippi?"

"Spent pretty much most of my first ten years here."

"Well," he said, scratching his sandy hair, "look like to me you'da
been smart enough to get outta this state a helluva lot sooner.
Anyway, welcome home. I reckon you can see ain't too much done
changed."

Certainly, the blues haven't changed; they never do at heart. The
feelings I experienced the first time I lay in bed listening to Cab
Calloway or Johnny Mercer singing "Blues in the Night" from the
radio next door in my parents' bedroom weren't much different
from what I felt when Miles's unbelievably beautiful "All Blues,"
served up in deliciously brisk 3/4 waltz time, got ahold of me the
way the train along the tracks across the street used to do in Ocean
Springs when it rumbled past in the night with its lonesome whistle moaning: *Ooooooweeee!* "My mama done told me. . . . "

The album *Kind of Blue,* I'm told, was more pianist Bill Evans's
conception than Miles's, but what does it matter now that all these
eerie years have sprung up around whatever plot first seeded it?
Physicists will tell you that the color blue absorbs red, orange and
yellow rays at the same time that it radiates green, violet, indigo and
its own stately hue. And having been haunted by "All Blues" these
many years, I can tell you there's no way to even begin quantifying
the infinite qualities of blueness.

Sky blue, ocean blue, lake blue, ice blue, blood blue, vein blue,
neon blue, flame blue, periwinkle blue, steely blue, nipple blue,
royal blue, true blue, moon blue, midnight blue, mountain blue,
snow blue, powder blue, algae blue, devil blue, heavenly blue, blossom blue, Nile blue, stocking blue, moldy blue, radiant blue, electric blue, shadow blue, twilight blue, navy blue, star blue, movie
blue, misty blue, ribbon blue, fox blue, feather blue, and on and on

into the blueness of your very essence—not even to mention exclusively human kinds of blue.

No, I didn't think I'd ever get over these blues; not until I woke up one night in the middle of a troubling dream and it hit me there was a realm beyond the blues, reds, oranges, yellows and all the rest of the spectrum. That was where I needed to be: brilliantly blended back in with the dazzling iridescence of the very force that powers life itself. That's all. That was all the blues had taught me and all I needed to learn from years of living with the blues, the whole blues and nothing but the blues.

SKETCHES OF SPAIN, 1960

Wandering around Madrid in the early sixties, I saw Gil Evans's gorgeous orchestrations being acted out, with Miles's inspired trumpet blowing like a coastal wind above it all. I wove it into the Spain I'd dragged to Spain with me, a Spain I had in fact invented from Don Quixote, Sancho Panza, Lorca's *Gypsy Ballads,* flamenco music and dance, images of solemn yet lovely Andalusian women in lace mantillas, the Carthaginians, the Romans, the Moors, the Inquisition, expulsion of the Semites in 1492, *El Siglo de Oro* (the so-called Golden Age of empire and culture), Goya's paintings, Unamuno's *Tragic Sense of Life,* philosopher Santayana's essays on solipsism, the films of Luis Buñuel, Salvador Dali's brand of surrealism, the Spanish Civil War, the Communist and loyalist activist known as La Pasionaria, Generalísimo Francisco Franco, fascism, persecution, Lorca's unexplained assassination, Picasso's *Güernica* and folk song piled atop folk song (Hello, Germaine Montero!) in the part of my head that warehoused such things.

I figured nobody on the Iberian Peninsula had ever heard of Miles Davis or American jazz, and yet one rainy night, stopping by a little bar in a working-class section of town, I stood by the jukebox with a tall, cheap rum and Coke in hand, and punched up Louis Armstrong's version of the African song "Skokian" along with Cozy Cole's old hit "Topsy: Part Two." The instant the music began drenching the little joint with warmth, I looked up to see a table of young black men who'd been sizing me up. Suddenly they were nudging each other and flashing friendly smiles. They motioned for me to join them. Their seeming leader, cheerful and in his early twenties, told me in Spanish: "When you played the right stuff on the box we knew you had to be one of us!"

They were Africans from Spanish Guinea who were studying in Madrid, some of them air force officers. They opened up completely to me and accepted me into their fold. We'd get together afternoons, and sometimes at night, to discuss everything under the sun except politics. Oh, they let me know in so many words that they were hip to the colonial scheme of things but that the wheel of history was still turning and turning, don't you see? Philosophy they loved and were well versed in the classical version of it. But that didn't stop them from being themselves nor from pausing between salient points in our chats to playfully firm up some assignation or rendezvous with one or another of the frisky Spanish women who either worked the place or worked in it as barmaids or waitresses. I perceived that the cat-and-mouse game of life goes on all the same under repressive or permissive regimes.

They told me about Africa. I told them about the States. I told them about Miles Davis and *Sketches of Spain*. They asked if I'd like to act in a movie some Cuban woman was making about the people of color in Madrid, and would I like to come to dinner sometime? I felt funny about both invitations because I was poor and living in a ridiculously cheap room at the Pensión Galápagos on the wrong side of the Gran Via. I simply didn't think I'd be able to reciprocate their hospitality, and so I never took them up on it. I chose instead to limit our relationship to a bar/café setting. I thought of us as latter-day Moors; they saw all black people the world over as an oppressed but gifted race with a special contribution to make to mankind.

It was all so singularly beautiful and warm that—even now, having dissolved from the third into the fifth decade of my quiet residence on earth—the lush and breathing strains of *Sketches of Spain* are enough to send me meandering through the streets and rooms and rest stops of an ancient Madrid that's probably only the product of an unhurried stroll I took once through a Prado Museum of the mind.

Fever & Ooh Poo Pah Doo

Little Willie John, 1956
Jesse Hill, 1960

THE DEAL was you worked eight to twelve hours a day, beginning at four in the afternoon and quitting whenever you were told to go home. This was at the docks, as they were called, down on Seventh Street in Oakland, California, and it was the whipping winter of 1964.

I had passed the so-called exam which required, as I recall, that you kneel before a snickering examiner and hoist a hone-hundred-pound sack to your shoulder and stand back up without buckling in his presence.

"Congratulations!" the chipper man told me. "You're a mail handler now. Report to work on Monday."

And so began three months of working for the U.S. Postal Service again, only this time it was as one of society's mules rather than as a clerk. Our job was to tackle and drag sacks of mail off the loading docks and stack them into the trucks backed up there. I never ached so much in my life.

We worked in teams of eight to ten, and there were two supervisors: a stocky gent named Jones who was brown-skinned and jovial, and a giant named Brown whom I prefer to call Red because of his light, freckled, reddish complexion and also because he was something of a devil. Jones, who ate a lot on the job, wore a greasy work jacket and a felt hat with the brim upturned. Anytime the sandwich man wheeled by, Jones flagged him down and grabbed himself a po'boy or a pie or something. I was skinny then but I liked to do that too, never suspecting, not until somebody pulled my coat weeks later, that I'd become a favorite of Jones because he liked a man who liked to eat.

Red was altogether something else. He came on duty around eight at night when Jones punched out, and he came on hungry and mean. Red carried around with him an old newspaper clipping preserved in plastic that told of the time shortly following the Korean War when he'd broken the record for a mail handler by working something like six months in a row, with no days off, for twelve full hours a day. The Postal Service had apparently seen fit to give this workaholic a salutory citation instead of telling that such a performance was actually threatening his health and well-being. He was made to see himself as a hero when he should've been reprimanded. Call it capitalism, call it socialism, call it the work ethic, call it whatever you want. I called it one sad day the night I locked horns with the Old Red Devil.

It was well known to everybody that worked on the docks but me that you didn't so much as whisper to Red when he was having his lunch. Lunch for Red took place at ten every night, and his passion was gumbo. He could probably consume it by the bucket, but he had to settle for two nightly quarts of the stuff which was served up by a joint close by known as Esther's—a rhythm and blues bar and lounge that also specialized in barbecued ribs, chicken, chitlins, greens, gumbo and all the usual soulfood.

Little Willie John was hanging out after hours in Esther's in those days, but he was on his last legs, having fallen on the proverbial evil days. No longer the perky, churchy-throated kid who had written and recorded the hit tune "Fever" in his teens, Little Willie was tired now and seemed a little lost. He'd turn up at Esther's to drink and goof and cut the fool; a superlative artist, still in need of more than the two, maybe three hits he'd enjoyed, and frustrated, I suspect, in an all-too-soon kind of way. There's no telling what might've been rushing and curdling around inside Willie John by then. Not long afterwards I happened to catch him as the opening act at a Jackie "Moms" Mabley show at the Oakland Auditorium, but in no time he'd killed a man and landed in the state penitentiary up in Washington, where he died. Details, as they usually are in such situations, are blurred. What isn't blurred are my memories of him being there at the peripheries of that short-lasting gig situation in the depths of Oakland, in the heart of what later came to be romantically known as the ghetto.

Believe me, there was nothing at all romantic about it. Sometimes, waiting for the last bus home in the very entrails of darkness, I'd be watching patterns my frosty breath made in the icy night air, then look up and catch a tableaux being played out across the street involving some hooker who'd been accosted or mistreated by some john. Suddenly her pimp and some buddies would appear on the scene and smash the shit out of the offender before my eyes. The funky bus would pull up and I would board, still trying to absorb what I'd just seen. The bus would roll away. I'd go home and dream tired, uninspired dreams.

Red had his rules. I broke one of them without knowing about it until it was too late.

One night when he was meditatively slurping gumbo with a plastic spoon, I tapped at the partly opened door of Red's hideaway room. All I wanted was to ask if it was OK to take a break. Red was sitting with his back halfway turned to me in the half-dark. From a glance I could tell that eating was a religious ritual with Red. Hunched over his gumbo in that checkered, tattered, plaid woolen hunting coat and baseball cap, his eyes, half-closed behind steamy glasses, rolled my way with a tilt of his head. I saw the scowl on his face, but that scowl was Red's natural expression. When he wasn't scowling, his leathery face wavered between a totally deadpan expression and a slow burn. Red was one miserable specimen of *homo afro-americanus.*

Just as I was about to knock again, still very much the innocent bystander, one of the guys from the crew, an exboxer named Brick, just happened to be stomping down the narrow hallway. In a flash, Brick sized up the situation, grabbed me by the elbow, and dragged me along with him until we'd reached a spot that was safely out of Red's earshot.

"Young," he said in a gruff whisper, "you lost your mind?"

"What're you talking about?"

"I mean, I know you one of them Ninety-Day Wonders, but you bout to get your block knocked clean off."

"Hey, Jones kept me working through my break when he went off-shift and I needed to ask Red if—"

Brick had a way of flailing his arms and wrists about, as if he might be loosening up for a sparring session or something, and he did this vigorously as he explained, "I don't care what the hell you need to ask. Ain't nobody told you don't be fuckin with Red when he greazin?"

"But all I did was knock! I wasn't about to get him in no big conversation."

"Man, what you was *about* to do was rile Red up and get him mad!"

"Mad about what?"

"Listen, you must don't know so I'mo try to tell you. Whenever you see food in fronta Red and he gettin ready to chow down or even if it's just him and cupa coffee and he be off by hisself, you don't say boo to him!"

"What's the matter with him?"

"What's the matter with him? Hell, I ain't no psychiatrist but I do know this much—the nigger crazy and he just might get it in his head to kill you."

"You jivin."

"All right, you think I'm jivin, you walk on back there and knock on that door one more time. We'll read about it in the *Tribune*— 'Champion Muthafukkin Dock Foreman Go Berserk and Waste Ninety-Day Wonder!' "

"You *are* serious, aren't you?"

"Serious as a heart attack, Jack! You stick around here and last out your few weeks, you gon know about Red when they spring your educated ass loose! I done saved you this time, but you better put some kinda restraint on yourself next time you go pullin that shit!"

There was no next time. Innocent though I often was on this job, I was fast at catching on once I'd pieced a sticky situation together. It became perfectly obvious that what the veteran dockers said about Red was true. But I did manage to run rather seriously afoul of another one of Red's unwritten rules. Put into language, it would probably run something like this: *Pull anything you wanna pull, just don't let me catch you at it.*

As Christmas grew closer and closer, and the mails heated up to the point where it was all we mail handlers could do to help slide the sacks down the roller conveyors and chunk and heave them onto the trucks, everyone began working so many extra hours that at any given time we were punchy and wiped. While others worked and kept watch, one or the other crew guys were given to taking naps on those sacks that were wedged deepest inside the trucks. This was common stuff. Jones knew about it, and I imagine all the other supervisors did. After all, this was the Post Office, which, in those days, had its own peculiar friendship and kinship network, to say nothing of the curious manner in which it was managed. It wasn't at all unusual, for example, for a particular male worker to be shifted into a new slot and for his on-the-job girlfriend to be shifted at the same time or, in any case, shortly thereafter. These people looked out for one another.

Then, too, you've got to remember that the scene was predominantly black, and not just black but invisibly divided up into native territories. There were Texans, Louisianans, Arkies, Okies, Northerners, born-Californians, and so forth. It got even tinier than that: Among the Louisiana Negroes alone, there was an intense and muttering rivalry between New Orleans, Baton Rouge, Lafayette, Shreveport and St. Charles Negroes. "Them niggers outta St. Charles," Brick might grumble, "they think they the slickest niggers in the world and don't nobody else know nothin!" Or you might hear a native St. Charlesean such as the olive-skinned, straight-haired Handsome Tony say, "The average muthafukka you see workin here couldn't make it in St. Charles cause they got the I.Q. of a bunion." And that pretty much told you the score.

On one of those nights I happened to be the one copping a few Z's atop the more recondite truck cargo. It seems I'd begun my snooze while Jones was on duty. As a matter of fact, I'd dozed off thinking about how much Jones reminded me of that old album organist Jimmy Smith and guitarist Wes Montgomery teamed up on, the one with a jacket photograph that shows them face to face, practically nose to nose, munching on twin hero or po'boy sandwiches. Somebody's transistor radio was blatting out Jesse Hill's "Ooh Poo Pah Doo," one of the biggies on KDIA, the black music AM radio station that called itself Lucky 13. And from here to eternity, "Ooh Poo Pah Doo" will always conjure back up what happened that night.

Red, who had evidently moved the crew from my nap truck to work another one down the dock, clunked up inside the truck in his John Henry workshoes, spotted me snoring there, and started screaming at the top of his voice: "Well, well, what do we have here? Nigger! Nigger, get your ass up from there this minute! I said get the fuck up! Who the hell you think you are anyway? Get up and get outta this truck!"

I got up at once and got out. Red, in all his not-to-be-believed ugliness, was trembling as he smacked the fist of one hand into the palm of the other. "Young," he said, "you know I done just about had it with you! I want you to get your ass over to Special Packages. You gonna be workin with Cowboy for the resta the night!"

And that's where I went. Cowboy was an old-timer on the docks; a lean, jeaned, work-shirted man who sported dark glasses, a vest, a wiry, full beard and a chewed-up, ridiculous cowboy hat. He didn't talk much, and he worked you hard and fast. But I could tell he had a sense of humor buried someplace beneath that blind exterior of his. If Red gave off a junkyard dog vibration, Cowboy's was more like that of the silent wrecking yard hand whose job it was to reach into the bowels of some not quite totally cannibalized auto and tear out, say, a pair of heater boxes from an old Volkswagen Bug. And whenever Cowboy would strut along the docks on his way to lunch or on a break, regulars would inevitably turn to one another and say, "Yon go Cowboy. Go on, Cowboy, with your crazy, bad self!"

Cowboy and I got along just fine. I did what he instructed me to do, and, from time to time, he'd give me one of those paternal smiles that meant everything was in order and moving right along.

Red was off in Hothead Heaven and Cowboy was rounding up everything that needed to be fed into the grander and more practical scheme of things.

Eventually I was brought back to work with my old crew, but Red, I noticed, left me alone. I couldn't figure out why until Brick told me one night what had taken place the Sunday I'd chosen to stay home.

"You missed it, Young, you missed it!" he said gleefully.

"Missed what?"

"The night you was home, Red come in here all worked up and went to gettin on Cowboy's case. Now, Cowboy, mind you, he just as ignorant and ready to die as Red, only he don't make no big thing outta that. So Red jumped off up in Cowboy's chest bout some bullshit that wasn't none of Red's business in the first place and Cowboy he give Red one of them smiles of his—you know that grin—and when Red wouldn't take the hint and back off like somebody with some sense Old Cowboy pulled a pistol on the nigger and you know what Red did?"

"What?"

"Red punched out, that's what!"

"Hunh?"

"That's right, Red who spose to be so bad and ready, he throwed up them hamhock handsa his and punched out, that's what he did! See, Red wasn't thinkin bout meeting his match. See, it's bad niggers and it's quiet niggers and sometimes it's hard to tell which is which."

I let go of the sack I'd been lugging when Brick told me that; let go of it and laughed in the shadows of the truck, thinking about the way Jesse Hill had been shouting over the dock radios all fall about how he was going to "ring a few bells in your ears" and how he wasn't going to stop trying until he could create "confusion in your mind."

My ears were ringing, my mind was messed up, and, having become a zombie who got home in the very wee hours to scrawl out a note for his nine-to-five working wife, I was aching to move out of all the Red zones of the world and cross innocently into the ever-elusive green.

▌I Got Rhythm

George Gershwin, composer

▐MAGINE, IF YOU CAN, endless choruses of "I Got Rhythm" stretched out back to back with seductive, bludgeoning blues from the 1920s clean into the very next century, and there you got it, man, there you got this thing called jazz squirming by the scruff of its neck stretched out far enough to reach anywhere, far enough to poke its warm, wet nose smugly into the snuggest corners of the world with a grin that can either end or begin just about anyplace you want it to.

Say, what?

Say, there's absolutely no telling where this stuff'll put you if you let it. My mama used to say, "All that crazy music, it's gon drive you crazy you aint careful!" And she was right. But I was careful. Bluesman Jimmy Reed said, "All them musicians played that bebop, they all either ended up dyin early or else they went insane." And he was right too. No getting around it. Look at the record. Listen to it close. Think about all the people with ears unchecked in love with this dangerous music who wound up on dope or unable to get up in the morning; humans who married outside their race or lost their place in line at the Supermarket of Life. Think about people whose inner ear led them to the far edges of Earth and inner space. Think about vast, cosmic surges of blues pouring down over your hot, troubled soul like a worldly, liquidy balm of tropical rain whose spiritual cousin is that same old sun the Aztecs and Egyptians knowingly worshipped.

When Mr. George Gershwin sat down and knocked out "I Got Rhythm," did he have any idea what the Negroes and the Negrophiles would do with it; how they would dress it up and mess with it and test it to its outer limits? Never mind the Negrophobes. That sound crept in and got to them too, even those among them who later had the nerve to ponder and cogitate the dire prospect that there might not have even been such a music had it not been for the brilliant compositional efforts of this Jewish gentleman named Gershwin.

Well, let's face it, the thoroughly lovable Mr. Gershwin had plenty sense, enough to go directly to the source: to the Negroes, that is, for inspiration. No Negroes, no "I Got Rhythm." No Negroes, no American music. No Negroes, no America. No America, no jazz. And that's just for openers.

Even Dr. Joseph Goebbels, Hitler's Minister of Propaganda—an unsuccessful novelist, playwright and liberal journalist—had enough insight to observe in what remains of his diaries: " . . . The Americans have the ability of taking their relatively small stock of culture and by a modernized version to make of it something very *à propos* for the present time. . . . The Americans have only a few Negro songs, but they present them in such a modern way that they conquer large parts of the modern world which is, of course, very fond of such melodies. We have a much greater fund of cultural goods, but we have neither the artistry nor the will to modernize them. That will have to be changed."*

But if it's true that much of the Nazi high command turned to heroin, morphine, cocaine and other heavy drugs when dark days came toward the end of the War, you wonder what might've happened had they given jazz and peace a chance. You wonder.

*The Goebbels Diaries, 1942–43; edited, translated and with an introduction by Louis P. Lochner; Doubleday & Company, Inc., New York, 1948.

Imagine, if you can, endless choruses of this sprightly thirty-two-bar tune, "I Got Rhythm," probed by some of the world's finest musicians: the Master Race presided over by His Master's Voice.

Imagine it all being transformed into something else again and again and again.

Come On-A My House

Rosemary Clooney, 1952

AT THIRTEEN, I'd listen to anything. Well, almost. I wasn't crazy about Lawrence Welk or Guy Lombardo, but the gates of my mind were still swinging wide open most of the time, and when I read somewhere about how much Louis Armstrong loved the sound of the Lombardo band before it migrated south from Canada, I was ready to open my ears and give even the Royal Canadians the benefit of a doubt. Besides, there was no particular sound back then that was supposed to be hipper than any other. The concept of hip might've penetrated the strictly jazz world, but it hadn't made much headway yet in the middlebrow midwest where everything was still in flux.

My favorite disk jockey from that matchless, pre-smoking era was a fellow named Bob Murphy who billed himself as the "Tall Boy, Third Row" and broadcast weekdays over WJBK in Detroit. Murphy's idea of putting a show together was to line up a stack of records that suited his fancy, no matter what the genre, and take it from there. His theme song, of all things, was Boyd Raeburn's "Dalvatore Sally." Now, it must be remembered that, of all the far-out big bands of the day, Raeburn's was probably the one that stood the least chance of ever being rounded up and brought back into the fold of convention. His band was to Stan Kenton's what I suspect Fletcher Henderson's had been to the Duke Ellington orchestra—an inspiration. It wasn't unusual to snap on my little metal-encased Arvin bedside AM radio and hear Murphy open a show with Sonny Rollins performing "The Stopper," then jump to the Four Aces and Johnnie Ray or those harmless Chordettes of Arthur Godfrey's Talent Scouts fame. Then the Tall Boy, Third Row might turn around and drop a Nat King Cole trio side on you, or a Charlie Parker—or, right smack dab in the middle of that groove, he might crank up Rosemary Clooney's "Come On-A My House," her early fifties runaway hit staged by Columbia arrangement and repertoire man Mitch Miller, and composed by a couple of amateur songwriters named Ross Bagdasarian and William Saroyan.

William Saroyan. That's the name that set off a buzzer in my busy head. I couldn't believe he'd been in on the making of this jumping pop number laced with quasi-immigrant Eyetalian lyrics (or were they supposed to be Armenian?) that spoke of "figs and grapes/and a pomegranate, too." There was a jazzy harpsichord churning up sand and grit with the rhythm section accompanying Rosie, as she's called by showbiz intimates, and that too—given the Saroyan connection—sounded entirely appropriate and very much in the spirit of everything I'd read by then of this eccentric California writer whose homemade prose style was profoundly endearing to a gangly, gawking pubescent like me. My very awkwardness seems to have ripened me for the kind of unbridled bravado and enthusiasm for life that Saroyan's short stories and conversational soliloquoys championed.

Routinely, I read everything I could get my hands on by Saroyan, and when the World Stage—a theater-in-the-round company in Detroit's Highland Park—put on his play, "Across the Board in Tomorrow Morning," I was right down front on opening night. And I made it back for a second helping. By then I was in high school and rather inclined to think of myself as a writer. I was publishing in *The Central Student,* our school paper for which I was features editor, and in a local jazz and cultural tabloid known as *Idioms.* Along the way I'd managed to wangle an actual press card as an occasional columnist for something called the Detroit *Tribune,* a black newspaper with a Christian Science slant whose publisher was a man named Fruehauf, of the trucking corporation Fruehaufs. So I figured I wasn't doing badly for a teenager. Like all adolescents with artistic leanings, I took myself seriously, too seriously, and, as Saroyan once said of his youthful self, I was intense. Poetry poured out of me like leaky fountain pen ink, and—to use the parlance of standard, not black English—it was *bad!*

William Saroyan's the one who showed me it wasn't always necessary to go by the rules. That is, it was more than possible to say in writing what you and you alone had to say about your own comings and goings, your own experience in the world, and say it in your own voice, even if that voice quavered at times and what it had to deliver was almost unspeakably dumb and wrong-headed. In short, style, zeal, enthusiasm, sincerity and bravado could carry you a long way when it came to getting your heart and mind down on paper. "In the time of your life," he says in his best-known play, "live!" I got the message.

The clock, indeed, is always ticking loss, loss, loss. The idea, as I got it direct from the Daring Young Man on the Flying Trapeze himself, was to relax and have fun while you're out there on the page. As a fledgling scribe with no sense whatever, and as one who has yet to come to terms and make his peace with form and structure, that message was worth at least half the world to me; a hemisphere anyway. It whisked me out of step with many of the knowledgeable and well-schooled writers I came to know once I'd slipped into the University of Michigan at Ann Arbor, but it also kept me going.

Over the years, I continued to fall in and out of love with William Saroyan's work. His output was tremendous, and only recently did I learn how much the man actually wrote. I heard his daughter Lucy on the radio one morning—a morning not long following his death—telling about how she and her brother Aram, as children, were forbidden to interrupt Daddy at home while he was working. She further mentioned that his published work is only the tip of the iceberg, so to speak, and that the unpublished manuscripts far outnumber all the work that's ever seen the light of print. Gradually, poring over his stories, novels, essays, memoirs and the letters literary scholar and historian James D. Hart had shown me, I've been able to piece together more than I care to know about the man who, because of American tax difficulties, took up residence in Paris in the late 1950s at 74 Rue Taitbout.

For years that address has remained in my Rolodex file under Saroyan's name. Something told me I'd be running into him one day. It was only a matter of time and timing. I thought about him a great deal when I moved from Michigan to the San Francisco Bay Area in the early sixties, and for a time I was traveling to Fresno to play a coffeehouse gig one weekend a month. The day after President John F. Kennedy was assassinated, my guitar whiz buddy Perry Lederman and I were wheeling into Fresno to knock down fifty bucks apiece as folk and blues performers. It was a Saturday night—November 23, 1963—and I can still reconstruct the unspoken sadness that hovered over the meager crowd we played for. It was even more acute than the malaise we'd felt the night before at the Cabal in Berkeley when nobody on the bill had felt like going on, and least of all myself. Something had ended or was about to end. Every one of us could sense it. The minute we pulled into Fresno, which I'd only known through Saroyan's eyes and ears and childhood grasp of the town's meaning, I turned to Perry at the wheel of that beat-up Studebaker and said, "Saroyan's town."

"What'd you say, man?"

"Said, Saroyan's town, this is William Saroyan's town of grapes and sun and immigrant Armenians."

"I don't see no grapes," said Perry, "but I'll bet they'll have some wine at the club. You really like that guy's stuff, don't you?"

"He's taught me a lot." And at that very moment, unbeknownst to Perry or anyone else in the world of Hello-Out-There, I was quietly transported to a place that didn't so much exist in time as it did in one of those intuitive flashes in which past, present and future fuse. In that instant I took in the winking neon lights of downtown Fresno, focused on the memories locked up inside me of two

Armenian women I'd secretly loved in high school and at college—
the one, a zaftig, brown-skinned girl whose beauty was only rivaled
by the black and Jewish beauties in the immediate community; the
other, a sleek, black-haired, fair-skinned honey who used to work
the check-out counters in the food lines at East Quad, Ann Arbor,
the University of Michigan, back when I'd been a busboy there in
1957.

But also playing around the edges of this stopped yet quivering
vision of timelessness were all the musty, forever-renewable seed im-
pressions of Armenian-American life that William Saroyan's nutri-
tive prose had planted in my fertile mind of long ago. *Life*—that's
what those stories and sketches and vignettes and plays had all been
about; the untellable history of the human spirit. Of course, of
course! Saroyan had *created* all this stuff about his childhood and
youth in Fresno and elsewhere. Sure, it was all based on actual
events and real people—whatever that meant—and yet the key to
understanding that world somehow lay in knowing, nay, *realizing*
that Saroyan was at all times only being himself, an artist, a writer
with a generous yet fragile point of view or slant on things that was
inextricably tied to his own delicate and complicated hunches, insights and beliefs.

It would be years before I found out about the problems he'd had
dealing with his own family as father and husband. It would take
even longer to learn that the man who wrote so winningly about
family love and warmth had never had an easy time of it himself.
Certainly those painfully formative years Saroyan spent in an
orphanage must have affected him enormously. And the heavy
drinking, compulsive gambling, monumental restlessness and
globetrotting were doubtless symptomatic of a deeply disturbed
personality. That's one way of looking at it.

But Saroyan was also a compulsive writer and a compulsive ob-
server of life and the human condition whose works are still read
and loved all over the world. Often his views were refreshingly
naive, even dead wrong, and he wasn't beyond waxing sentimental
or maudlin at the drop of a hat. He recorded the human comedy as
he saw and felt and lived it, and—when you come right down to
it—the world is far richer than it might have been had he never

traveled this way at all. He was willing to take extravagant risks that, more often than not, paid off handsomely. Imagine holing up for a month in a room to simultaneously write a whole novel *(The Adventures of Wesley Jackson)* and, over the same period, keep a diary about that experience *(The Adventures of William Saroyan),* both of which would appear in a distant volume called *The Twin Adventures.* His award-winning play, *The Cave Dwellers,* was composed in eight days in a New York hotel room. The speed with which these projects were executed is no measure, of course, of the works themselves, but the spirit and gusto that prompted them still stuns me. Why not sit down with a songwriter and come up with "Come On-A My House"? It might just turn out to be a hit.

When my son Michael was five, I took him to see a Jackson Pollock retrospective at the San Francisco Museum of Modern Art. For me the exhibit provided an opportunity to take a fresh look at one of the declared masters of that long-lasting vogue known as abstract expressionism. Like bebop, so-called "action painting" was a cultural phenomenon that had thoroughly permeated my adolescence to the point where I'd almost grown up believing this was the only true way to paint, making all other approaches seem misguided or, worse yet, academic. Fashion is like that; licks and modes have a way of shaping whole eras whose participants sincerely believed that the only way to play jazz was like Charlie Parker, the only way to sing a pop ballad was like Frank Sinatra, the only way to write poetry was like T.S. Eliot, and the only way to paint was like Jackson Pollock.

I walked with my son around the museum, gazing in my late thirties at Pollock's frantically executed swirls, dribblings, spatterings and fat brush strokes which, at one time, I'd felt intimately at home with when it came to appreciating visual art as culture. Culture, what was that? After you get past yeast and yogurt, it can get awfully tricky, particularly when the vernacular civilization you move in is profit-motivated.

When fatigue set in, I sat with Michael on a long marble bench and sighed. "Well," I asked him, "what do you think?"

"About what, Daddy?"

"About Jackson Pollock's paintings."

Michael looked around the stately, immaculately organized room and then at the immense canvas that took up the high wall before us. I imagined how Pollock had probably donned a tall ladder, set up canvas and pots of pigments, dipped his brush, swathed it liberally, then slam-banged and splashed and re-splashed his way across the blank wilderness of canvas. What a way to make a statement!

"Well?" I asked my son.

Not having yet learned to fidget at such questions, Michael looked at me and at the mammoth painting again. "Daddy," he said, "I paint too, you know."

At that, I laughed and hugged him until he squirmed and wiggled loose. He had no idea what his innocent comment had meant. As far as I was concerned, this was art criticism at its finest and most revealing.

On our way out, by the late Sunday afternoon ticket-taking door, who should pop on his way in but William Saroyan himself. He was dressed for the weather in a London Fog raincoat and floppy gray hat with a black umbrella at the ready. It was the lavish mustache that did it, though; the 1890s mustache and the eyes, those eyes, as sad and twinkly as the eyes of a child about to be dragged from the circus grounds at closing time. O he looked to be about as world-weary as they come, this graying man of letters and notions who was wandering, as if by some divinely silent cue, in our direction.

Just as he stepped within comfortable earshot, I said, "You're William Saroyan."

"Yes, yes, that's me all right." His smile was ready, warm, polite and bright. "And who, if I may ask, are you?"

"Al Young, and I'm delighted to finally meet you at last. I've been a fan of yours since I was a kid."

"You're a writer, aren't you?"

"Yes, I am."

"And what do you write?"

"Novels, poetry, all kinds of stuff."

"Is this your son?"

"This is my son Michael."

"What a handsome lad. How old are you, Mike?"

Michael laid his best sociable giggle on the old man and said, "Five. Well, five and a half, really."

Saroyan shook both our hands and said, "You must tell me the names of your books."

"I wish I had copies of some of them on me. It would be a pleasure to inscribe them for you."

"Don't worry about that. I know how it is. Just give me some titles." He tapped at his temple. "I won't forget because I'll make a point of finding and reading those."

"You still living in Paris on Rue Taitbout?"

Saroyan laughed. "You really have been keeping up with me, haven't you? Sure, but I've got it worked out so I spend a few months over there and few over here. It's more interesting that way, you know?"

"Of course, I understand."

"So give me some titles."

I felt embarrassed but all the same I mentioned *Snakes, Who Is Angelina?* and *Sitting Pretty,* all the novels I had come up with by then.

"Great titles," he said. "And you say you're a poet too?"

"Listen," I said, "I'll send you copies of each of those books."

"No, no," he said, "I'll find them somehow and I'll read them. I'm still a big reader and I won't miss these."

I believed him and I didn't believe him.

Bunched up in my mind, ready to unravel, were all the topics I wanted to rush out and have coffee or beer with him and discuss at reasonable length—playwriting, publishing, San Francisco, Hollywood, the thirties, the forties, the fifties, travel, Fresno, memoirs, spontaneity, Armenian food, music, that picture he'd posed for from the 1950s in front of a piece of sheet music composed by himself and expatriate American writer and songster Paul Bowles, and, quite naturally, whether there was a connection between music and storytelling and record-spinning and, well, how did he and Ross Bagdasarian just happen to come up with "Come On-A My House"? If only I could get him over to my place!

But there was no time left. The museum was about to close and

Saroyan looked as if this might very well have been the last scheduled stop in a long day of making his San Francisco rounds.

With Michael tugging at my sleeve and the clock tocking and ticking and signaling as always, I was forced to understand that this was going to be either the nourishing end or the very beginning of a long-anticipated moment that, like the rest of life, would forever be receding like bubbles into the roaring, sloshing sea of memory.

We shook hands again before Saroyan disappeared into the crowd with me watching the top of his salt-and-pepper head every inch of his way.

American through and through, all I could think to remember at that moment was how beautifully timed his arrival and departure had been.

Straight
No Chaser

Thelonious Monk, 1960

THOSE WERE NIGHTS when the Baroness would pull up in her gleaming, other-worldly Bentley to fetch Thelonious and motor him away between sets at the Jazz Gallery. The scene was simply not to be believed, unless you happened to be there to see it for yourself as I was for as many nights as my lean, practically non-existent budget would allow. Somehow I never worried about money. It came my way in dribbles, but mostly it went. It went for foolishness, and foolishness was a staple for me in those summery times when I was so much older than I am now.

Foolishness sustained me. Foolishness was rambling around the whole of Manhattan, mostly on foot, but also on buses and by subway. I went it alone and I ran in crowds, thinking it possible, as a matter of course, to hear all the music there was, see all the films, read all the books, meet all the people, and, in my idler moments, write reams and reams of prose and magical poems to celebrate the wonder of it all and, naturally, just to keep my writing chops up.

Oh, and there were languages to learn, and girls; long philosophical chitchats into the night, and entire days whiled and gladdened away in Hoboken and Brooklyn; ferryboat rides to Staten Island, funky weekend parties, airy beach parties on Long Island, tuning in nightly to radio bard Jean Shepard, wanderings through museums, hanging around the docks and parks, crashing in strange friends' and friendly strangers' rooms and apartments, learning new things on guitar and ways of deepening and stretching the singing voice, sitting at a Village curb with Dennis Rosmini (guitarist Dick Rosmini's pint-sized cousin) and sketching on cheap paper with cheap pencils the disappearing world as it zoomed and wobbled before our eyes.

Am I romanticizing? Am I licensing myself to poeticize what, after all, were only quotidian, dissolving events in the formative era of a simpleminded kid whose head and eyes and ears and nervous system all needed shrinking at the time? Perhaps I am. But that's only because this was the way I lived it when and while it seemed to be happening—these things, these foolish things that continue to remind us of ourselves when we're in the sorcerous process of becoming ourselves.

And Thelonious Monk was as much a part of me then as he is now. All kids who listen to Monk's music seem to love it at once. It's a child-like music; compelling and attractive in a fundamental way. There's no way, really, to put this all in language (spoken luggage), but when has being at a loss for words ever stopped a writer?

On one of those nights, one crazier than usual, I spent a rapt three sets at the Gallery with my guitar buddy Perry Lederman and with Gordon Hope, a drinker with writing ambitions. We had put away a gang of ale and cheese, crackers and onions over at McSorley's Irish Saloon, and now we were checking out Monk, who had Coltrane with him just then. It was also a night when Steve Lacy was sitting in with the group on soprano saxophone. Charlie Rouse was the other horn man. Actually, Monk and Trane were being featured separately as a double bill, but Trane's energy level was such at the time that he managed to ease in on Monk's sets with no apparent strain.

The setup was fascinating. Lacy had just recorded his first album on Prestige, which included the Monk compositions "Bye-Ya" and "Trinkle Trinkle." For formal reasons, Monk had Lacy sit all by himself off to one side of the little stage, and when it came his turn to solo, Lacy would stand and play while the rest of the band provided him with serious, intensive backing. It was like a microcosm of the kind of situation you'd expect to run up against in old Johannesburg or in Monk's native North Carolina, but not at the Jazz Gallery.

I don't know why that detail of spatial arrangement registered with me so deeply. Black soloists, after all, had long been featured with white bands as island performers, you might say; in fact, it had become something of a tradition. I could tell, though, that Monk appreciated Lacy's playing and ideas. That Steve Lacy had also chosen Monk as an inspirational ace and mentor must have accounted for his presence on the bandstand at all. It never left my mind, however, that bop itself had been pioneered by ingenious musicians, some of whom had as their express purpose the creation of a music white players weren't going to be able to steal. And, for a time anyway, Bird and Diz and Monk and others like them managed to pull the wool over the white boy's ears, and some colored ears too. Fletcher Henderson's arrangements had helped float the Benny Goodman band to glory; Sy Oliver had cut the kindling and stacked the logs for the Tommy Dorsey band's success; Glenn Miller had borrowed his reedy, lead clarinet-above-the-saxophones sound from the lesser-known Negro band of Eddie Durham, and so it went.

This is how the rest of that night went at the Jazz Gallery with its cozy decor of abstract expressionist paintings: Perry sat there stunned set after set, drifting into the music from a folk music and country blues perspective. Gordon kept disappearing into the john to sneak little nips of gin from a half-pint he'd packed. The minute the last set ended, Monk disappeared. He didn't dance offstage the way he'd later do nightly once he landed a long-running gig at the Five Spot. Perry, who wasn't a smoker yet, rushed outside for air. I had no idea where Gordon had gone, but since he was basketball player height, I figured he wouldn't be that hard to locate. Monk, I imagined, would be outside the club at curbside, climbing into the Bentley with the doting, glamorous Baroness Pannonica Rothschild de Köenigswarter at the wheel. To the press she was the Jazz Baroness, but to the tight côterie of musicians she was Nica. Monk had written his soothing "Pannonica" for her, and she had inspired Horace Silver's sultry "Nica's Tempo" and other jazz compositions. It was in her apartment that Charlie Parker had died.

I rushed out into the leafy, downtown summer night, blinded by its artificial brilliance. That's when I glimpsed the scrawny black man being chased, hounded by a pack of white hoods. I blinked and then saw him drop to the pavement, scroonched up in the fetal postion with nothing on but briefs, occasionally flailing his arms and kicking to ward off blows. He was bleeding and kept groaning.

"This is what he gets," one of the hooligans busy kicking him shouted to the crowd. "This is what he gets for goosin a girl in the park!"

The assailants were scuzzy-looking, sallow and ugly like hooligans everywhere. And, like their movie counterparts, they were playing to the flashing camera minds of the crowd gathered at curbside. "For goosin a girl in the park," they shouted. It was a litany.

They kept saying it, all six or seven of them, as if it justified their every savage move: "For goosin a girl in the park, for goosin a girl in the pahk, fuh goozin a goil in da pahk, f'goozin a guheeeyull innapahk, f'goozinagoilinnapahk, f'goozinagoilinnapahk!!!"

What goil? What pahk? What offense justified any of this? Right away—the music forgotten, the notion of getting another look at Monk and Nica dissolved, the whereabouts of my pals shattered into glassy bits and pieces of meaning like the night with its thousand eyes—I wanted to pull a gun, anybody's from anywhere, and blast them all away, slowly, each by each, as the flames of my anger inched toward insanity—Choom-Choom-Choom-Ka-pyowww! Thunk! Fight fire with fire!

In slow-motion instant replay, unknown back then, I can almost chart this pitiful event frame by frame. Suddenly there Gordon stood, cursing and on the verge of exploding, right there on the curb. In real time it was all coming at me so fast I didn't know where start finished or where ended began. Hatred heated the moment. A big old American car was waiting with the engine running and a nervous driver, ready to make the getaway. At first I stood transfixed, trying to size up the scheme. What had really happened? Who was the girl? Who was the young man being stomped before my eyes? Had it all begun in Washington Square Park? When? How? What were we looking at? "Quit it, stop!" I screamed.

Without thinking, I pushed my way through the crowd toward the victim. I didn't know what I could do, but I knew I had to make my way to the front line and let whatever was going to happen happen. The minute I reached the curb, the thugs turned tail and raced into the street to squeeze inside the getaway car, one of them yelling out one last "That's-what-he-gets-f'goozinagoilinnapahk!"

I turned to see Gordon moving toward me from out of the crowd. He looked practically sober with concern and fright. "Al," he said, "thank God, you're OK. I thought it was you they were kicking the shit out of!"

The two of us automatically got to work at once and, with Gordon taking the man's arms and me lugging him by the feet, we lifted the bruised, bleeding man from the gutter and stretched him out on the sidewalk. Someone must have already phoned the police because in no time we heard a siren and could see the twirling colored lights approaching the nightclub. That's when Charlie Rouse, a mainstay with Monk's band, walked out of the Jazz Gallery, his saxophone case in hand. He strolled to the curb and looked down at the victim impassively.

"What happened?" some latecomer asked from the crowd.

Rouse shook his head slowly from side to side and said, "Humph! I reckon the cat musta fell down. Yeah, he musta fell down."

Gordon got down on his knees and put his ear to the man's face and heart. "He's still breathing," he announced. "But they sure did do a number on him, poor guy."

Perry popped up then from out of nowhere. He said, "If I had me a gun I'da shot the muthafukkas. This is Mafia shit, that's all it is, but I'da shot 'em!"

The cops arrived and dispersed the crowd and cleared the way for an ambulance to park. We were all told to stand back and to go home, the authorities were going to take care of it.

The three of us took the subway to our respective digs, and we spent a lot of time talking about the crazy, disgusting wrongness of it all.

"I'm gonna get me a gun," Perry kept saying. "Can't believe I grew up around here and still don't have a gun. You gotta protect yourself against shit like this!"

Gordon sipped from his bottle and said, "Yeah, that's some terrible stuff. I'm just glad it wasn't one of us."

I don't remember what I said, but I do remember how passive and resigned the crowd had been, and I couldn't get it out of my mind that this had taken place in New York City in the liberal, permissive ghetto of the East Village; not in Alabama, Mississippi or the Georgia backwoods.

"Who were those guys doing the kicking?" I asked Perry.

"Local Italians," said Perry. "They never have liked all these outsiders coming into the Village, and Negroes in particular. I'm telling you, man, you better pack yourself some heat!"

What a way to end a night of beautiful, exciting music!

The subway sped uptown to our separate but equal worlds, each of us locked into the pain and anger of that night.

Later I heard that there were repercussions; that a black gang known as the Chaplains—the very ones reputed to have once challenged the New York Police Department to a rumble in Central Park—poured into the East Village in taxi cabs and got out dressed in suits and ties, toting neat little business-like attaché cases. Inside those valises were bicycle chains, knives, pipe wrenches and other urban artillery. The way I heard it was that the Chaplains—whom many whites called the Mau Mau Chaplains—proceeded to avenge the brutal beating that'd taken place outside the nightclub by slashing out at any white man who even *looked* street tough.

Although I come from a family of pistol-packing Southerners, right on down to my elderly grandmother and aunts, I never felt comfortable with guns. But Perry did, indeed, get himself a gun, and that's another story. They actually sent the Baroness up the river on a narcotics possession rap. Steve Lacy, like dozens of American jazz artists, moved to Europe. John Coltrane and his music flourished, even to the point of inspiring one devoted cult to build a church around it. Monk quit playing in the 1970s; simply stopped with no explanation and died in 1982. A year later, Gordon died of chronic alcoholism. Charlie Rouse, a beautiful player and wit, took leave of this gig called life on November 30, 1988.

And, as you can see, I lived long enough to get this down onto paper, knowing well that—like notations on musical score paper—it'll go on being strictly dead stuff, an artifact, until another human being runs it through that most marvelous of instruments, imagination, and transforms the look of it into sound by breathing sense and meaning and feeling back into these blues.

My Boyfriend's Back

The Angels, 1963

ONE DELICIOUS AFTERNOON in the middle of my twenty-third year, I'm stomping out of Tad's Steak House in midtown Manhattan, not bothering nobody, pricking my gums with a mint-tipped toothpick, when suddenly—point-blank—it slaps me upside the head like a number 10 paintbrush saturated with hi-gloss nail polish!

Are they Polish? Are they Bohunks? Are they the ghosts of all those glandular girls who used to bunch together in the hall outside the school cafeteria to nasalize "Crazy Little Mama" by the Penguins? No, these tootsies are rolling in pure, sticky, pubescent syrup—American through and through—and what they're doing to me *live* right there on the sidewalks caked with transistorized sound is shrieking at me rhythmically in tones so primal and insouciant, it's all I can do to hold back and keep from bursting out in gritty falsetto yelps to keep up.

"Hey, la!/Hey, La!/Muh boyfriend's back!"

What's that they're saying?

"Hey, la/Hey, la!/Muh boyfriend's back!"

Are they actually singing about that region of the vertebrate body located nearest the spin, in man consisting of the rear area from the neck to the pelvis?

No, not at all.

Finally you catch on, the way you always have to catch on or forever remain silent once you've been flung against your will into the bowels of some dumb song and have to hear it out before you can work your way full circle back up for air. No, what these vibrant fillies are champing at the bit about is revenge. Yes, revenge, my man! It's as simple as that, and almost as simpleminded.

Of all the ninny songs mindlessly inhaled during my ultra-cool and prolonged I-know-what's happening phase, this one comes lunging at my adenoids and gonads the way those old doo-wop ditties used to do back when rhythm & blues was news.

The Angels, I figured the minute I heard them, were the white girls' answer to the Shirelles; that is, somebody else's answer to record producer Phil Spector's relentless string of money-making smash records fueled by girl groups. Years later, when the sidewalks I haunted had shifted to another coast, an unsentimental California scribe—a man sympathetic to classic jazz—would lean across a sunny luncheon table and tell me: "Queen of the slut groups, that's what they were!"

I couldn't agree.

It's all lopsided and odd here in America, the ways we wiggle and wobble from era to era. "Give us your hungry and your poor," we cry, then turn around and do a Dr. Jekyll for a decade in the Robber Baron mode. Maybe that's the way it is with these youthful, schizoid, upstart nations. And maybe it's the same with the nubile and restless daughters of blue-collar aristocrats who don't know anorexia from the corner Rexall Drugstore. All they know is they're hungry for a hit.

The Angels, The Shirelles or the Shangri-La's (as in *La la la la la la la la lahhh-ahhh-la, I love you!*)—like all the others—were only giving the people what they figured we'd like and—so help me Mitch Miller!—they were right on the money.

Somebody Done Hoodoo'd the Hoodoo Man

Junior Wells, 1967

I GREW UP in homes where the verbal jam session was a floating and usually festive fixture. Clusters of people were forever talking with one another, telling stories, sharing experiences, observations, jokes, riddles, conundrums, and swapping lies. Our talk was musical. The old folks often quoted scripture and we all mimicked the voices and gestures of others, marbling the fat of our utterance with lean strips of proverbial wisdom: "A dog that'll *carry* a bone will *bring* you one." Much later I would become aware of the Kenyan proverb that goes: "Talking with one another is loving one another." For then it was enough to take delight in the pictures and emotions that flooded my imagination as I went about learning, by ear and by heart, the nature of the world that lay beyond my childhood walls and fields.

I used to curl up on floor pallets in a corner or in warmly quilted beds with the door ajar and, while pretending to be asleep, listen to the grown folks carry on into the night by kerosene lamplight—with crickets or rain or wind in the background—way back up in rural Pachuta, Mississippi and other distant settings.

Language and its stitched-together patterns of sound and beat and melody and pitch was real for me. Those crazy-quilt patches of bright and somber and giddy sound formed the literal fabric of my tender world. They were to be taken every bit as seriously as the very tree stump by the side of the dust road winding into town, that stately chinaberry stump where Uncle John, my maternal grandfather's brother, boasted that he'd once seen a hair-raising haint trot past one autumn long ago, hundreds of midnights before I was born. "He was ridin on a moon-white steed," said Uncle John, "and he was as close to me as you sittin from me now. Old Jack seen it too, like to sked him half to death. Rared back, commence to buckin and jeckin so bad I got gooseflesh!"

But I knew Old Jack. He was still alive and he was Uncle John's favorite riding mule. And I knew what Papa, my grandfather, meant when he'd haul off and say in the dead of winter, "I'm tireda hurryin down there to see bout John's mules. Only thing John's mules sufferin from is the miss-meal colic."

It was all as clear and mysteriously evident as lightning bugs pinpointing the summer-starved nights, winking out their starry morsels of code. My cousin Jesse and the other kids even held long discussions about this. That was probably the way fireflies talked with one another. We figured there had to be some luminous cipher involved that was none of people's business. All the same, we spent hours trying to break the lightning bug code; that is, when we weren't dashing around trapping them in Mason jars to make our own special flashlights. The rise and fall of locust choirs on sizzling afternoons was equally magnetizing. Locusts, in fact, provided the background music for a signal incident that buzzes through my memory circuits to this day.

I'd just finished feeding the chickens and was resting on the edge of the back porch, lazily scrawling letters in the yard dirt with a prized stick, when an old, raggedy, smiling hobo appeared out of nowhere. He wore a faded, floppy straw hat and was carrying a burlap croaker sack. I stood, startled, and looked at once to see what

Claude was going to do. Claude was our sleek, black farm dog whose jet, keen nose usually picked up everything. But Claude didn't stir; he didn't let out so much as a low grow. That tattered stranger, armed with nothing but a grin, crouched at the porch steps where Claude had been dozing and, nodding a friendly "Hi do?" in my direction, patted the dog on his tick-tortured head just as gently as anyone in the family might have done.

Mama, my grandmother, was coming from her garden with an apronful of fresh-cut okra, snap beans and green tomatoes. I could see she was as puzzled as I was. Nevertheless, she put on a smile, walked around to where we were, and she and the hobo exchanged pleasantries. He wasn't asking for a handout or odd jobs to do; he was only passing through and had somehow lost his way. Mama, her gold tooth fittings flashing in the late sunlight, patiently re-routed him, invited him to pluck a few figs and gather some pecans, then sent him on his way. He seemed harmless enough. But when he was gone, she studied Claude and looked at me, then stepped into the shadows of the porch. Narrowing her lucent brown eyes, she said, "I do believe that old rascal musta hoodoo'd that dog." She said this low under her breath, just loud enough for me to hear.

"Hoodoo!" I said. I must've been seven, maybe eight, and I'd heard the term but never from her lips until now. Its meaning had long been hidden from me. "What's hoodoo, Mama?"

"Hoodoo?" she repeated with a slow smirk that wasn't easy to read. "Aw, that's a kinda magic, whatchacall conjure. You burn candles, you mix these powders, get a holt to a locka somebody's hair or a piece of they clothes, say these words over and over. It's magic, but it's the Devil's magic. See, God got his magic and the Devil got his. Myself, I don't like to be foolin with them hoodoo people, never did."

"Well, how come you say that man done hoodoo'd Claude?"

"Cause that dog ain't got no business layin up and lettin that Negro pet him like that. Didn't bark, didn't even budge hardly."

"But how could the man put a hoodoo on him if he hadn't even seen Claude before?"

"That's what we don't know. He coulda slipped round here one night while we was sleep and sprinkled around some goofer dust.

Mighta even had some in his hand or up his sleeve just now for all we know."

"But, Mama, wouldn't we'da heard him sneakin round the house here at night?"

"Don't know that either. Them kinda folks know all this low-down stuff; that's all they study. The man coulda run up on Claude back there in the woods someplace and hoodoo'd him then."

"But why would he wanna hoodoo Claude in the first place?"

Mama trained her gaze on the chickens and the chicken coop and said, "Can't answer that neither, but I can tell you one thing. If I hear any kinda devilment goin on in the night, yall'll hear me shootin my pistol."

This was the same woman who moaned and hummed and sang spirituals all day long while she worked, and who taught me table blessings and the beautiful Twenty-Third Psalm.

It was in such settings that poetry began for me. Perhaps it is children who understand poetry best. I know for certain that, unlike most people, I never outgrew the need or magic or the curative powers of language. The quiescent greenness of those pastures in which I pictured myself lying down is more vivid than ever, and I can see the shapes of cloud and sky reflected in those still waters. I do not take John lightly when he declares, "In the beginning was the Word, and the Word was with God, and the Word was God." Even now in the Nuclear Era when we're constantly only a micro-chip blip away from graceless extinction; even at a time when the functions of poetry have been denigrated and trivialized, when post-literate societies largely regard poetic expression as a mere amusement at best, I've come to view Creation itself as the actual-ized speech of the Divine: the unnameable, dream-like essence of some marvelous cosmic presence. Sustained and intensive personal experience and involvement with language has opened both my ears and eyes to the magnitude of the Word and its power to transmute perception and consciousness: reality, if you will.

Such lofty realizations have never been uncommon among tra-ditional pre-literate peoples, nor among the so-called civilized. Hindu, Taoist, Judeo-Christian, Buddhist and Islamic cosmologies abound with them. Leslie Silko opens *Ceremony*, her fecund novel about Indian life on a New Mexico reservation, with a poem that begins: "Ts'its'tsi'nako, Thought-Woman is sitting in her room/and whatever she thinks about/appears." And in his moving book, *Eskimo Realities,* the humanist anthropologist and filmmaker Edmund Carpenter notes: "In Eskimo the word 'to make poetry' is the word 'to breathe'; both are derivatives of *anerca*—the soul, that which is eternal, the breath of life. A poem is words infused with breath of spirit. 'Let me breathe of it,' says the poet-maker and then begins: 'I have put my poem in order on the threshhold of my tongue.' "

It took me quite some time to learn how poetry has always functioned and flourished among all peoples in all times and places, customarily as a natural component of song, dance, work, play, prophecy, healing, exorcism, ceremony, ritual or communal worship. It was the printing press, among other innovations—to say nothing of altered notions about the place of the individual in the scheme of things—that helped change the way we think about poetry and the Word.

Long before the printed word and stuffy ideas about literature turned up in my life, and certainly long before I became the willing ward of schoolteachers, I was sleeping with words. I fondled and sniffed and placed my ear to their secret meanings. I soaked up the silences between syllables, tested them, tasted the saltiness or sweetness of them, and stared off into their bottomless eyes and down their dark, rosy throats. In a world innocent of ABC's, I dreamed in word-pictures and word-objects and word-feelings. And, like most children who live poetry all day long, I disappeared in between the spaces words made. It is this early enchantment with electrifying speech that abides with me still, in spite of the literature industry, in spite of poet-careerists and their ambitions, and quite in spite of the poetry scene itself.

"I always knew you were gonna be strange," Mama reminded me. She lived to be one hundred years and six months; a tough and beautiful little country woman whose light-drenched eyes could still see clean through me. My father's long gone from this world, and my mother has slipped away too. I've wandered and rambled from

Mississippi to Michigan to California; all over this country, all over the world. And for a long time Mama was still there, telling me things I needed to hear. "Always knew you were gonna be strange. From the time you could babble, you had your own way of talkin and understanding. We would put you on the floor with a funny-book or a magazine while you was still a baby, and you'd start turning pages and feelin on 'em and drift right off into some other world. Never would cry hardly. Long as you had them books to look at, you was happy. I never seen anything like it."

All my life I've been trying to hold onto and expand the joyous purity of those early moments and the magical talk that nourished it. Word by word, line by line, season upon season, poetry keeps teaching me that the only time there is, is now.

My Funny Valentine

Richard Rodgers & Lorenz Hart, composers

NOT LONG AFTER she'd roused him in the dark to tell him her water had broken, he caught up with himself in the waiting room on the hospital maternity ward. One other father-to-be lay napping in work clothes on a nearby sofa.

He was trying hard to focus on the Sunday morning football game, but his attention kept shifting from the warm colors of the screen to the black-and-white bleakness outside where rain and mist were washing out another kind of picture. It wasn't always easy to tell which world was real and which was imaginary. The love of such mysteries had made a writer of him.

Birth, death; arrivals, departures; yesterday, tomorrow; dreaming and wakefulness—where did any of it end or begin?

"Well, any score yet?"

The disheveled napper was sitting up and yawning at him now. "Zip."

"Good." The man squinted at his watch. "I been here all night waiting for this game to start."

"Is this your first time too?"

"Nah, the fourth time around for me. My old lady's gonna get her tubes tied."

When the nurse appeared to lead him into the delivery room, he felt shaky and vaguely jubilant. The middle of November, he thought. The heart of the rainy season. What a time for a kid to be coming into the world! What if something goes wrong? One of his sister's children, his nephew, had been born retarded. A bit of oxygen at the right time might have worked wonders. Was there ever a right time, though, to die or get born?

Seeing her convulsed in pain with her long legs up in stirrups made his stomach quiver. Her tears weren't at all like the ones she'd shed the time he'd proposed to her at the train station in Madrid. Thoughts of time and distances began to overwhelm him again when he thought about the places where they'd started out and stopped—Mississippi, Massachusetts, Michigan, New York, California, Mexico, Morocco, Italy, Portugal, Spain, France and now California again. What distance did a soul travel from eternity to paternity and maternity?

He became so caught up in coaching her to work and relax, push, breathe, just as he'd been trained to do in Lamaze class, that he had to remind himself to relax. Contractions were coming rapidly now.

"I—I can't do it anymore," she cried.

"Sure, you can, angel. You're doing just fine."

But he was no longer seeing his wife Arl; he was looking at woman in a wholly new light, and the beauty and miracle of her was blinding him with a radiance that outshone the antiseptic brilliance of that hospital chamber.

Meanings of labor, meanings of love—and the meaning perhaps of the labor of love—exploded upon him the way entire lifetimes are said to unfold before the secret eyes of the drowning. And wasn't it one of life's oldest secrets or mysteries that he imagined he was glimpsing? What had once been invisible was blossoming in the seeable world, but what was the hidden force that gave it life? Where did it come from, where did it go?

"C'mon," he said, "I can see the head poking out! The hair's all black and wet-looking!"

Her tearful flash of a smile made him think of sunlight; sunlight reminded him of rain, the day: November 14.

The nurse and obstetrician egged her on. "We're practically there," they announced. "One more big push."

"Sweetheart, you've done it! Now, give it all you've got. Atta girl!"

"It's a boy!" yelled the doctor as he pulled the glistening infant from its dark and nurturing shelter.

All pure cliché, the writer in him was thinking by then. But the man was helplessly observing how flimsy words were when it came back down to ultimate truths. One of his own mother's favorite sayings took on a powerful, fresh, deep meaning: "Everybody is somebody's child."

The whole world, in fact, felt like an afterthought. The snipping of the umbilicus flushed him with images of navels, oranges, vegetable and fruit flesh, sailing, boats, salt, the incubating sea; the oceans of eternal bliss that mystics say are real. Just as he'd always intuited, the so-called real and the imaginary eventually connect, for when the doctor slapped him gently on his tiny behind, the baby opened his eyes, saw at once what he was up against, and began to bawl.

It was only after he'd kissed her and left the hospital, when he was back on the freeway, driving into serious needle-slanted rain, that he remembered how perfectly timed their son's arrival had been after all. He switched the windshield wipers to high gear, snapped of the radio, and thought about the distant day in February, nine months ago to the night, when it had all begun.

What a Little Moonlight Can Do

Billie Holiday, 1935

I CAN'T TELL YOU what my daddy was up to in 1935 when this joyous little ditty first came out, but I know good and well he couldn't have missed it because Ben Webster was on it with Benny Goodman, Roy Eldridge and Teddy Wilson, and Dad was a Webster listener from way back.

I can tell you for a fact, though, when "What a Little Moonlight Can Do" finally hit me smack in the solar plexus. It was on a totally lunar night on another side of the world, down in Western Australia, a little spot in the bush that went by the aboriginal (read: original) name of Wundowie. Sounds like someplace secreted way back up in the piney woods of the Delta, don't it? Wundowie, Mississippi. But never mind, there's a whole new moon that's got me talking in tongues, for the moon can be so milky and moveable on certain warm nights in tropical regions I swear you can almost hear it moo.

Close to half a century after she'd recorded it, Billie Holiday's wonderous "Ooo-ooo-ooo!" caught up with and wafted me away deep into one of those primal nights nestled at the heart of all nights. We're talking root nights here; we're talking summertime in Australia—what we'd still regard as winter on this side of the globe—when skies of the Southern Hemisphere are crammed with planets, stars, shooting stars and astonishing constellations. Not only did it take my breath away; the upside-down and all-turned-around view of the heavens available Down Under was enough to melt and freeze my subtlest feelings, fix them in amber, and press them under the kind of glass that will always be more spirit than they ever were the connect-the-dots menagerie of pop astronomy I'd been trained to remember.

At one point that night the sky became so alarming and magical in its magnetism that every single one of us gathered there at Brian Dibble's ranch—Sherry Hopkins, Fran Richardson, Altamira, John and Chris Allert, Jan Berry and poets Roger McGough, Rosemary Dobson, Chris Wallace-Crabbe and Phil Collier, among others—cut our loving talk short, set down our beers, and got up to check out what was going on up above us. That's when Billie Holiday started playing through my American brain.

It was also the night I'd been traipsing around the surrounding paddocks with my feeble Instamatic camera, hoping for a kangaroo to show its face. Everyone had been making fun of me, the poet as tourist. Jan Berry, a lovely blonde New Zealander immigrant and interior decorator, said, "Al, if no kangaroos turn up for you to photograph, do you think you'll ever come back?"

"Shoobee-right-might," I told her, striving for coolness in my Yankee approximation of the all-purpose Aussie rejoinder: "Should be right, mate!" From what I'd observed during my whirlwind visit, the phrase seemed to cover everything from "How's it going?" or "Do you think it's going to rain?" to "Do you think she'll survive?" and "What say we call it a night?"

That night I wanted to resurrect Billie and give her a big hug for having transformed that otherwise neglible pop tune from the Depression thirties into something lasting. I still haven't heard anyone else who's been able to bring it to life the way she did. But that's genius for you. Billie could sing the words *lonely* or *flower* or *heaven* or *flame* or *soul* or *happiness* or *sky* or *romance* or *kisses* or *love* or *moon* like no one else. She'd make you taste them on your secret tongue the way she lived and loved in the bittersweet world we share in this dreamy wakefulness where word and touch and glimpse and fragrance and flavor and feeling keep dissolving, melting us into that eventual ocean of bliss we seem to be looking to drown in on the sly.

Billie, if you're out there listening somewhere, I just want you to know about one lovely night in Australia, of all places, when the sound of you at the back of my heart rose to the surface and helped the moonlight do what moonlight does so simply and gloriously.

Talk about your love at first sight, it was a little bit of all right. Ooo-shooo-be-dooo-be—right. Might.

And, as if that weren't amazement enough, some kangaroos actually showed up.

The Big Hurt

Miss Toni Fisher, 1960

FRESH OUT of Michigan and crossing the Bay Bridge into San Francisco on the lonely F Bus, it seemed I could see the whole color of the world once and for all. I was in my early twenties. It was windy and sunny. Openings to the universe were loosening up for me, for I was in love with something very special, or perhaps it was with everything at once. From this bend in time, it's hard to say which, because poetry kept seeping out of everything I squeezed.

Rooms I inhabited, for example, were sleepy-headed expanses with nothing but oceans shining out of their windows, lighting the sky and all its doubles.

Why it took Miss Toni Fisher and "The Big Hurt" so long to seep up from my subconscious sea and roll over me like a sympathetic wave is also mystifying, particularly when I look back and survey the flood of sweet- and not so sweet-nothings I gave conscious attention. I rather suspected that Sam Cooke's "Chain Gang," Brook Benton and Dinah Washington's "You've Got What It Takes" and The Drifters's "Save the Last Dance for Me" might be around for a few seasons. But what was it about Brian Hyland's "Itsy Bitsy Teeny

Weeny Yellow Polka Dot Bikini" or the Hollywood Argyles's "Alley Oop" or the Everly Brothers's "Cathy's Clown" or Elvis's "It's Now or Never" that could possibly last? I was wrong, of course, just as I was wrong about Marty Robbins's "El Paso," Brook Benton's "Kiddio," "Walk Don't Run" by the Ventures, and Brenda Lee's "Sweet Nothin's."

And who in the world did I think I was anyway? Certainly no Tin Pan Alley shaman or shaper of wham-bam-thank-you-ma'am runaway hits. It was all I could do to pull my own act together enough to hit the road and make the right bus connections.

Dreaming out the bus window midway over the Bay Bridge, swimming in the electrifying violet-blue of twilight, far from the homey simplicity of the flat Midwest, I could feel it begin. Twilight to dawn. California, there I was; right back where I'd started from; alone with myself and face to face with a sea of possibilities.

"The Big Hurt" surfaced like a nourishing lament. It zithered across the evening sky like a shooting star, its smoking tail a trail of quivering sparks.

"The Big Hurt" was pure theater; a dramatized sadness that began in the mind and played to the heart of some odd need to applaud that fragile part of myself that liked to sit in the dark and feel blue.

Moonlight Serenade

Glenn Miller, 1939

WHAT HAD BROUGHT me back, of all things, to a clear recollection of the dreamy part of my Gulf Coast childhood was the silvery sound of Glenn Miller's "Moonlight Serenade," that slow dance jewel that had hovered around me for over forty years like the aura of memory itself incandescent and audible and calming like balmy waves washing a shore on a festive night in late summer.

This comforting sound had always resided in a posh dance hall by the sea—all of it imaginary—on certain moonlit nights with all-American couples, elegantly suited and gowned, partying and gabbing and gliding and sliding toward dawn in movies and radio shows and comic books. Images of Archie Andrews and his arch rival Reggie horsing around with Betty, Veronica and Jughead continue to play in the Tuxedo Junction of my mind. Like countless other sub-American kids, hot-house-bred in ghettoes, on farms, near coal mines or across the tracks, I felt cheated and left out of these lunatic good times.

All this sentimental glitter flashed into my head the night I boarded a Houston bus in my early forties. The sign posted above the driver's seat for all to see said: NO SMOKING, RADIOS SILENT. But, of course, the driver himself was puffing on a cigarette and had his AM/FM radio going. All the way from Holcombe Road, where I'd got on, to Fannin Street where I got off at the Medical Center, we were the only ones on the bus. The driver was roundly tuned to the local nostalgia station airing "Moonlight Serenade." I sat in that seat up front across from the driver and basked in the reediness of the Glenn Miller Orchestra.

"That's some soothing stuff you've got going there," I commented politely.

"Well, yeah," he said. "I try to keep it a little on the listenable side."

He was gray-haired, paunchy and ornery-looking; the kind of guy who might actually draw you into a heated argument about the weather.

I said, " 'Moonlight Serenade' just keeps on coming at you, don't it? All my life it's been like that."

"You know," said the driver, "I believe in giving the passengers a break from this rock and roll. This old boy that works the morning shift, hell, he wears 'em to a frazzle with that boogie stuff he blasts. The way I figure is people get enough of that junk, so my idea is to calm 'em down and relax 'em some."

"This is certainly relaxing," I told him.

"Lemme tell you something," he said, leaning forward as he cut his wheel to make a sweeping lefthand turn onto Fannin Street. "Out here where I live—and I wanna tell you it was white people living next door to me when I first moved in, before I went away and come back, then they'd slipped some colored in on me—buddy, lemme tell you . . . they keep that jungle beat goin all day and all night long."

Mind you, the driver, a white man, was telling me this while we were still the only two people aboard, passenger and driver, bumping along in the cool Texas night. Perfectly aware of my color, the shape of my nose and the tight, spiraling texture of my salt-and-pepper hair, he was telling me this.

I let a few more bars of "Moonlight Serenade" slip by before I said, "Blacks aren't the only people who go in for rock and funk these days."

That's when the driver's face lit up and he turned to face me fully as we approached my stop.

"Hell," he said, "I know that! We're gettin to be just as bad!"

All the Things You Are

Jerome Kern, composer

OVER THE YEARS I've stopped keeping track of the worlds crammed inside this blossoming song of praise. But I'll never forget September of 1983 on a slow, thunderous afternoon in the Arizona desert, an afternoon crackling with lightning and bracing winds, when this song broke open like a bud of a saguaro flower for the wind to catch and dispatch its fuzzy seed messages and send them parachuting in all directions.

After watching blue lightning dance in the distance against a wall-flower backdrop of mountains, Lois Shelton and I motored back from the Desert Museum to her cozy house in Tucson, a house she shared with her husband, the poet Richard Shelton. There in their glassed-in living room I could look out and see that a storm was brewing. I sat to tinker at their grand piano while Lois ducked out to the kitchen to make coffee. A perennial beginner when it comes to piano, I began plunking out notes and mashing out chords to the most hesitant, reluctant and thoroughly rudimentary version of "All the Things You Are" imaginable, with no thought of how it was sounding. When Lois meandered into the room with a gleam in her eyes and her arms outstretched, singing Oscar Hammerstein the 2nd's actual lyrics in bell-like tones, I almost fell off the bench.

She sang: "You are/the promised kiss of springtime/that makes the lonely winter/seem long," and somehow I managed to make the opening changes. By the time we reached the bridge, however, I had grown so intensely involved with rising to her level, which was obviously professional, that to this day I can't tell you whether I was hitting the proper chords or simply inventing them as we went along. My head was saying: F minor 7, B, B-flat minor 7, E, E-flat 7, A-flat major 7, D-flat major 7, G7, C major 7 and all like that, but my fingers were strictly on their own.

When we'd reached the end of it, I sighed, looked up at Lois, and said, "Where did you ever learn to sing like that? What a shock! Why didn't you tell me?"

Once she got through quivering with laughter, she flashed me her earthy "Hey, Sailor!" smile and said, "My training was in opera."

I promptly apologized for my lumpish accompaniment but Lois, gracious soul that she is, said, "You were fine, just fine. I couldn't resist coming in on you like that. I love that song."

"I love it too," I told her. "It wasn't until I heard Beverly Sills sing it years ago on TV that I realized it didn't always have to be done in pop or jazz style."

Then Richard Shelton walked in the door, just in time for some fresh, fragrant coffee. He bet me it wasn't going to rain; this wasn't the season. He lost. I told him about "All The Things You Are." He was tickled and rightfully proud of Lois's voice. She'd been starring in Southwestern musical productions for years. I'd already met Richard in California and had long admired his work. Lois was the one who'd guided me patiently to the Tucson Airport and picked me up there after I'd booked myself into Phoenix. At the University of Arizona Poetry Center, which she quietly directed, I'd seen smart photographic portraits of writers she'd taken. Beyond that, I'd had no idea of all the things she was.

Late that night, peaceful in my campus bed, a visiting writer and guest of the University, I lay thinking about all the things we truly are, thinking about the vast, crystalline silence of the desert and how it restively nurtures reflection. While crickets chirped in the bathroom at Poetry House, and an occasional unconcerned lizard zipped across the floor of my snug bedroom, I lay remembering "Bird of Paradise," Charlie Parker's version of "All the Things You Are" and the chord it had set quivering in me years ago. For nights and mornings on end, I'd never wanted those changes to change.

Whether I'd been thinking birds or flowers, the paradise Parker had pulled me into, I realized in Arizona, was all intact. It was all still there, omnipresent in a finely muted region of spirit, the basis for everything, where nothing ever changes or moves or comes or goes or withers or blooms. It was all too divinely simple for my rambling, self-centered human mind to grasp just then. Yet the meaning of it all, like my scrambling at the piano to keep pace with Lois Shelton's vocalizing, pianist that I wasn't, was beginning to ring clear all the same. Like everyone else, I vaguely identified with all things, and it was only my awareness of this that needed sharpening. There existed a part of me that already knew all there was to know; it was only a matter of connecting with it.

That night, just before shifting from wakefulness to the middle of dream, I slipped into that delectable state where the thinker who's still busy calling out chord changes makes blissful peace with the player who's already playing. As I lay in this state, there appeared before me, in effortless recall, that portion of wall in the next room where guests had taken turns scrawling a highly specialized graffiti, and these words in flawless English of the Russian poet Yevgeny Yevtushenko:

> *I bless all those unblessed by God;*
> *Those with shoes and those unshod.*

The surprise of all surprises, however, came when I happened . upon a note I'd written in 1977 titled ALL THE THINGS YOU ARE.

The mind-blessed bend of a rainstorm aiming in a hurting direction, it's almost as if we were all fake piano players smoothing out mistakes with a false, facile flourish. You are the wash of a wave over stones left wet. You are the way wheat looks after it's been mauled. You are another afternoon.

Tell me about promised kisses, springtime, September, the desert, lightning storms, rain, the power of poetry and song, and why the lonely winter seems long. Slowly tell me all the things you are, we are, I am—and sing it.

Set Three

I'll Remember April

Gene DePaul, composer;
Don Raye and Pat Johnston, lyrics

EVERYONE THINKS drivers are wary of hitchhikers, but it works the other way around too. When the driver backed up almost a full block that morning in Berkeley to pick me up, I didn't know what to think. He was driving a beat-up car, and, climbing into the backseat, the first thing I noticed were the books on raw foods and other esoterica. As for the driver, he was balding, white-haired, had big bushy white eyebrows, seemed to be in his fifties, but the most salient characteristic was the glow he exuded.

He and his teenage son sat up front and as he chugged uphill, away from McGee and Dwight Way, where they'd backed up to get me, I had a feeling deep in the center of my solar plexus that something was up.

"What do you do?" the driver asked.

"I go to school," I lied.

"Up here at Cal?"

"Yes."

In the rearview mirror I watched his eyes squint curiously at me while I wondered why I was telling him this. It wasn't his business, I rationalized, and besides, in a sense I *was* going to Cal. I was working for a Ph.D. candidate in psychology, a man who was setting up experiments in conformity around town in various public schools. And I was, after all, a student of life.

"And what is it you study up there?"

"Anthropology," I said without missing a beat.

"What's that?"

"It's the study of man."

"The study of man, eh? Well, that's interesting. I never got beyond the fifth grade myself, but I've been studying hard to make up for it. I read a lot—histories and dictionaries especially. I've got five kids and I gotta leave 'em something, something they can use.

"So you study anthropology?"

"Yes," I said, beginning to feel uneasy.

"I don't know anything about that, but I have had some of these U.C. students babysit for me and, from what I can tell, they don't know much of anything."

I laughed at this and so did the driver's son. We were approaching Dwight Way and Telegraph, where he would be dropping the youngster off at the vocational high school that used to be there.

"From what I can tell, all they seem to be teaching those kids is more stuff to keep 'em ignorant." He glanced back over his shoulder at me. "There's a reason you got this ride, you know."

"There is?" I had picked up the ancient volume on raw foods and had nervously begun to flip through its well-thumbed pages. It looked and felt like the kind of item you'd find in the cheapie sidewalk bins in front of a good used bookstore.

"Yes. You notice how I backed all the way up like that? I almost missed you. We saw you out there with your thumb stuck out, and I told my boy, 'We have to go back and get that guy.'

"Listen" he said suddenly, "you've read a lot and studied a lot, haven't you?"

"Yes, I have," I told him, feeling more tentative than I ever had before.

"That's what I thought." He took one hand off the wheel, his right hand, and thrust it back toward me with his palm open. "So," he asked, "can you give me 'A'?"

"I beg your pardon? . . . "

The driver wiggled his fingers at me. "You heard what I said: Can you give me 'A.' Just give me 'A.'   "

At this, the driver's son, a tall, handsome lad, turned to face me fully. I've never forgotten the wry smile on his face and the way his eyes twinkled at me as if to say, "You don't know what you're in for, do you? This father of mine is something else." What he really said, however, as his father slowed and pulled to the curb for him to gather his own schoolbooks and notebooks, was: "Pleased to meet you."

While his son was getting out, the driver motioned for me to move up. "C'mon, up front," he said.

"No, thanks," I told him, "I'm comfortable back here."

In no time at all, we were back in traffic.

"Where you headed?" asked the driver.

"LeConte Elementary School," I said.

"Oh, is that where you work?"

"For today, yes. We move around to different schools."

"What do you do in these schools?"

"I help conduct a psychology experiment."

In a low, gentle voice, the driver put another question to me. "And what are you doing with those kids?"

"We're working with them."

"But are you teaching them anything helpful or useful? Or just playing around with 'em, helping keep 'em ignorant?"

At once the way I really felt rose up into my throat in one big awkward rush of confusion and guilt. What *was* I doing? When I thought about it, it seemed to go something like this: At each scheduled school, we would arrive early, set up our electronic circuit boards and little booths, our screen and projector, tape player and P.A. system. The kids—who had either volunteered themselves or were urged to volunteer for the project by their teachers—would come into the room, then sit and listen while I gave a little talk about how this little experiment was going to run.

"Don't worry about a thing," I'd tell them. "When you sit in these little booths next to your pals and classmates, you'll have a little board in front of you with lights that light up to tell you how your cronies are reacting to whatever we flash up there on the screen or play over the loudspeaker. All we ask is that you don't push any buttons until it's *your* turn, and the board will tell you when it's your turn to answer. You got that? OK, so now just relax and have fun."

And that's what we'd do: get them all rounded up and seated in these tiny stalls—seven or eight kids at a time—into little slots with a partition between each one and a light-dotted board in front of them. The stalls were just high enough for the screen to be seen. So, say my boss Ron Mack or his other assistant Sherwin. Sherwin snapped on the slide projector and flashed onto the screen a line marked Line A that extended perhaps two feet along the length of the screen, then, in rapid succession, flashed Line B, which was obviously a full foot shorter than Line A. What I would genially ask the kids to do was indicate, by pushing a button, which was the longer line. And that was exactly what they'd do but, precisely because it was a psychology experiment, I needn't tell you that there was something funny about the whole setup.

This was how the thing really worked: Each student, going by fraudulent information dished out by their circuit board, was being led to believe that everyone else had answered before them and that he or she was the last to be registering a response. When we got down toward the end, down to the music part of the so-called test, where Ron would give Sherwin the cue to play twenty-eight measures of Beethoven's *Fifth Symphony,* then three measures of Sousa's "Stars and Stripes Forever," then ask the kids which piece had lasted longer, the air in the room would usually be crackling with emotion. Working through a host of factors and cross-factors, my boss Ron's objective was to find out which kinds of students surrendered fastest to majority opinion and which ones held out in favor of their own perceptual judgments. What I found curious was that the more middle-class and white the community's school, the less apt students were to cause trouble or make waves. In the marginal or lower-class or black neighborhood settings, you could count on someone acting up in the middle of the experiment. They would either bust out of their stall and look over at their neighbors' circuit boards, or yell something like: "Hey what the fuck is goin on? Y'all deaf or blind or somethin?" And, I must confess, I liked those kids.

This is what whooshed through my mind while the driver, the quintessence of the mysterious stranger, sat waiting for my answer. What could I tell him? Obviously what we were up to wasn't helping those youngsters in the least. Not knowing how to reply, I allowed my own uncomfortable silence to do the talking for me.

"Like I said," the driver went on. "I've got all these kids and I need to leave 'em with something they can use. They need to know the truth. How much truth do you know? If you had to, could you explain God to an eight-year-old?"

By then we had reached the very corner where I was to get out. The driver parked in front of the school and, there in the dewiness and sunniness of a warming April morning, he turned to me and said, "You still don't know why you got this ride, do you?"

I shook my head.

"You're looking for something," he said again, "and I'm gonna try and give it to you—if you'll let me." He clicked off the engine and turned to look directly at me. "Don't you know why you suffer?"

"Well," I began, but that was as far as I got.

"You suffer because of your desires," he said, looking into my eyes with such feeling and depth that something inside me fell away altogether.

Then, recalling the language of the many books and texts I had been devouring of late on Eastern mysticism: yoga, Vedanta, Buddhism and Taoism—books like Alan Watts' *The Joyous Cosmology*, W.Y. Evans-Wentz's translation of *The Tibetan Book of the Dead*, and Paramahansa Yogananda's *Autobiography of a Yogi*—I managed to utter a single word. "Karma," I said, reluctantly of course, because it seemed to be inappropriate given the person I was saying it to; given his plain-spokenness.

He smiled and said, "All right, well, karma, yes—if you wanna put it that way. But it's like this: There really isn't any such thing as hell, and certainly not the way you've been thinking about it. You know where that comes from? Comes from those days back there when they used to drag all those dead bodies off to the edge of town and set 'em afire and burn 'em—that's where. Don't you remember?"

Honestly, I was scrunched into that backseat, as scared as I could be.

"They'd have a slow, steady fire of those bodies going all the time," he continued, "and that's where the concept of hell comes from. You're going through hell right now, though."

And it was true; I'd inwardly reached one of those blind alleys where—or so I thought at the ripe age of twenty-four—I'd looked down every street and back road there was to examine and, no matter how closely I scrutinized mapped-out paths, they all led to nothing, and nothing added up to zero. A few days before this hitchhiking interlude, one of the grand events of my youth, I had been feeling lonely and hungry for something unnameable. During a lunch break, I had excused myself from Sherwin's and Ron's company to go and have my sandwich on the Berkeley Pier. And, standing there at the railing, in the tepid sunlight and the fibrous, mind-stretching offshore winds of high spring, I remember looking out across the choppy, troubled blue-green-muddy bay waves and the way the gleaming noonday light was speckling and coating and riding them. Aha, I had thought, so that's how Jesus walked the waters! Something was happening inside me; some soulful craving was beginning to unravel and unfold. I hadn't understood it. I had gone home and drunk copious quantities of a friend's home brew to try to drown it out, but that soul-hunger I felt kept right on expanding; it wouldn't go away. Later, in a poem, I would refer to it as the craving for infinity. Yes, I had begun to look for something, and with an intensity I must've been broadcasting obsessively.

"And so," the driver said. "What you must do is study and think. Study and think, that's what you must do. This situation is awful; it's a mess. You've got eyes; you can see. We've got a lot of my kind messed up in this thing, and a lot of your kind."

If I said anything after this remark of his, I can't recall it. Mostly I remember wanting to get the hell out of that old, beat-up car and on into the school to start setting up the first morning experiment, even though I now knew I wasn't going to be sticking with that job for very long.

"You know," the driver said, peering, I swear, down into every nook and cranny of my secret self. "You've been to a lotta schools and read a lotta books, right?"

"Yes," I told him, baffled about what he was driving at.

"Nobody's ever been able to tell you *nothing*," he said. "You were always ahead of 'em. And now here I am, the first one to come along and kick your ass."

I had no idea then what he meant, except in a broad, generalized, you might say college outline kind of way. It was true that I had usually been rated and placed in the accelerated classes along with all the so-called smart and high I.Q. kids. But all along I had known that the kind of intelligence that fed me wasn't the kind that produced mathematicians and physicists and paleontologists and political strategists and literary structuralists and demographers and business tycoons. I always worked out my answers to problems and questions in a roundabout fashion, slipping up on truth through the side door, as it were.

Acknowledging my discomfort, the driver beamed at me and said, "Poor guy. You've been through a lot and you've still got a lot to go through. But you know what? One of these days you're gonna slip right out of that cloud you've been buried in and find out for yourself what's really going on. In the meantime I want you to study and think. When you can explain God to an eight-year-old, then you'll know something.

"Oh, just look at you," he said. "You're so frightened of what I've been telling you about yourself that you've just about had it—right here." He touched his throat. "Had it right up to the gills. But don't worry."

He pulled the front passenger seat forward to enable me to climb out of the car. After I'd gotten up, he stepped out too and stood beside me next to the cyclone fence and, beyond it, the playground.

"I know I said all that stuff about kicking your ass," he said with the oddest of smiles, "but in a moment I'm going to shake your hand, then you'll realize I didn't really mean that. You'll know what I really meant."

At this, he placed his warm hand around mine, which might've been trembling, and shook it with a sureness I had never before felt.

"Good luck to you," he said, "and think about what I've been telling you."

No sooner had his thick, hairy fingers slipped from mine than I felt myself becoming light and balloon-like, but not in the head. It was my body that felt as if some enormous bone-crushing weight were being lifted from it. I waved to the old man—being twenty-four, I thought he seemed rather advanced in age—and watched him motor away. In fact, I stood there in a daze and kept waving, knowing how Ron was going to give me, heh, heh, hell when I stepped into that classroom, twenty minutes late at least. But the giggly high that was puffing up past my throat and into every cell of my self just then said: Man, aren't you sick and tired of going around worried and anxious about stuff that couldn't be helped anyway? Frankly, I didn't care if Ron fired me on the spot; I'd get by. Something would turn up, the same way the sky was opening up for me and those treetops and birds and the sunlight itself seemed intimately aware of what I was feeling.

The beautiful fact is that I wandered about for days in this blissful condition. But it was that night, going for a walk, standing on the sidewalk and looking at the full moon, that I realized—*realized,* that is, *knew* and could *feel* as distinct from understood—that there was no distance whatever between that lighted orb hanging out there above Sacramento Street, above the Bay, above Berkeley, Oakland, San Francisco, California, the West Coast, North America, this whirling ball of mud and stone and greenery we called the Earth, and myself. The moonlit blood my heart continued to pump throughout and around my bodily constellations was winking to me that there was only one distance anywhere.

Did I go looking for that bushy-eyebrowed, gray and balding gentleman again? But of course. I stood on that same corner morning after morning, two blocks from the cottage my wife and I shared, and never laid eyes on either him or his son again. Every time I'd walk by that vocational school when classes let out in the afternoon, I'd look for his son in vain. For years I kept an eye peeled for them. Gradually, though, I came to realize how useless it was to keep scouting out the messenger when the message had been all I'd needed.

Every time a band or a singer strikes up "I'll Remember April," or when I rudely pick it out on piano myself, and for more Aprils now than I care to remember, I've been meaning to tell this little story. Except to a closed handful of sympathetic friends, I've figured it might be best to keep my mouth shut about it. But now that an entire horizon of clouds is beginning to break, when at least I can feel the warmth and nearness of that cloud-melting sun, I'm ready to sing it to the world.

"This lovely day will lengthen into evening" is the opening line Don Raye and Pat Johnston came up with back in 1942, describing, without meaning to, an unforgettable life in the day of a poet who, twenty-two years later, would remember Edna St. Vincent Millay's "Second April" and poet Bob Kaufman's "Second April" and the wistful melody of Gene DePaul's timeless "I'll Remember April" (from the motion picture, *Ride 'Em Cowboy*) and all the people who've played it and played with it and played to it and danced and hugged or kissed and made love to it to the thunder and lightning, in their souls or outside. And, facing the music, how could this poet forget the people who've gone to war remembering that song, who whistled and hummed it absentmindedly in the trenches of duty or ignorance or tipsy or dead drunk at the edges of some soft, breezy, terrifying daybreak or black hole of night or while stitching up a stomach or sitting in the cockpit of a high-flying bomber, pressing a button to unleash enough computerized missiles to wipe out an entire village that will neither see nor hear its coming and going as it whizzes overhead in the rural sky of some Buddhist countryside while the pilot listens in the comfort of his cabin, his luxurious stall, to Miles Davis or Lee Konitz or Charlie Spivak's Band or Ella Fitzgerald or Linda Ronstadt doing "I'll Remember April"?

And that poet, no longer able to masquerade as an innocent bystander, the victim of circumstance, a helpless but worldly hitchhiker, will have to swallow hard and face the music, then put his own words to what he has seen and heard and felt and done and learned and lived before he can know what to go back and tell that eager, wide-open, moon-pulled part of himself that never grew older than eight.

I'll Play the Blues for You

Albert King, 1977

THERE'S SOMETHING unalterable, unutterable and yet perfectly if not totally expressive about feeling-states the blues instill. I mean this from the ground-zero center of my heart—arteries, blood-run and blood count.

Having reached the turning point in my life—that thin bend in time where you turn the corner and twist inexplicably down some other street, an altogether unmapped street as unfamiliar to you as tomorrow, except you can sometimes see exactly where and how it's been blooming from seeds you've been sowing all along—having reached that intersection of Earthly Street and Heavenly Avenue, such ripened beauty as Albert King sings about comes to my ears as the blues. And the blues are about as soothing an expression of the basic human condition as ever there will be.

It's true that there are nights when you're so lonesome, so lonely, that it just wouldn't do for anyone to show up to befriend you or to try and startle you out of your solitude. On the same wavelength, there are times when you're so horny, so randy for the world that even the most intimate and prolonged contact with it—say you get close enough to the woman of your dreams to be able to verify from candid observation that it's got to be jelly 'cause jam don't shake like that—well, such closeness could only leave you feeling unfulfilled.

So what's all this got to do with Albert King? When Albert King in his gruff, tender way promises, "I'll play the blues for you," you go for it headlong, the way a simple mackerel snaps at fishing-pole bait. And when, in his easy cocktail lounge intermission manner, he makes good his promise, plays the blues so plangently and directly—gathering momentum chorus after chorus while he rolls down the hillside of your sorrow, rounding off the edges of your sadness—you know that by the time this Saturday night dissolves, you'll be fifty bucks in the hole, but all those green wigs of moss that love to make their home on stone will have rocked down to sea level. And by the time that's happened, you'll be as chilled out as the sand and grit and gravel at the bottom of King's hilly voice.

Go right on, Albert, with your multidirectional self! Play the blues for me. And you can pour it on because I'm already up to my ears with major blues. But I'm so tickled with the sound of your minor blues, I'm thankful I was born with ears.

Last Tango in Paris

Gato Barbieri, 1973

FORGET ABOUT Marlon Brando and Maria Schneider and the buttered-up sex and mooning. Forget the title shot and also the sadly erotic tawdriness of tit and ass pavilions. What you really want to concentrate upon is how it must feel to be rushing around the streets of St. Germaine des Pres with a fluttering at the back of your skull that's opting for joyful, frontline hits.

Add all this up and hear how Gato Barbieri scored. Listen to the lush but simple bandoneon statements of melody he's penciled into the arrangement. People are driving around America with bumper stickers that read: PLAY AN ACCORDION, GO TO JAIL, THAT'S THE LAW, but they don't know how beautifully particular players can squeeze those boxes. This bandoneón is from those gritty streets of Gato's childhood, where time was tapped to shoe measure.

Remember, if you can, those warm-throated pre-Peronista nights, an evening barely begun. Violet light is flooding the eye's heart. Overcome with desire, that light is neither sure nor understands why it is being set daffy with longing.

So where does this tango lead? Where do all tangos lead? No place but up to Gato's place, that space just in back of his heart, yellowed with taxis. And if an August rain's begun to fall in April or in May, this could make it an even juicier visit. This could send the tango wandering into some smoky shadow of a corner to find its partner, to do what it takes two to do.

Ah, the tangles and entanglements of love let loose like light let in, whisking and snatching you gently and crazily every broken-legged way but loose!

Imagine all of this for background while you listen to *Last Tango in Paris*. Put yourself in the picture. Expand to the *duende* of this intoxicant, the movement of the music itself. At long last you've got your damp palms wrapped around each other's waists; the feet are working, doing whatever they should; the mustachioed musicians are all but winking at the both of you from between the wheezy cracks in the squeeze and shudder of keys and buttons, the sounded breeze the bandoneón makes. The wind is so slow-moving in the flowered room that you can take your time breathing in the smells of smoke and drink, perfume and sweaty euphoria. You make that little ethnic pass around the floor. What's that they call it? Tango's as good a name for it as any.

The crowd, such as it is of a week night, looks on. The light even glistens in the elongated sliver of scalp your partner's parted hair reveals. For sure, it's a perfect match for her now-lowered, now-undulating cleavage, all dew and shine in the heave of her smart yet simple blouse. These are not champagne and chauffeur people; these are the descendents of cowboys, gauchos, laboring people and scufflers. Both your busy foreheads are lathered in salt. The moon is nowhere to be seen, but the tide of the tablecloths you keep brushing from your laps and the glide of the tango are the only things spilling from this ardent moment now, like fruits and vegetables from an old-time horn of plenty.

The tango is everything, all this moment is made of. It's almost as if there's never been anything else in any season of your sweet and bitter passages. Along the giddy edges of your stomach and the nape of your neck, you sense this moment isn't going to be your last. But you aren't certain about how you mean that. Last as in "last night"? Last as in "there ain't no more"?

The sting of demon time is poisoning your blood. What will become of this casual passion about to wane and recede like practically everything you've ever tried to clutch or make last?

Saxophonist, songwriter, epic builder Gato Barbieri—perhaps with Pharoah Sanders and John Coltrane at the back of his inner ear—has picked up all the pieces and saved them for you, that's what. Barbieri saw his shot when director Bernardo Bertolucci sent for him. Yes, of course, that's got to be it. It could only take an Argentine out of Buenos Aires to coax the last ounce of romance from Parisian myth musically for all the rest of us.

Forgive me, Gato. And listen, reader. Nobody knows about any of this except you and me, and I swear I won't say any more about it if you don't.

Flyin' Home

Lionel Hampton, 1942

Somehow are we not forever flying home somewhere? Speeding there in our automobiles, tooting our own horns the way we do cocaine, or smacking our way home on a spoon of heroin, coming or arriving soon? Decisions, decisions. To be or not to be.

To be a kid and listen to the sound of Lionel Hampton's "Flyin' Home" was to be grounded firmly in the twentieth century of arrivals and departures by way of rhythm and being. And rhythm was a matter of being with 'em, if you'll excuse my Afro-boa-constricting loa, this spirit that rides and rides its lordly horse.

Tell my horse about the time when you were growing up in Detroit, Michigan and Lionel Hampton would come to Detroit. I'd be riding that crowd so hard when Hamp's band struck up "Flyin' Home" that even after he'd walked down off the stage and led them all out into the streets and around the block for a musical walk in under the stars, they'd still be so charged and ready it was all I could do to try and restrain them so they wouldn't tear up the theaters the way managers reported they did after Hamp's band had trouble getting booked back in at the Fox and the Graystone and the Paradise Club and those other theaters the following year.

What was it about "Flyin' Home"? What was it that made them want to boogie in the aisles and all out on top of parked cars at the curbs and in the parking lots and all on top of each other so hard they forgot it was only a tune—highly charged, admittedly—and took it perhaps to somehow mean more than Hamp had meant it to mean?

Wasn't it because of the yea-saying, life-affirming ring of Hamp's vibes and Illinois Jacquet's and Arnett Cobb's church-like voices reaching toward some kind of heaven? We even memorized and would sing Jacquet's solo, note per note, and as recently as 1980, when Jimmy Carter invited Hampton to play at the White House Jazz Festival, Zoot Sims got up and swung that classic solo of Jacquet's.

Even if it was smoky and boozy and jazzy and coarse; even if it did hover above the band's brass and saxophone choirs and all those palpitations out there in the pulpit, this heaven at hand that Hampton evoked was rapidly reachable. To get there, you didn't have to crawl, limp, walk, swim or row. You didn't have to hitch up no wagon to no mule, or sit up all night on some train with a boxed chicken lunch, or doze while you drove there on some bumpy highway where, when you got hungry, you had to go around to the back of some God-forsaken greasy spoon to get a bite to eat. And don't talk about the times the only thing that kept you driving into that night were the dark spots along the road where you could hide behind a tree to pee and let well enough be.

No, you didn't have to go through all that to get to heaven with Lionel Hampton's band. You plunked down for your ticket, you got yourself either an aisle or a window seat, and, depending on your needs, you either clicked your seat belt into place or took your own sweet chances, but, doggone it, you took the trip direct, the same way you posted your letters Air Mail Special. You closed your eyes and patted your feet and let the music pilot your body to heaven and, before you knew it, you were flying home.

Keep On Truckin', Mama

R. Crumb and His Cheap Suit Serenaders, 1970

THE TOPIC of Angelfood McSpade had popped up somehow on that steamy afternoon at the Café Mediterranean as I sat with pal Leslie Perry over coffee and Italian sodas. I was telling him about something mildly unbelievable I'd been reading in the latest issue of *Zap Comix*. It turned out Leslie had never read or even heard of cartoonist R. Crumb.

Crazier Than Thou was the name of the game everyone was playing, it seemed, in Berkeley by 1970. There was so much grotesquerie to behold and acknowledge that it was easy to get anyone's attention, but practically impossible to hold it.

As I told Les about Crumb's inky black amazon Angelfood, he began to get restless. Finally he leaned across the wobbly, little round table and said, "Where'd you say you saw this funnybook?"

"At Moe's," I said, "right across the street."

Les smacked his cup down, dragged the paper napkin across his beard, and jumped up. "C'mon," he said, "let's go!"

"Go where?"

"I can't believe what you're telling me. I gotta see it for myself."

I could see he was steamed up, but it wasn't always easy to tell with Les because he tended to be dramatic. After all, he was an actor. He had also just written a play about Frederick Douglass that he would later star in and become something of a Bay Area celebrity.

I followed while Les jaywalked across Telegraph Avenue and straight into Moe's Book Shop.

"Where?" he asked.

I pointed to the underground comic book section. Les's eyes got big and then narrowed as he surveyed the racks that bulged with all those gaudy and often racily illustrated covers of *Slow Death Funnies, Young Lust, The Furry Freak Brothers, Fritz the Cat, Yellow Dog,* and other scuzzy favorites.

"What'd you say this thing was called?"

"Zap Comix," I said, reaching and handing him a crisp new copy of the very issue I'd been describing over refreshments at the Med.

With flaring nostrils, Les leafed through it, and I could see he wasn't taking lightly the outrageous and unsavory shenanigans of Angelfood McSpade and all her dwarfish and doofus-looking sexual partners, to say nothing of the reprehensible and sometimes swin- ish antics of Crumb's other characters. Here was Angelfood engag- ing in coitus with some wimpy white loser. And here was Mr. Natural with his snowy, long beard, jumping nasty with some sweet young thing. And how about this drawing of one of Crumb's big- legged young hippie females in a miniskirt as she crouched to pay lip service, right there on the sidewalk, to some pop-eyed black pimp flashing regulation gold teeth and sporting gassed, patent- leather-looking hair?

Les didn't crack so much as a smile at any of it. Not even at the spectacle of the zaftig Lenore Goldberg, her copious blue-jeaned behind spread all over the seat of the roaring Harley between her legs, on her way to terrorize a cowering roomful of effete East Bay intellectuals with the cutting salutation: "Hi ya, smarties!"

"Hey," Les said, comic book in hand, "I'm calling 'em on this shit!" And turning on his heels at once, he stomped over to the ponytailed clerk at the cash register.

The clerk said, "You gonna buy that?"

"Hell no," yelled Les. "I wanna file a protest!"

The clerk, who had probably witnessed by then every manner of madness go down in Moe's, looked more irritated than surprised. "A protest about what, man?"

Les whacked the *Zap* flat down on the counter. "This so-called funnybook your store is selling."

"What's wrong with *Zap Comix,* man?"

"First of all," Les told him, "quit calling me *man!* You got that?"

"Shit, are you ever uptight!"

Les's intensity was even taking me by surprise, for I had no idea he would ever carry the thing this far. But there was nothing to do now except stand back and watch.

"You're goddamn right I'm uptight! Just look at this! Look at the filthy and obscene ways black people are being depicted in this racist publication! I don't find this shit funny worth a damn!"

The clerk's ponytail swung as he looked on and turned the pages of the comic. To me he looked absolutely lost and dumbfounded.

Leslie Perry opened up the *Zap* and started pointing out specific drawings he found offensive. "Look at this," he raged. "And look at that. Don't come telling *me* this isn't racist."

The clerk patiently noted each illustration as Les's finger fell upon it, yet he still seemed not so much alarmed as puzzled. "Yeah," he said. "So?"

"So we want this kinda garbage outta your store. It's racist and it's disgusting, and that's *all* it is!"

"Hey," said the clerk, "I can't do that, man, uhhh, I mean . . . "

"What!" Les hollered. "What the hell you mean, you can't do it? Then lemme talk to the boss. Get Moe over here!"

"Moe's gone home for the day."

"Well, *some*body's gonna have to do *some*thing!"

Trembling, the clerk snatched the comic out of Les's hands, then spread it flat on the counter again. "Look," he said, obviously trying to be as calm and as reasonable as he could, given the circumstance. "I'll agree with you that this publication might be sleazy and it might even be sick, but there's no way you can say it's racist."

"How's that?" I asked, curious to hear what the clerk would say, even though I didn't believe in censorship.

He nervously brushed at the *Zap* page on display with one hand and said, "How can I say that? See for yourself. Everybody in this magazine is sick—and that's the fucking point! They're all sick, Robert Crumb is probably sick, you're sick. Fuck, it's a sick fucking society! And you," he raged on, turning to Les, "you're coming in here telling me we oughtta stop selling it. Shit, that's sick too!"

Suddenly Les, who's fair-skinned, turned a deep, incendiary shade of red. His gray-green eyes were smoldering. He did another about-face and pushed past me. While the clerk was still holding forth and turning *Zap* pages, Les raced back over to the underground comics section and pushed and flung and kicked every item on display on the floor.

Heads turned.

I took a deep breath.

The ponytailed clerk's voice was quivering as he shouted, "Don't you ever come back in here again, you sick sonofabitch!"

"Keep stocking those racist funnybooks," Les yelled over his shoulder, "and see what happens!"

And with that, Leslie Perry, his handsome face aflame, stepped unhurried out the front door.

When I caught up with him outside, Les patted my shoulder and, smiling, said, "Hope I didn't embarrass you too much, man. But somebody's gotta show these peckerwoods we know what's going down. . . . I'm glad you told me about that stuff."

The Avenue, as they call it in Berkeley, was jammed with people, and as I took a quick look up and down the street, absolutely everybody my eyes fell on looked as if they'd just stepped straight out of a *Zap Comix,* including the fragile professor clutching a copy of *China Reconstructs* who was emerging at that very moment from the Café Med, which old-timers still called the Piccolo.

And somehow I sensed that if Les and I stood out there chatting long enough, Lenore Goldberg or Mr. Natural or even Angelfood McSpade would be certain to turn up too.

Moody's Mood for Love

King Pleasure, 1952

WHAT WE LIKED to do at Hutchins Intermediate School in Detroit was get together—a whole gang of us, say, half a dozen to ten kids—and either walk through the halls, or hang out by the grocery store over there off Woodrow Wilson, or step through streets singing "Moody's Mood for Love" in loud unison with a vengeance calculated to blow grown people and other squares clean away; keep them right there where we wanted them—at a distance and out of our business.

In the motion picture soundtrack of your mind, you can easily envision and hear us all silly and feisty, arrogant as city mice out to pull the rug out from under our slower, country cousins; that is, anybody who didn't know the words to this tricky vocalese version of an alto saxophone solo James Moody had cut on Prestige Records. From beginning to end, Moody never stated the melody line of the tune whose chordal layout he was bouncing from—Jimmy McHugh's "I'm in the Mood for Love." One wonders why he didn't bother claiming composer credit, for this was how the beboppers had learned to fatten their royalty checks—when they were lucky enough to even get royalties—from record companies and from BMI (Broadcast Music, Inc.) or ASCAP (the American Society of Composers and Publishers). The copyright office said you couldn't copyright a chord progression, only a specific melody. So Moody, living in Europe, had borrowed an alto saxophone from Swedish bopster Lars Gullin and made this three-minute cut, which might have gone the way of many a fine but forgotten jazz solo if it hadn't reached the ears of a mystic and singer named Clarence Beek out in East St. Louis. Clarence Beek changed his name to King Pleasure.

"There I go/There I go/There I go/Therrrrre I go/ . . . is what Pleasure had heard Moody whispering as he began to poeticize the urgency of his emotions in a solo that gathered candor the way an object approaching the speed of light accumulates mass, grows tinier and tinier until time stands still. That's all Einstein had been talking about, and there Moody was—like any other outstanding jazz artist—telling such a story in musical notes and tones that Pleasure broke down into language that was far from sounding like the airy sweet nothings we'd been brought up to expect from popular songs: "A. You're adorable,/B. You're so beautiful,/C. You're a cutie full of charm," sung by Perry Como or Doris Day—and don't get me wrong, Doris Day could sing—but there was something about this invisible collaboration between James Moody and King Pleasure that was irresistible to us as adolescents.

There are rumors that the lyrics were really Eddie Jefferson's. But whoever wrote them, these were love lyrics that cut across neat little bar lines and formulas; that were lofty yet earthy—"Pretty baby,/You are the one who/Snaps my control." There was something awfully close to real about them, and, because they followed the heated build-up of Moody's soar-and-cruise, the way stories in jazz are traditionally laid out, these were also words that we could taste in our mouths as we sang and said them. By the time we each felt the first climax approaching, the whole gang of us would stop in our tracks and flail our arms toward the sky. All we could do was peep around at one another in anticipatory glee an instant before the beat told us it was time to belt it right out: *"Ohhh, baby,/You make me feel so gooood!/Lemme take you by the hand. . . ."*

Singer and lyricist Jon Hendricks, whose first record was a vocalese duet rendition of Stan Getz's instrumental, "Don't Get Scared," has told me how shocked he was to go into the studio with Pleasure to find out that Pleasure hadn't written words for Hendricks to sing. On that recording, Pleasure sings Getz's tenor solo and Hendricks sings baritone saxophonist Lars Gullin's. But when Hendricks had asked Pleasure where were the lyrics he'd have to sing, Pleasure had to remind him that this was still jazz and that Hendricks was going to have to write his own.

I don't know whether Blossom Dearie had to do the same thing for the passionate but cool response to Pleasure's wolfish plea on "Moody's Mood for Love," and we didn't even think about anything like that back at Hutchins. All six or ten of us would simply shift from baritone or tenor into falsetto register and gurgle out the girls' part too. And who can ever forget how she opens? Perhaps Dearie's coyness suggests what we were all probably too macho or unconscious to accept or understand: namely, that the seducer and the seduced are always in cahoots, and usually there isn't much question as to which has the upper hand, not in "Moody's Mood" anyway. Dearie, taking Swedish pianist Thore Swanrud's piano part, sings: "What is all this talk/About loving me,/My sweet? . . . "

And, on that sly note, just when they're off to find "a place where we can use a loving state of mind," Pleasure, like all good Victorian storytellers, draws the curtain on the ensuing scene, leaving to the imagination what didn't need to be said anyway. Then, telling James Moody that he can come on in there, man, and he can blow now, "we're through," the song ends as breathlessly as it began.

Most of us didn't really know who James Moody was, but there was a kid at school named James Moody, a rather prominent gang leader himself; he was the neighborhood head of the Shakers, a hardball pack of youths, ranging in age from thirteen to thirty, that terrorized Detroit in the early fifties. The story of how I, who belonged to no youth gang, managed to coexist on turf that both the Shakers and their rivals the Ooloos warred over regularly, and yet steer clear of both gangs diplomatically, would make a novella in itself. James Moody happened to like the song, though. He basked so completely in the reflected glory of this musical salute that he actually grew to believe that he'd composed it, or something.

The truth is that we were all composing it, over and over, everytime we sang it. Even now when I listen to Aretha's version, still regarded as offbeat and too jazzy to be commercial, I remember how it was played over the rhythm and blues station, WJLB, on "Rockin' With Leroy"—a show upward-looking Negro parents didn't want their kids listening to, even though an awful lot of grown-ups' auto radios were glued to that 1400 spot on the dial. Leroy Holmes, the deejay, spun out a powerful line of jive, and when he put on "Sixty Minute Man" by Billy Ward and the Dominoes or "Baby, Don't Do It" by the Five Royales or Hank Ballard and the Midnighters doing "Work with Me, Annie" or their outrageous sequel, "Anne Had a Baby (Can't Work No More)," my folks would voice concern about what the world was coming to, but they were fascinated all the same. Only the most daring of white kids at school knew anything at all about it.

"Are you guys making that up?" one kid asked us in the locker room one morning while we were doing a round of "Moody's Mood for Love."

"No," some wisecracker told him, "James Moody wrote it."

"Oh," the curious kid, onlooker and listener, said, pulling up his sweat socks, "I didn't know he did anything but fight."

It was all about territory, I suppose; physical and mental, cultural and emotional; what was pure versus the adulterated and the adult, you might say. But, above all, it was still about square versus hip. Mainly, our feeling about what we sang and how we sang it and where it came from was this: It wasn't nobody else's business.

Bohemia After Dark

Oscar Pettiford, composer

THE STORY, as I got it, was that Oscar Pettiford, a magnificent bassist and cellist, used to get a kick out of getting people to try to play the bridge of this song of his, popularized by renditions Cannonball Adderley, George Wallington and other jazz colleagues recorded across the years. O.P., as intimates called him, was part Cherokee, and the bridge to "Bohemia After Dark" has an Amerindian tribal tom-tom trickiness about it that floored most players the first time they tried to read the actual notes he'd scored, and this is said to have given Pettiford considerable pleasure. But it isn't so much this story that floors me as it is the mere notion of Pettiford's having titled a piece of music "Bohemia After Dark," which always makes me think about bohemia.

In *Who Killed King Kong?*, an unpublished collection of essays that won him a Hopwood Award at the University of Michigan in the fifties, the poet X.J. Kennedy—known to intimates as Joe—included a memorable essay about bohemia and its origins. Joe had tracked it back to the European Middle Ages, to the days of the Goliards and other wayward students and scholars: drunken boisterous types, defrocked priests among them, who would gamble away everything they owned, including their books, and whose overriding characteristic was the din, the racket, the noise they kept up. All traditional bohemias, according to Kennedy, were noisy.

The bohemia I fell into in my teens certainly grew loud at times. Music—and jazz especially—was very much a part of it. For the most part, bohemia for me meant running with an older crowd, people five to fifteen years older than myself, who knew about art and literature and Marxism and Freud and Zen Buddhism and African primitivism and Leadbelly and Scots-Irish balladry and Hindemith and Thelonious Monk and the fact that prizefighter Jack Johnson ran around for a spell with other American expatriates in Mexico and wrote a little poetry himself. As a matter of fact, boxers have always been a part of America's black bohemian scene. Sugar Ray Robinson and bop singer Babs Gonzales rubbed shoulders in the clubs, and one of the things that attracted amateur boxer Miles Davis (who had recorded "Ezz-thetics," composer George Russell's musical tribute to Ezzard Charles) to pianist Red Garland was the fact that Garland had fought professionally.

There was no more professional musician than Oscar Pettiford. He played hard, drank hard, lived hard, wrote hard-to-play tunes, and, even though I was a very young man when he died, I still miss him. Sometimes in the bohemian night when I'm humming his most famous song or listening to some bass player tackle his composition, "Tricotism," I think of hand-some, balding, brown-skinned trickster figure Oscar Pettiford, who probably knew all about Coyote, fighting his way through the music jungle, dragging his bass into Greenwich Village's Café Bohemia for a three-night stand.

Heroic in the midst of all that noise and smoke, for unlike their classical brethren who do their performing in genteel settings, jazz musicians are expected to create beauty and ply their wondrous necromancy in taverns and saloons, I can picture images of the Indian reservation in Oklahoma playing through Pettiford's head, and early days when he tap-danced with his father's territory band,

and what it must have been like for him to study tailoring on the side, just in case showbiz became too threadbare and raggedy. And, thanks to all the lovely music he left to warm and tickle us, Oscar Pettiford's artistic, intellectual and athletic bohemia grows lighter and brighter as the years get shorter and my ears get bigger.

⊞itch Hike

Marvin Gaye, 1963

"I'M GOIN' TO CHICAGO/but my next stop/just might be L.A. (L.A.)/Now, what I say? (L.A.) . . . "

The calls and responses of Marvin Gaye didn't end when he stopped leaving space for listeners to chorus in their own rhythmic fillers. Right after he was killed, I happened to be in L.A., out on West Adams where a cornerful of black people'd gotten together with tapes and records right out there on the street to commemorate Gaye's passing. If there ever was a singer who spoke directly to most of the people all of the time, it was Marvin Gaye. Those lines of his echoed on into the hungover dawns and sparkling pharmaceutical afternoons of that poignant appetite Gaye's energy conjures up in us.

When he sang "Hitch Hike," his first Motown smash, you not only danced to it, you could smell the grease along all those exit ramps just off the freeway of love—which is all Gaye ever sang about—and not just those "hot dogs and french fries" the Coasters croon about in Carole King's "Under the Boardwalk," but the bacon and smoky links and the flame-broiled Whoppers and the donuts and the Church's chicken and the fried okra and the hot sauce on the tacos and the chuchifritos and all those Colonels still to visit.

And when, down in the mouth and pitiful, he sang "I Heard It Through the Grapevine," you could practically reach out and pluck the grapes, bite down past their thick, bitter skins and end up in a juice-squirting sweetness so delicate and musky you could spit the seeds out right there in the middle of the dance floor—unless you happened to be outdoors, or a migrant farm worker.

What got me about that neighborhood commemorative gathering in L.A. was the spontaneous look and feel of it. While Marvin whined and moaned and purred from the speakers of ghetto blasters set up in store doorways and at curbside, young and middle-aged men and women danced along with boys and girls right there on the sidewalk. Try imagining the sound of two hundred people all singing the words to "What's Going On" or "Inner City Blues (Make Me Wanna Holler)" or "Pride and Joy" at the same time.

One 1980s night outside Detroit at a party of journalists and writers that had finally reached the dancing stage, somebody put on that cut of Gaye's from that album he cut in studios all across Europe, where, through multiple tracking and synthesizers, he sang and played almost all the instruments you hear—*Midnight Love*. To the rhythm of the hook on "Sexual Healing," *L.A. Times* reporter Itabari Njeri (soon to become famous as the author of *Every Goodbye Ain't Gone*) closed her eyes and moved out onto the floor with a satisfied smile. As she began to move as if she were snug and encapsulated in a magnetic field, or in a state of suspended animation, I said to her, "Marvin Gaye's lyrics don't leave much to the imagination, do they?"

"No, no," she answered from some place deep down inside her entrancement. "He didn't have but one thing on his mind. All the time. And that's what he sang about."

Listening to that sensual voice, you know it couldn't have come from any place other than from church, and you know too that the pain that Marvin Gaye was capable of singing about in a way that almost made the hurt feel good, you know that this pain must've been genuine.

What we hear in Marvin Gaye goes deeper than the words to "Can I Get a Witness?" or "How Sweet It Is to Be Loved by You" or "Ain't That Peculiar?" or "Mercy, Mercy Me (The Ecology)." It's that same primal cry you hear in tribal religious music all over the earth, and although it might sound like a cry, it's really at the source of all joyfulness. It all seems to depend on whether you want to listen to it in the shadows or out in open sunlight. But it is the very thing Coca-Cola, for all its extravagant advertising and geopolitical leverage, can never be: the real thing.

Boogie Chillen

John Lee Hooker, 1949

"ONE NIGHT I was layin down," John Lee Hooker tells us while he lets his fingers do the walking along his guitar-strung street, a Hastings Street made of rhythm and memory alone. "I heard Mama and Papa talkin. I heard Papa tell Mama to let that boy boogie-woogie. She said, 'It's in him, and it's got to come out!'"

And when Hooker came out with "Boogie Chillen", he'd been playing house parties, but that was the end of that phase of his life. "The thing caught afire," he told Living Blues editors Jim and Amy O'Neal years ago, "it was ringin all across the country. When it come out, every jukebox you went to, every place you went to, every drugstore you went to, everywhere you went—department stores, they were playin it in there. I felt good, you know." Hooker quit his factory job in Detroit and never looked back.

After "Boogie Chillen," this blue-throated mesmerist recorded "In the Mood for Love," "Hobo Blues" and "Crawlin' King Snake." Like Lightnin' Hopkins, who worked out of Texas, Hooker recorded for everybody, under any pseudonym that popped in his head. As Johnny Lee he did "I'm a Boogie Man"; as John Lee

Booker he made "Stuttering Blues"; as Birmingham Sam he did "Low Down Midnight Boogie"; as The Boogie Man he did "Do the Boogie"; as Johnny Williams he did "Bumble Bee Blues"; and as Delta John he made "Helpless Blues."

I grew up with Hastings Street very much instilled in my consciousness. As a member of a family that had emigrated from Mississippi to Detroit, lived on the East Side, then made the jump to the West Side, I was forever hearing some figure of authority— usually my mother or an aunt—tell me: "Hey, straighten up! You act like somebody that was brought up over on Hastings Street!" What this meant is that Hastings Street was rough, possibly even rougher than Memphis's Beale Street had been, or Chicago's South Side. Hastings Street was hard to beat for boldness. You could go down there any night of the week and buy leg, dope, cheap bootleg hooch, hot merchandise, eat chitlins and ribs, listen and dance to the funkiest of funkybutt blues, and probably even get a contract out on somebody for $29.95.

Earl Williams the drummer lived up the street from me; we were at Central High together. His father, tenor saxophonist Paul Williams, had made a record called "The Hucklebuck" back in the forties, which had been a colossal hit. Some say he'd gotten it from Charlie Parker (Parker's "Now's the Time" and "The Hucklebuck" happen to share the same melody), but what whetted my curiosity about all of that was the way gut-bucket and blues and swing and bebop and country stuff and doo-wop and gospel were all mixed up with one another.

Paul Williams had also recorded something called "Hastings Street Bounce," and when I'd go to visit Earl, I would see this clipping from a French jazz magazine Earl had on his bulletin board. Because I was a language buff, Earl was always trying to get me to translate it for him. When I did, with the help of a dictionary, it turned out that the French were paying tribute to Williams as an outstanding jazz musician. This mystified the both of us. The author of the article had actually made a pilgrimage from Paris to Detroit and straight to Hastings Street to gather background and color for the piece. He might have even dropped in on Henry's Swing Club (which Hooker on the record of "Boogie Chillen" pronounces to sound more like "Henry's Swank Club"). I've never forgotten the way Earl looked at me when he heard this. He looked at me and said, "You mean, a Frenchman came all the way over here to check out Hastings Street?"

"That's what it says here," I told him.

"Well, I'll be damned. My old man made all that money off that record, and he'd have a fit if he heard I was hangin out or even giggin over on Hastings."

And yet when Willie Mae Thornton came out with "Hound Dog" in the early fifties, it didn't surprise me at all to see Dizzy Gillespie, working in front of the Stan Kenton band at the Fox Theater, put his horn aside in the middle of some brisk number, push his hands to his hips, and roll his eyes and cry out to the crowd, all gruff and skunky: "You ain't nothin' but a hound dog/ Come a-snoopin 'round my door." We fell out, every last one of us.

I'd heard John Lee Hooker as a child, but it wasn't until the late fifties and the so-called folk music craze that he landed on my eardrums with both feet and full force. And what was he singing? Hooker was singing things like "Boogie Chillen," "Crawlin' King Snake," "Hobo Blues," "I'm Bad (Just Like Jesse James)," "Bumble Bee," "House Rent Boogie" and "Got the Mad Man Blues."

"You know," I heard Hooker tell somebody during that period, "I been playin the same stuff all my life, and they keep on changin the name of it on me. Now they callin it folk music, but it used to be rhythm and blues and just plain blues. No tellin what they'll be namin it next."

When I caught up with him again, in the eighties, John Lee Hooker was living in Gilroy, California, which was where he said he had to go to get away from his wife. Giving her the car and moving from Chicago to San Francisco hadn't created enough distance. Crossing the Bay Bridge and settling into an apartment in Oakland hadn't done the trick, either. It wasn't until he'd made it down the Peninsula to Gilroy, a little town south of San Jose on Highway 101, that he finally found the kind of distance and solace he needed. Anyway, that's the story he used to tell.

He was working with his youthful, all-white band at Keystone in Palo Alto. I decided I'd go down there that night. And when I got there, they were playing nothing but what Hooker calls "fast boogie" numbers all night long. A couple of times during the sets, Hooker would come forward and sit on a chair and play something solo, but mostly it was strictly rock and roll with a heavy blues backbeat. John sat up there on stage in his suit and tie and dress hat and listened to the band while he comped on guitar. It was as if he were saying, "Well, y'all got it and y'all can have it." The crowd, of course, was largely white, but there were a few black fans scattered throughout, older people mostly, people who probably used to actually dance to John Lee Hooker before the while folks had discovered him. Or so went the thoughts I was making up there on the spot.

During one of the breaks, I saw Hooker over at the bar and I made a point of going over and asking if I could join him, even buy him a drink.

"Sit down," he said, "but you can't buy me no drink; it's all on the house for me."

"How're you feeling?" I asked, alluding politely to news that he'd been ordered by a doctor, following a mild heart attack, to lay off performing.

"Not bad," he said. "I'm feelin all right. I got to kinda, you know, take it easy."

"Well, you sure have given me a lot of enjoyment over the years."

Hooker acknowledged the compliment by giving me an automatic nod, then he sort of sat there with his hat on, drank some of his soft drink, and looked at me as if to say: "Say, Blood, can't you tell I don't feel like bein interviewed or anything? I'm tired."

The take I got was that Hooker couldn't figure me. Maybe it was because, as Lonnie Johnson once put it in one of his thirties blues, I was too old for the orphanage and too young for the old folks' home. Either way, I had enough respect for this world-class bluesman to leave him alone after that. Besides, there was a young woman loaded down with expensive cameras—a girlfriend perhaps—who came over and told him it was time for his supper, that his food was ready. She seemed thoroughly custodial. As she was leading him away, Hooker nodded at me again and shook my hand and said, "Pleased to meet you, sir. Thanks for dropping by."

It was after this that I read what he'd told Jim and Amy O'Neal in a *Living Blues* conversation when they'd asked him it he thought his music had changed since he went to California. "No," said Hooker. "A lot of musicians, they have to have a band—they can't play by theirself. But I can sit down and do it by myself and then I can do it both ways. . . . But we got so many young kids comin up now, they want to dance, they want to buy records, somethin with a beat to it. So I can make them kind and then turn around and make somethin that's slow-goin like folk blues. And then you get two different sales. So, I mean . . . sometimes you have to change with the times. If you want to survive. I play a lot of stuff now I really don't particularly like playing. You know, just all this fast boogie."

Everything I'd heard that night has boogied on back into being a memory, but as we close in on the twenty-first century, I'm still listening to "Boogie Chillen" and thinking how wondrous it is that Hastings Street played its part in inspiring such a record. In the fifties they were still calling it slum clearance, and in the sixties it was known as urban renewal, but now it's being called gentrification. Hastings Street was leveled and gentrified long ago. But the blues by any other name is just as bittersweet. People still get the blues, and people still boogie. The basic sound of John Lee Hooker is still around; it helps us keep in physical touch with our natural selves and the Earth.

Nostalgia in Times Square

Charles Mingus, 1958

IN THIS CHARLES MINGUS version of urban renewal, you can hear trucks rumbling and traffic moaning and somebody's heart that seems to have gotten run over in the scramble. For me it's all so clear, not unlike the way life is when you've just turned draft age in a world laid out for one-way wandering.

No wonder I respond to the power of this music by letting my shoulders shake ever so vibrantly, and by letting my boodie move while my ears pick up the huffy he-bump and the shadowy she-bump that's busy dislodging itself in there. And like that crazy feeling my ears are picking up, I too refuse to grind to any halt that a city runner of red lights wouldn't. This means: There comes a time to sit down and recall in slow motion all this one-wayness, a process that seems to see each moment as one of a kind.

Even my deepest confusion back when this record came out often sounded so delicious it threw me. Take the days I was reading the New York papers in Spanish and hungering for the only friend

I had in Manhattan at that point: a London-born undergrad I'd met at a gig in Oberlin. She was sophisticated, beautiful and spoke in lilac. Afternoons I'd drop by her East Seventies digs (her girlfriend's uncle's triple-decker townhouse) and, madly jabbering the only kind of jive I knew to lay down—serious conversation—I'd land with her in the lovesick hotseat of their bottom-most deck and we'd pet like mink until the sky turned ink and we never bothered checking whether the stars came out.

One night we were walking to her place through Times Square—back before genitals and orifices were being packaged—and she turned to me and, letting go of my hand, shaped her lips to say something I sensed was going to be urgent and deep, but changed her mind.

It is this remembered silence of ours that has hovered for decades in a secret part of me that would come out sounding—were it ever orchestrated—like Mingus's subway-grounded, wounded, slash-and-burn landscape of love. Sometimes, standing at the edges of "Nostalgia in Times Square" and listening to it without regard for history or time, this piece sounds to me the way God might've described how it might feel to go spirit-slumming and wind up sidetracked and unheard from on some festive back street. But I know I can always pull out of this mood because those choo-choo strains in the background of this blues come right out of Jimmy Forrest's "Night Train." I know I can always hop that load of freight and bum a ride home. Besides—and even Mingus will tell you this—it all started back there at the roundhouse with Duke Ellington's "Happy-Go-Lucky Local."

Love, where are you now? And what was that you were about to say before we were so hauntingly interrupted?

Perhaps

Charlie Parker, 1948

DEAR BIRD,

Sometimes it's hearing the blues in all the music of North America that makes me think of you again, that brings me back to your effervescent lines and soarings. Other times it's specific occasions that carry me back to you. This is one of those, for I'm about to be hired as the writer to write a movie about you that a British production company wants to make. They aren't half bad, either. To their credit, they've produced a couple of cinematic successes. *A Room With a View* is one of them, and *My Beautiful Laundrette* is another. These pictures are made first for showing on Channel Four Productions in London, then put into theatrical distribution. Yours would be one of those, and, from the looks of it, they're serious about making this a good, honest movie.

Tell me, Bird, where should I begin? How should I structure this story, your story? Or is it your story, or a story at all to be told? Sometimes when I listen to Max Roach, who's a consultant on the project, when I listen to him talk about the things you used to do and say, I realize that you were and must have been at heart a very personable man. How else could you have gotten away with all that stuff they say you got away with? He told me the story about your knocking at some door late at night, in the wee hours, and when nobody would come and answer, you'd change your voice by lowering it, then knock harder on the door in a belligerent fashion and shout, "Police, police!!!" Presently the door would open and a head would stick itself out and somebody would say, "Bird, is that you? What you doin, man?" And then you'd get the smack you'd come for, or whatever it happened to be. "That's a strange sense of humor," Max told me, shaking his head.

There's also the story he told about your dropping by his place at four one morning—explaining that you never slept and would often stop by friends' homes to nap in their easy chairs or on their sofas and sit up dozing and reading all night. That particular morning you went down the hall at Max's, according to him, to use the john. After awhile, he says, you yelled for him to hurry into the bathroom. "Max, Max! C'mere, you gotta see this!" And when he got there—and, mind you, you two weren't gigging together or anything anymore—he noticed, besides the evidence of blood in your stool in the toilet, he noticed you standing in front of the mirror with your clothes off staring at yourself. This would be the full-length mirror directly in front of the commode, according to Max, and you pointed and said, "Look at that, Max, just look at that, would you?" He said he looked and saw how bloated you were, your hands and feet and everything; how awful you were looking by then, which would've been just a couple of months before you disappeared.

"Max," he has you saying, "I done wore this motherfucker out!"

"So," I said to Max, "Bird was a spiritual person, huh?"

"I don't know about spiritual, Al. All I know is I'd never heard anything like that before."

What I like to remember about that story is what kind of vision it takes to see the body as something that can be worn out, and to know at the same time that there's something, some presence quite apart from the physical apparatus of a human being, that's capable of witnessing what the body experiences but without necessarily identifying with it.

They're playing Billy Strayhorn's "Take the A Train" on the radio at the moment, making me think about the time Duke offered you a job in his band, a story Mingus tells. Duke must've known what he was letting himself in for by doing that, but then again I have to admire the way he managed to bring all those gifted eccentrics together in one band, in a succession of bands for all those years— Johnny Hodges, Bubber Miley, Harry Carney, Cedric Hardwicke, Paul Gonsalves, Sonny Greer, Cat Anderson, Juan Tizol, Clark Terry, Jimmy Blanton, Ben Webster, and all the others—in a reasonably smooth way. Those who know the true ins and outs of that would doubtless tell another side of that story, but this is the way I see it from the outside. You would've fit into that band the way Duke would've wanted you to, but the catch, of course, is that you weren't the type—not past age twenty-two anyway—to do much fitting into anybody's band but your own.

One thing I know: This movie will open with a flock of birds, city birds, fluttering out of some fountain, maybe around the old Times Square of the forties during some early morning excursion you might happen to be on—unshaven, wiped, horn case in hand, wending your way someplace or somewhere in a state of thorough fascination with what it is you're beholding as those birds fly off. Maybe they'll be pigeons. Heh, maybe they'll *have* to be pigeons.

There will also be an early scene that will catch people totally by surprise: a scene in which you do the unexpected, like walk out of some all-night movie house imitating the tones and movements of one of your favorite actors. You must've done a lot of that, going by the way you could come from out of nowhere with such lines as "Why, you cur!" or whatever it was Dizzy has you saying in his account of that fight that broke out in some club where some redneck sailor is hitting him in the face and you're standing there calling the dude a cur. Diz is wondering if the joker even knew what a cur was.

Maybe this scene could have something to do with a black crowd's reaction to hearing about some prizefight victory on the radio, even a crowd of musicians with a radio in the back room of some club. Or we could have you reading an article on Einstein or his theory of relativity or something like this. I have no doubt that you would've known a great deal about what Einstein was up to, just as he might've known about your existence. It's a safe bet, wouldn't you say? This opening scene could virtually involve you doing anything, for, if Art Blakey's to be taken at his word, you knew about everything: geopolitics, modern and classical art, Persian poet Omar Khayyam, Islamic culture, all the stuff Schoenberg and Berg and Stravinsky and Webern and all the avant-garde European composers were doing, chess; and so on.

Perhaps (and we'll work with that tune title too) this opener could encompass some of the experimental living that was going on in the American forties, which was this country's true workshop period, not the sixties, wherein we get a glimpse of how you might have viewed what was happening during the Cold War era with the Rosenbergs or the Communist Party or something equally unthinkable to the average jazz fan or scene watcher who equates bebop with apolitical, straight-ahead 4/4 time, or suchness.

It's a little on the ironic side, wouldn't you agree, that I should have written you so long ago under the influence of your "Confirmation" about my feelings about the Hollywood film they were thinking of doing on you back then with Richard Pryor, and that I should now be the one sitting in the catbird seat, so to speak? The word now is that Clint Eastwood is going to direct a movie about you.

Chasin' the Bird. How's that for a movie title? Like it? Or do you think it sounds too much like J.C. Thomas's book on Coltrane called *Chasin' the Trane?* I'll do some more thinking about it, but I rather like the association of the duet you used to do with Miles and the title, which would sound good on the sound track. I must say, there's something altogether confirmative about the energy surrounding this project; it's been there from the beginning, since August, grave month of your departure in 1955. It's coming from something as simple as walking out of a SoHo artist's studio with Horace Ové, the Trinidadian Londoner who'll be directing the film, and whistling Miles's line, "Donna Lee," and having Horace say, "Oh, you know that one, do you? I grew up on Bird's stuff. Isn't it beautiful. 'Barbados,' that's the one I like. Do you know 'Barbados'?"

How many ways did you know how to play the blues, Bird? And this brings me back to beginnings, everything that's opening this letter and sustaining it and, for all I know—or will soon find out— ending it. My intention is not to make a movie about some junkie who happened to be black and a genius, but to make a movie about a sensitive genius of a musician who happened to be a junkie and all that stuff they like to celebrate, but stuff they leave out when they make official stories about Mozart, Chopin, Franz Liszt and all the others. My pal Betty McGettigan swears that Liszt must be the pre-incarnation of Duke Ellington. "Just read Liszt's story," she tells me, "and then pick it up with Ellington in the late nineteenth century, then tell me what you think. I think you'd be amazed."

Who were you the reincarnation of? I'll bet anything you took time to look into occult stuff too. As a black man, I *know* you did. The hidden, what's hidden, is simply a great part of the legacy. I know you hid more than anyone else can ever know. But you didn't hide the joy, thank God. I can hear it pushing its way out of you on all those old sides—from the beginning to the end.

I'm going to tape everything I can get my hands on, all your records and comments, and see where that takes me. The music should be the guide, agreed?

> As always,
> Al
> (Winter 1986,
> New York City)

I'm the Zydeco Man

Clifton Chenier and His Red Hot Zydeco Band, 1982

IN THE SEMI-RECLUSIVE AUTUMN of 1982—on ice but alive and incubating in Texas—I went rather suddenly one night with poet Lorenzo Thomas directly from "Sound and Space," an avantgarde jazz concert performance by a Roscoe Mitchell ensemble out in Lawndale Annex, to the Continental Zydeco Lounge in Houston's principally black, working-class Fifth Ward. Featured there that Friday night .. as a threesome called the Sam Brothers.

I liked Cajun music, but only knew about zydeco largely through those early recordings of Clifton Chenier that music explorer Chris Strachwitz had tracked down and produced for his marvelous Arhoolie label. One night I had caught Chenier's band during one of its swings through Northern California, an outpost for emigré Louisianans, and I'd danced to their music until, it seemed, my body was going to melt and leave nothing hanging out there on the dance floor but infrared light molecules.

"What you got to eat?" I asked the tall, dark waitress once she'd seated us in a listening corner that reminded me of sections some of the jazz clubs used to rope off for minors and nondrinkers when I first started catching live music. As a matter of fact, "For Minors Only," trumpeter Art Farmer's brooding melody, had been playing on Houston radio quite often that November, making me lonely for big bebop cities I rarely lived in anymore. It was a mood, it was a groove, and now the groove was zydeco and, while the patient waitress stood assessing me, I said, "You got any gumbo left?"

"Ain't nothin left," she told me in a hurry, "but *boudin*—that's all we got."

"Hmmh, *boudin*," I repeated, unfazed. "How much is it?"

"Three dollars," she said. "You want some?"

"Sure."

"And what to drink?"

"I'll have a beer."

I let Lorenzo and the couple we'd come with, a baritone sax player and his date, order their drinks before I asked Lorenzo, "By the way, what is *boudin?*"

Lorenzo laughed and said, "Just wait, you'll find out." He laughed again. "Gonna get you some *boudin,* huh?"

Because he knew everybody there, Lorenzo was up and at it on the dance floor in no time. Mike, the horn player, was quick to follow his example. I sat there with the beautiful woman, Mike's girlfriend, feeling awkward. She felt awkward too, so we focused our attention on the music and watched the sweating dancers in the half-darkened area right out there in front of the band. When one number ended, the dancers sighed or laughed or shouted, then the Sam Brothers, with an accordion at the lead, would glide right into another Cajun two-step or a bayou-flavored blues.

"They don't clap," Mike's girlfriend said. I want to call her Susan.

"No, it isn't necessary," I said.

"Isn't necessary?" she repeated, pushing a partition of blonde hair from her eyes to peer at me.

"No," I said. "Why should the dancers applaud? You might as well have the band applaud the dancers. I mean, it's the same thing; it's like a symbiosis."

All Susan did was continue to peer at me. I myself couldn't believe that I was coming on so pedantic. In a flash it hit me why the hostess had put us down there in that roped-off section in the first place; with the possible exception of Lorenzo, who was also sporting a tie and jacket, we probably reminded her of anthropologists. Two colored dudes and a white couple, college types, let's put 'em over here. Chances are good that the poor woman hadn't been thinking that way at all, but it was an all-black scene, and it was the Southwest, the underbelly of Houston, and it was pushing the wee hours.

After awhile, the impassive waitress came back with my order. When I saw the sausage-looking items on my dish, I knew I might've done well to do some checking around beforehand. I took a swig of beer and cut into one of the sausages.

"What's that?" Susan asked with her nose wrinkled up.

"Boudin," I told her, as if I'd been putting the stuff away by the plateful since early childhood.

"I don't know French," she said. "What is it in English?"

Laughing, I said, "That's what I'm about to find out."

It turned out to be a spicy, bready mixture—a little like turkey dressing—stuffed into a sausage casing. It wasn't bad; in fact, it was awfully tasty—but, really, three dollars?

I forked up a bit of it for Susan to taste, then Lorenzo and Mike came back to the table.

"Look at you, Al Young," Lorenzo said in jest. "Sitting up here studying this stuff. I used to be like you when I first moved down here to Texas from New York, but now I've cut all that out. Now I've just fallen on off down into this shit."

With this, Lorenzo loosened his tie and hit the dance floor again. Once the music got going, some perky little woman, who looked sixteen at the most, actually walked over and asked *me* to dance.

What the hell, I thought, and proceeded to shed my coat and tie right then and there. It didn't take long to get back to that state I had experienced while dancing to Clifton Chenier in California. Soon those feelings of being on the verge of turning infrared or blue seemed only a matter of temperature and gyration. What was that old line about everything being one percent inspiration and ninety-nine percent perspiration? It felt good to be moving with all those kids and old folks and people my age, people who had obviously come here to forget about the rest of the week and who weren't much for conversation at all.

"Where you from?" my partner asked.

"California," I said.

"Yeah," she said, "I knew you musta been from *some* place 'cause you don't act like nobody that live around here."

And that was the extent of the conversation.

When I excused myself to hit the men's room, I had to pass the jukebox. While I was waiting in line there at the back of the Continental Zydeco Lounge, I pored over the titles of the selections. It didn't surprise me to see that half the numbers on there were Chifton Chenier's. A framed, smiling picture of Clifton was hanging on the wall above the jukebox.

"You know what?" Lorenzo was saying. By then, Mike and Susan were driving us both home. "You notice how it took Roscoe Mitchell and Gerald Oshita and Tom Buckner and them all night to finally get around to the blues? You notice that?"

"Sure did," I said.

"And the Sam Brothers, they played the blues all night. They started with 'em and they finished with 'em. Now, how come it is that Roscoe Mitchell, the Chicago Art Ensemble, Ornette Coleman, Sun Ra—all of 'em, they're playin' the same thing, but it takes 'em *all* night to get down to it?"

"I know what you mean," Mike looked back and said.

"I thought they kinda treated me funny at first," I said.

Lorenzo said, "That's 'cause they aren't used to you. You keep going back, then they'll get used to you. By the way, how was your *boudin?*"

"I was disappointed."

"It was kinda late to be ordering food; that's probably all they had left."

"That's what the waitress told me. That was fun, though. We'll have to do it again."

"Yeah," said Lorenzo, "only next time, let's don't go to no art opening or jazz concert first."

Nuages

Django Reinhardt, 1935

MONDAY STRUCK ME as being an unlikely day for a near-capacity crowd of 1,800 to shell out as much as $14 a ticket for a lecture and slide show, but UCLA's Royce Hall was packed to capacity. People of every age had turned up to catch Gary Larson, creator of "The Far Side," now syndicated daily in close to six hundred newspapers worldwide.

One enthusiastic ticket-holder, a bearded man who looked to be in his early thirties, was carrying a stack of paperbound books, all Larson titles. They including *Bride of the Far Side, Valley of the Far Side, It Came From the Far Side,* and *The Far Side Gallery.*

"I intend to get every one of these rascals autographed," I heard him tell a friend.

When I mentioned the story I was there to cover, he rested his books on a windowsill, pulled his finger through his beard, and broke out into a loose, sloppy grin. "Larson's so great," he said. "He takes me to another level, puts me in some other place. You know, it's kind of like music . . . like jazz. Gary Larson *draws* jazz."

All I could do was smile while I let that reaction roll to the back of my head. Remembering my early days of listening to jazz, early jazz especially, but also the music of people like Thelonious Monk, Ornette Coleman and Cecil Taylor, performing composers who play by their own rules, and with delightfully eccentric results, I thought I knew what this person meant. But then again, I'm never quite sure what anybody means when they use the term "jazz." They could have Spike Jones in mind, or Homer and Jethro or Martin Mull or any number of musical satirists. It sounded good, though, so I made a mental jot: *Hmmm, Larson draws jazz. . . .*

Larson's appearance had also drawn a crew from ABC-TV's "20/20." On hand, too, were George Parker, head of Andrews, McMeel and Parker, Larson's Kansas City publishers, and Vicky Houston, publicist for Larson at Universal Press Syndicate.

"They make him nervous," Houston said, referring to writers like me. "Gary doesn't even like giving interviews. But, face it, when you've got three books simultaneously on the *New York Times* best-seller list, it isn't exactly easy to hide."

Judging by the crowd, everyone in Los Angeles who cared seemed to know Larson was in town that Tuesday night to take part in the UCLA Extension series, "The Many Faces of Humor." Splitting the evening with Larson was comedian Jay Leno. As for previous guests, well, there was Victor Borge, Whoopi Goldberg, George Carlin, Patrick Oliphant, Gail Parent, Professor Peter Schickele (PDQ Bach), Dick Cavett, Chevy Chase, Mark Russell and David Steinberg. I was impressed, even though a New York friend, when I told him about it, snipped, "Wow, a college seminar on humor! Only in California!"

The theme for that night was "Laughter in the Eighties!" Addressing himself to this in a prefatory talk was Joseph Boskin, professor of history at Boston University and author of *Humor and Social Change in 20th Century America.* I couldn't have been the only one in the audience that night eager to laugh with Larson rather than be told about the humorous aspects of "scarcity and shared resentment in this decade of American disillusionment."

In his scholarly commentary, the jocular Boskin made a lasting point about humor itself. Automatically it slipped into the same mental drawer where "he draws jazz" had gone. "At its basic level," Boskin concluded, "humor wards off the darker side of ourselves and our culture by providing one of the most important elements of living; namely, a rewarding release and, through release, perspective."

I sat there in the darkness of Royce Hall, wondering why adjectives such as dark, bizarre, oddball, quirky, irreverent, surrealistic and whimsical always crept into discussions of Gary Larson's lucid, good-natured cartoonery.

My inner file drawer had no sooner slammed than the voice of Harvey Mindess, the UCLA professor moderating the evening, reached me. It was showtime. People in the auditorium were clearing their throats and leaning forward. Our boy was about to be summoned to the podium. Sensing all the restlessness that had built up during Boskin's lecture, and knowing a little something about show biz, Mindess kept his introduction down to the length of a TV commercial.

" 'Jiggs' typifies the laughter of the forties," he offered. " 'Blondie and Dagwood' the laughter of the fifties, 'Peanuts' the laughter of the sixties, 'Doonesbury' the laughter of the seventies, and 'The Far Side' the laughter of the eighties."

To rollicking, hero-worship applause, Gary Larson approached the podium. Then came the moment when I had to decide whether I wanted to join the people who were suddenly getting to their feet, quite as if Larson had already knocked us out in concert and we were avidly demanding an encore. Had he been Tina Turner, he would've gone straight into "What's Love Got to Do With It?" Or had he been Chick Corea, it would've been "Spain." I thought about the panel he'd done of a checkered-jacketed cocktail pianist saying to his fellow senior citizens, drink-clutching listeners gathered around the keyboard: "Hey, thank you! Thank you! That was 'Tie a Yellow Ribbon.' . . . Now, what say we all *really* get down?"

But Larson was charmingly himself: blondish, clean-cut, collegiate-looking, casual. He certainly didn't look 36. To me he was vaguely remindful, in manner anyway, of the early Dick Cavett. I could tell he was shy. In fact, he looked a tad stunned by all the uproar. All the same, there was something magnetic about his soft-spokenness as he peered out uneasily at the rows and tiers of well-wishers.

"A lot of people," he began, "think I'm going to be like someone who's stepped out of one of his own cartoons. And maybe I am. But I sure have a hard time analyzing it. I've tried to be introspective and ask, 'Why is this happening to me?' I never have been able to understand where the humor comes from."

What he had to tell us about how he does what he does sometimes made Larson lapse into a kind of dignified embarrassment, not unlike the bewilderment that blooms in the faces of improvising musicians pressed to articulate the fragile particulars and imponderables of their performing art. I thought about the diplomacy skills of someone like blues great B.B. King and all the times he's been asked, "Now, tell me, how do you go about constructing those marvelously expressive guitar solos of yours that reflect so poignantly the suffering and pathos of your people?"

"What makes or breaks a cartoon," Larson explained, rather tentatively, "comes down to an expression on a character's face. There are these nuances, and these tangible things. I just try to know when it *feels* right. I've drawn some things that have fallen very flat. Sometimes I'm convinced that one day I'm going to draw the cartoon that offends *everyone,* and that'll be the end."

Since its troubled, seedling beginnings in 1979 as a weekly feature in the *Seattle Times,* Larson's single-panel cartoon—first known as "Nature's Way"—has flowered into a bona fide phenomenon. "The Far Side" is now read throughout the English-speaking world as well as in France and Japan. *The Far Side Gallery 2* is the third book-length anthology of Larson's dazzling panels to hit the *New York Times* bestseller list, where they've resided for a cumulative total of three years. But there are ten "Far Side" books in all, and the ever-swelling quantity of copies in print is currently well over five million. A line of products, designed around the peculiar appeal of Larson's panoply of unpredictable characters—animal and human —has emerged. Among other marketables, these include sweatshirts, T-shirts, mugs, posters, greeting cards and calendars. Screen director Alan Rudolph is even talking seriously with Larson about the prospect of making a feature-length "Far Side" movie.

As someone who had early learned to read sitting on my parents' laps and paying attention while they read the funnypapers, as we called them during World War II, I had grown up with an affection for comics and a penchant for cartooning. The opening decade of my life, in fact, saw me picturing myself as a comic-strip artist. Nancy and Sluggo, Mutt and Jeff, Archie and Jughead, Scrooge McDuck, Moon Mullins, Henry, Plastic Man, Li'l Abner, Snuffy Smith. Blondie and Jiggs were among my childhood favorites. When *Mad* hit the scene in the early fifties and strips like Charles Shultz's "Peanuts" and Gus Arriola's "Gordo" began to make it big, I sensed, with all the glandular rebelliousness of a smirking adolescent who loved hard bop and cool jazz, that things were beginning to open up. My parents and other grown folks had trouble relating to some of that stuff—the first time around anyway—and so my pals and I were obliged to champion it. For me the fashionably scandalous underground comics of the late sixties and early seventies were strikingly like much of the shrill, cuss-and-tell avant-garde loft jazz of the period. The best of those artists survived and grew. Arguably the most influential cartoonist of that irreverent generation has been R. Crumb, whose *Zap Comix* characters like Fritz the Cat and Mr. Natural have been imitated and ripped off the world over. Crumb's original vision and drawings fertilized and emboldened the cartoon world the way Ornette Coleman and Cecil Taylor helped change the way musicians and their audiences experienced "jazz." Around the same time in the late seventies when supermarkets were beginning to flirt with bebop backgrounds, Crumb's "Keep On Truckin' " decals and bumper stickers had become entrenched in the national sub-psyche. The scene was set. It must've been a piece of cake, duck soup, or both, for artists like B. Kliban and Garfield's Jim Davis to waltz right in and get syndicated. That's how it seemed anyway.

But where did Gary Larson step into the picture? Where did it begin, this vision of his? How long had this process of transforming the usual into the unusual been "happening" to him before he went public with it? Individual "Far Side" readers are forever letting

Larson know how surprised they are that anyone else gets what he's doing. Obviously his work—like superior humor and music the world over—is capable of blowing the lid off of hidden, weeded-over, back-alley regions of ourselves.

Take the "Far Side" world I've co-created with Larson. Sometimes it's a world of mature wives, mothers, aunts and grand-mothers. Many of Larson's frowsy, no-nonsense women—astringent in their dowdy dresses, their upswept hairdos clamped glumly in place like helmets, eyeless behind opaque, oval glasses that waggishly exaggerate their long and drawn visages—are ringers for the relatives and neighbors of my childhood. From living-room couches they look on judgmentally, in dour disbelief, at buffalo scuffling to unstick themselves from "buffalo paper," or at cows encased like hamsters in rolling, see-through plastic globes. Other times it's a world where laboratory scientists—usually physicists, biologists or paleontologists—play, childlike, with plastic models of prehistoric creatures, or study their own hangnails under the lens of an electron microscope. And always it's a world where animals interrelate facilely with human culture and with one another in ways as outrageous and uproarious as they are breezy and matter-of-fact. Larson's cows, for example, are eternally frustrated in a gadget-obsessed world that presumes the use of opposable thumbs.

"The Far Side" is a continuum of the unexpected; less a comic strip than it is a sort of laugh-inducing Möbius strip, where surprises are endlessly surfacing as No Big Deal. The look on Satan's face, for instance, as he routinely ushers a new arrival in Hell, a symphony conductor, to his digs: "Your room is right in here, Maestro." And through the opened door you see the roomful of grinning, pathologically jolly banjo pickers ready to have at the poor, startled fellow. And there's Carl Sagan as a kid, high atop a hill with a friend, gushing as he points at the nighttime sky. "Just look at all those stars, Becky," he's telling her. "There must be hundreds of 'em!"

The point, of course, is that Larson's work is vibrantly pictorial. Its humor is encoded in the offhanded magic of the drawings themselves. While this might appear to be characteristic of all cartoon art, the appeal of many of today's most popular strips and panels is surprisingly verbal. Garry Trudeau, for example, will think nothing of running a static shot of the Pentagon dome in "Doonesbury" for five straight panels with tidy balloons of dialogue puffing out of it to set up the situation. With Larson, it's the other way around. Often I catch myself laughing up a storm before I even read a word of "The Far Side"—if there happen to be any words to go with it that particular day. Years ago I worked with a fellow who would sometimes, out of the blue, look across his desk at me and say, "Man, you can talk about your Wonder Woman and your Barbarella and all the rest of 'em all you want. But there still isn't *anybody* can draw women like Al Capp could. I mean, he made you just wanna somehow travel up into the page and be a part of what was going on in Dogpatch. You know, get to *know* Daisy Mae."

Like the characters in Capp's "Li'l Abner," Larson's cave folk, ancient Egyptians, Vikings, Norsemen, Einsteins, slobs, couch potatoes, reptiles, insects and single-cell amoebas aren't easily forgotten.

In one unpublished panel, Larson has drawn a pair of smug houseflies motoring through traffic, their offspring presumably in the backseat. The yellow, triangular decal on their rear window reads: MAGGOT ON BOARD.

This is one of the ways Larson's humor achieves its off-balancing effect. By depicting casual, everyday twentieth century foolishness in capricious contexts, "The Far Side" throws everyday behavior into sidesplitting perspective.

Gary Larson admits that he sometimes has to restrain himself while he's at the drawing board expressing himself. From the beginning it's been necessary for him to acknowledge his own fearfulness about what might be going on out there in the world. He and his older brother Dan—the one who used to hide in the darkness of their closet at bedtime and play scary tricks—were reared in Tacoma, Washington by an office secretary mother and an auto salesman father. Larson describes his background as "blue collar" and his childhood as "normal."

When I told Larson at his home in Seattle about how my parents had taught me to read, he laughed and mentioned, as he often does, that his mother read to him nightly when he was small. His favorite book was *Mr. Bear Squash You All Flat*. Of course, Mr. Bear was in for a surprise when he went to sit on Mr. Porcupine's house.

"I drew a lot as a child," he said, "but I never pursued art in any serious fashion. I never took an art or drawing class. Then I stopped for about ten years.

"After junior high, I fell away completely from drawing. I was drawn to music, jazz mostly. I love it, swing and some bop. And girls. I was crazy about Herb Ellis, Joe Pass and Count Basie's rhythm guitarist, Freddy Green. I started on guitar and then—a horrible mistake—I went on to banjo for years. In fact, when I got out of Washington State University in 1972, I played music for money for a few years. That was before I took a job in a music store in Lynwood, which was probably the death of my musicianliness.

"After eight or nine months, I was very frustrated. So around 1976 I took a couple of days off and drew half a dozen cartoons. I took them down to a wilderness magazine in Seattle, *Pacific Search* (now *Pacific Northwest*), and they bought them. When a check for $90 came in the mail, I was so happy! They'd bought all six at $15 apiece. I got inspired.

"Eventually I met a reporter from the *Seattle Times,* showed her my work, she showed it to her editor, and, in 1979, the *Times* decided to run my panel, 'Nature's Way,' as a weekly. It ran next to a little feature called 'Junior Jumble,' a crossword puzzle for kids. That was quite a collision!

"After about a year, I took a trip down to San Francisco and showed the strip to the *Chronicle.* When I got back to Seattle I got the letter that the *Times* had to cancel me because they were getting too many complaints. It was two or three days after this that I got the *Chronicle* contract. I thought, 'Geez, that was real close!' If I'd gotten that cancellation before I'd gone to San Francisco, I know I would've said, 'What do I think I'm doing?' Of course I was scared to death when they said they wanted to do a daily; I had no idea whether I could. But I was too scared to say no. I've never been a very assertive person. I couldn't get that thing signed fast enough."

After giving it a new name, the San Francisco paper ran Larson's cartoon for three months before its syndicate, Chronicle Features, decided to promote it. Takers were slow in coming, but Stuart Dodds, Larson's British-born editor at the syndicate, wasn't discouraged.

"Stuart," Larson says fondly, "was the guy in the trenches. He was traveling around the country with it. And the strip was generating sparks—at least in editors' offices. Editors themselves were saying, 'I really like this, but our readers might not be able to handle it.' Newspapers would pick up on it, then drop it, then reinstate it. One step forward and three back."

In 1984 Larson signed with Universal Press Syndicate. "In the last three years," he said with a complicated laugh, "the thing has really mushroomed. It's still a weird cartoon, though."

Larson's laughter over his zigzag beginnings was as puzzling to me as the fame and admiration "The Far Side" has brought him. All of it makes him uncomfortable. My questions about his income seemed similarly disquieting. "I'd rather not discuss it," he said, running a hand over his sandy hair. "I'm doing OK." But when I later sat and calculated—and by the most cautious of estimates— Larson's share of the syndication fees daily and weekly newspapers pay to carry his cartoon, the sum I came up with suggests that success has made him very comfortable, indeed. And that wasn't counting royalties from the bestselling books or income from other "Far Side" marketables.

"Contractually," Larson said, "it'll take a while. But I'd like to see this line of products trimmed. I'm not real big on some of them— the T-shirts and stationery, especially. I never want to see this stuff get on keychains. I don't want to see it junkified."

Despite his uneasiness in the presence of fans—many of them acolytes devoted to what they regard as the deep, inner meaning of his drawings—and despite his press-shyness, Larson, not surprisingly, has an uncommon sense for providing journalists with lively copy. Several are well documented. There's the time his Plymouth Duster hit a mutt when a pack of dogs dashed across the road while he was driving to interview for a job with the Humane Society. There are also the practical jokes he and his close friend Ernie Wagner, curator of reptiles at the Seattle Zoo (Larson's old rented house in the Ballard district just happens to have been located right near the zoo) used to play on one another. One of these involved Wagner dumping a jarful of live whip scorpions into Larson's sleeping bag. After Wagner taped a scissor-snipped string of frozen mice tails intended as python food across the rear window of Larson's automobile, Larson vengefully dumped fifty pounds of rhino manure into Wagner's bathtub.

"That was before Ernie and I both settled down," Larson explained.

Having digested some of this hearsay beforehand, I had stepped into Larson's house expecting to find snakes coiled around the chandeliers, iguanas under the sofa, cupboards and closets writhing with other kept reptiles. But settling down, on Larson's part, has meant getting rid of the twenty individually caged pet king snakes he once kept, including one python from the Seattle Zoo. "She was fifteen feet," he recalled, "and weighed one hundred and fifty pounds when I finally woke up to what I had. The snakes just got to be too much."

The only prominent retentions of his abiding interest in the species are the breath-stopping paintings of prehistoric reptiles by Seattle artist John Altweis that animate the living-room and dining-room walls of Larson's two-story, three-bedroom home in Laurelhurst, the stately neighborhood overlooking Seattle's Lake Washington. Larson still isn't sure what he'll do with the stuffed rhinoceros head that adorns the corner of one downstairs room. "I bought it from a guy," he told me, looking embarrassed, "who had it in his tavern and wanted to get rid of it."

"What's your interest in animals?" I asked.

"I was a biology freak from the ninth grade on," Larson admitted, seemingly comfortable enough with me by now to know it was OK to talk about it. "I squeezed in science electives everywhere; my brother was the same way. I loved to go to the neighborhood swamp in Tacoma, pick up salamanders, bring them home, and try to keep them alive for a few days. I was always drawing dinosaurs—and gorillas and whales. I didn't major in biology, though. I didn't know what I would do with a four-year degree in biology, so I graduated in communications. In the back of my mind I was thinking of advertising, the creative end. I was going to save the world from inane advertising. I'm flattered by biologists' interest in my work. There's this panel I did about a mosquito who comes home to his wife from a hard day of spreading malaria. Of course I got these letters reminding me that it's the female who does the biting. So, besides being sexist in some bizarre way, I was also biologically incorrect."

Last year's recipient of the Best Syndicated Cartoonist Award, Gary Larson is an ardent follower of his colleagues' work. He prefers, however, the company of musicians and his Saturday morning basketball buddies. As admiring as he is of artists like Roz Chast and *New Yorker* regular George Booth ("He's great. Everybody loves his dogs, and his artwork is so critical to bringing that off."), Larson admitted—with more than a hint of "Aw, gee!" in his voice—that his personal favorites, those cartoonists who have most influenced and inspired him, are Gahan Wilson, Don Martin and B. Kliban.

"I like Kliban because he's morbid. With Don Martin, it's that surprise last panel and also the way he draws feet. With Kliban, well, he's drawing cartoons. But they come very close to being something real. And it's those nuances that can make or break a drawing. Booth is revealing in this sense. And Roz Chast is wonderful. Stylistically you can be influenced, but the actual guts come from the inside. Garry Trudeau is primarily a brilliant writer, but visually not too interesting."

Even though he feels he works hard at drawing his ideas five days a week in his upstairs studio—from late morning until early evening—Larson doesn't see his cartoons as having any kind of conscious message. "I just want people to laugh and enjoy themselves."

Working one month in advance of publication, he posts at least seven panels to his editor Lee Salem each Saturday after his basketball workout. "I send ore if I can so Lee can pick and choose in case I get hit by a truck."

In the course of professional interviews, that interlude arrives when interviewer and subject know it's time to turn off the Sanyo and to simply kick back and get to know one another. Larson and I had clicked from the moment we'd talked on the phone.

"What other sort of writing do you do?" he asked.

"Oh, novels, poetry, essays, stuff on music."

His eyes brightened. "Music? What sort of things on music?"

"Well, a couple of volumes of my so-called musical memoirs are out."

"Oh, yeah? Give me some titles."

"*Bodies & Soul* is one; *Kinds of Blue,* the other."

At this, Larson laughed, jumped to his feet, excused himself, and raced upstairs. When he got back he was holding a copy of *Bodies & Soul* and beaming. "I've got it," he shouted, "I've got your book. A friend put me on to it. I read it; it's great!"

Tickled and embarrassed at the same time, all I could say was, "Hey, I figured since we liked the same music you had to be all right."

"Would you sign my book?"

"I'd be delighted."

"Come on upstairs to my studio."

And up we went, freed somewhat of the strictures of our previous journalist-celebrity relationship.

The first thing that struck me about Larson's cozy workplace—besides the placement of his cluttered drawing board by the window overlooking the street—were the bookshelves. They were packed with the likes of Ditmor's *Thrills of a Naturalist's Quest,* Robert Ardrey's *Venomous Reptiles and Amphibians,* and the Audubon Society's *Field Guide to North American Insects and Spiders.* His well-thumbed library also included literary classics, fine arts editions, a sizable collection of jazz biographies and discographies, and Norman N. Holland's *Laughing: A Psychology of Humor.*

Resting refulgent on its stand in one corner of Larson's studio was one of the five acoustical guitars he owns, all of them hand-fashioned and custom-built by the legendary Long Island luthier, Jimmy D'Aquisto, famed as the present-day Stradivarius of the guitar. On the music stand next to that particular guitar was a sheet of score paper upon which Larson had penned the chord changes to the evergreen jazz standard, "Nuages." "Clouds" is how we'd translate the title of this wistful, wordless ballad by Django Reinhardt, the fabled Belgian Gypsy guitarist.

It was also a cloudy afternoon in Seattle, even though Larson was radiant now that we were pretty much talking jazz, his music and muse. Everything around him looked classic: the stacks of virgin paper on his drawing board, the books and tapes and LPs, the sketches and pictures and notes pinned to the bulletin boards, even the sleek-looking word processor he'd recently purchased to give his cartoon captions "a professional look." More than anything else perhaps, it was rain-swollen Seattle I was glimpsing through Larson's barely opened window that looked so classic and timeless. Having once lived in that lovely, watery, Scandinavian-American city—just up the hill, in fact—I wondered about its lifelong influence on Larson. Instead of asking, which would've meant resuming our deep-talking-to-the-deep relationship, I treated myself to several hits of wintry air blowing through the window air wet and ripe with the smell of fallen leaves.

It was the tinkle of chimes, door chimes, that broke my Seattle reverie. They were just soft enough and loud enough to change the mood of the house altogether. Who could it be? Maybe I was going to get to meet Larson's girlfriend, the one who had just accompanied him on a scuba-diving trip to Indonesia and Bali. No, impossible. Larson had already told me that she hadn't yet gotten back from Spain.

No, it was three ten-year-old girls—one blonde, one brunette, one redheaded—and they had bravely undone the front gate and sounded the doorbell. When Larson answered, softly surveying his nervy young callers, I watched the friendly squint of his easy gray eyes and could tell how perplexed yet relieved he was to see them. Relieved because all Ashley, Maria, and Heidi wanted were autographs. From the name on the mailbox, they had figured it out. This just had to be the house, *the* house! But Larson knew they weren't about to ask where he got his ideas or his theories on the curative powers of laughter, or how much money he made last month. He seemed perplexed and later confided that this sort of thing had never happened before, not here at home.

"Heidi," I asked, butting right in, "what is it about 'The Far Side' you like?"

Heidi was the blonde. She ignored me and directed herself to her hero exclusively, even though Larson was already busy signing the single sheet of paper he would presently tear into three pieces.

"I don't always understand what your comics are about," said Heidi. "But I like the pictures. I *love* the pictures."

"Well, thank you," Larson managed to say as he handed each girl a signature, then excused himself. "I have to go now; I'm being interviewed."

"Oh," said Heidi, all wide-eyed, while Ashley and Maria stood by, looking scared. "Are they gonna do a bibliography?"

# Respect

Aretha Franklin, 1967

IT WAS WASHINGTON, D.C., more than thirty years after my mother decided not to marry Rev. C.L. Franklin and more than twenty years after his daughter Aretha, my old Detroit neighbor and schoolmate, finally switched from Columbia to the Atlantic label, slipped down to Muscle Shoals, Alabama, and cut that unstoppable hit, "Respect," that was still filling the sunny May air of a late Sunday afternoon on my way, this time by taxi, to National Airport, which is actually in Arlington, Virginia.

Leaned forward in the backseat, watching the querulous, lanky driver's eyes connect with mine in the rearview mirror, I was thinking about Leon Russell's line from "A Song for You," the one that goes: "I love you in a place/where there's no space/or time." That so many years had already passed and that I'd soon be landing again at Chicago's O'Hare Airport in the time it would take to listen to a Leon Russell and an Aretha Franklin LP back to back had me thinking in rhythm and patterns and clusters and slices. If, for example, I were ever asked for some reason to draw one of those demographic, statistical pies sliced up to indicate how I'd spent my time on earth, there would have to be one thin, barely forkable sliver of pie to represent the entire one percent of my life I've spent making plane connections at O'Hare.

But this was National, a departure, and I wasn't in any hurry to be anywhere except perhaps at home asleep, for it had already been one of the busiest springs of my life. I could've sat in the back of that taxi for hours and listened to Aretha's earthy, life-affirming tones. The driver must've sensed this too.

"Where's home?" he asked.

"California," I said.

"L.A.?"

"No, up near San Francisco."

"Must be wonderful," he said, "I got cousins out there. I'm from Brooklyn, but I been here a long time."

"Oh, yeah?"

"Yeah, I had one of them mothers in Brooklyn don't too many people know about. Most people don't, but black people do. I had the kinda mother who raised four kids on $75 a week. I don't know how she done it. She was a good-lookin woman too. Coulda had herself a sugar daddy, but it wasn't till I was fifteen that I even ever seen a man kiss her on the cheek."

He zigged and zagged through traffic the way Aretha's voice was cutting through the heated lyrics and backbeat of "Respect" and, as he blew his story to me, it didn't take too much high I.Q. to figure out the height and shape of the volcano rumbling inside of him.

"Told her," he began, "I told her, I told that woman, 'If it wasn't for God, you wouldn't be here. No, you wouldn't be here, cause I'da *been* done killed you!' Coulda taken all day to do it too. And it was all on accounta them three dogs. Yessir, God kept me from killin that woman, man. Fifteen years ago I was over in Vietnam, where it was my *job* to kill people. I got back here and people didn't treat me or any of the soldiers all that good. But that's just the way it is; I could understand where they were comin from. But I couldn't understand where this Humane Society woman was comin from. You catchin this? I mean to say, I get tireda these people sit up and look at television and think and actually *believe* that's the deal.

"All she could say to me was, 'You were unkind to your dogs. She kept sayin that till I thought I was gonna scream! And check this, man: she wanted me to clean up my act and get myself together inside of two weeks. Two weeks! I used to be the kinda guy would go through $7,500 wortha drugs in six weeks, and she wanted me to do drug and alcohol rehabilitation in two weeks! You know? I'd just lost my mother, and I couldn't get *her* back, so maybe I could get my loves back. I loved my mother. I loved my dogs too.

"Listen, man, some woman, a neighbor, filed the complaint with the Humane Society. They broke into my place; broke the door down while I was out and took the dogs, all three of 'em. I mean, I wanted to kill that damn Humane Society woman so bad it was all I could do to strain and hold back 'cause I was ready to spend the resta my life in prison just to teach her about respect.

"You know, here they are callin themselves the Humane Society and tellin me, You ain't takin good care your dogs, so we gon kill 'em. I know that's all they wanted to do was gas 'em. That's all I had: them dogs and my mother. I didn't have no father. I mean, sure, I *had* one, but all I have are about four picture-memories of my old man. He was killed in the sixties.

"My mother, so she was all I had. Like I say, she coulda had her a sugar daddy or turned tricks, but she respected us kids and was lookin out for us. I loved my mother, man, and I love my dogs. Sure, I didn't treat 'em all that well, and that's all that Humane Society woman could see. But, hell! Look what I was doin to *myself!*

"So the Humane Society wanted me to clean up in two weeks, so I went over here to St. Elizabeth Hospital and got myself cleaned up. Then the woman said she couldn't locate me, couldn't find me. Well, man, you know, St. Elizabeth is in the phone book! Then she said she didn't like my apartment where I was keepin the dogs; said it was too small and too messy, so I got another apartment, a whole new thing—six rooms—and she *still* wanted to take my dogs away and kill 'em.

"If it hadn't been for me lovin my mother so much—oh, man! That's the only thing kept me from killing that woman from the Humane Society. I called the city to find out what I could do and they said wasn't nothin they could tell me 'cause they didn't have jurisdiction over the Humane Society. So then I called the mayor, and the mayor told me wasn't nothin he could do 'cause he didn't have jurisdiction. I said, 'Then tell me, who in the hell does have juris- diction over them people?' And he said, 'Hey, it's a national organi- zation and way outta the reach of anybody in the District of Columbia.'

"Man, I mean, sir, the last time that woman come out to my place, wasn't nobody there but me and her and my girlfriend, and I know my girlfriend woulda got her told, but I wanted to kill her! She wasn't showin neither me or my dogs no respect.

"So I'm tellin you . . . All these people that lay up and watch TV and think life's the way it is on TV, they are sick! Life's more com- plicated than that. These people on television be solvin they prob- lems in thirty or sixty minutes or maybe, at the most, in a coupla hours or in a few nights on a miniseries. You know yourself life is deeper than that. I loved my dogs, not as much as I loved my mother, but I loved 'em just the same. I was attached to 'em, even though at the time I didn't have myself together. I was sick. But do you suppose that, even for one minute, you think she respected that?"

I flew back into Chicago, thinking about all the molten feeling that had erupted from the volcanic action of that taxi driver's soul: human connectedness in a way I'd never thought about it before. And when, on the connecting jetliner to the Coast, I remembered my own departed mother's favorite adage—"Never forget that everybody is somebody's child"—I knew I would never be able to listen to "Respect" again without thinking about human connect- edness and mutual respect, the glue of it all, in a light—the kind of light you only see from a car window crossing the Potomac at sun- set—I'd never felt affect my solar plexus in quite the same way. Now when I hear Aretha sing: *"R-E-S-P-E-C-T/Find out what it means to me/R-E-S-P-E-C-T/Take care of T-C-B,"*—well, I'm ready to R.S.V.P.

(Sittin' on)
The Dock of the Bay

Otis Redding, 1968

THERE WERE STORIES—and not even strange ones, considering the paranoid era that fertilized them—that Otis Redding had gotten too big for his showbiz britches; that the Mafia had somehow fixed his plane to crash when it did near glacial Madison, Wisconsin just when he was on the verge of making the leap into superstardom, whatever that meant or means. The truth is this: The man could sing. Although he was Georgia-born, Otis, in a sense, was a true Memphian. He grabbed hold of everything that floated down the river—Sam Cooke, Smokey Hogg, Ray Charles, Percy Sledge, any number of sub-American vocalizing gallants—then balled them all up into one big jolt of his own. Those early records of his on the Volt label went all through you the way electricity can make even the kinkiest of hair stand on end should you happen to be standing in a puddle of water and grab a live wire without thinking.

I hadn't thought about it before this record came out, but Otis Redding and Steve Cropper's tune—cut three days before Otis's plane went down, killing him and four of the Bar-Kays—conducted all the generative juice of my long-ago West Coasting directly to my inner brain by way of vibrational touch. For me it was Berkeley. It was weekends walking down the pier down there at the Bay with my beautiful wife, gazing at the shimmering waters that mirrored the sun's glint of greeny-blue Bay-pull from a California Bay Area of the tide-flattened soul.

Even if none of that makes sense, I just want you to know I loved you, Otis, and still do. I love you for finding me with your thunder-coated voice. My choice was to stay in California, to never go home—not back to Georgia, where I wasn't from anyway—but to Detroit and the rolling and remembered light of orange and blue and black industrial fumes: symbol of loneliness as something generalized and motorly and catching.

Wasting time had always been the sweetest move I'd ever made for all those wandering, rambling years I'd spent getting down, right down to the real nitty-gritty, to living in depth as a way of side-stepping death.

Otis, your flow was the perfect advertisement for deathlessness, for bone-wearying loneliness just wouldn't leave me alone, either. Alone, alone, alone must be where we go to be cured, and for me it was the dark hickory dock of the Bay—a good kindergarten-to-high-school chunk of years before they built that restaurant known as Dock of the Bay, which has become Skates and will likely turn into something else again. Your song soothed a part of me that must have been in love with its own suffering.

Let go, your whistling wave of a song said, and go back where you really belong. When it came down to that, I didn't have any choices left; all I could do was face up to the truth, and the truth was this: Pacific Oceans don't know anything Atlantic Oceans don't.

All of this I had to learn over and over between June and October of that first year away from lake-and-land-locked Michigan, and it took a lot of longing and timing and forgetfulness, to say nothing of Rainier Ales and chilling mistakes and oversights. But finally I seem to have gotten it straight: "To thine own self be true." It turns out that Shakespeare, whoever he was, was trying to tell me something. Otis, your whistling at the end of that side surrounds me gently now, or however it wishes, like the shy warmth of coming to terms with oneself in these relatively benign climatic zones.

The point? I never got over either you, the dock or the darkness and its way of trying to pass itself off as actual, edible light. But, as a resident Memphian, who had been watching it all drift down the Mississippi, you knew all along what floated and what didn't.

G**iant Steps**

John Coltrane, 1957

WHEN JOHN COLTRANE cut this side for Atlantic on May 5, 1959, I was an undergrad busy studying *Don Quixote* for Sanchez Escribano's graduate-level Spanish lit class at the University of Michigan, Ann Arbor. I was several steps ahead of myself and delighted that Professor Escribano had even let me into his advanced Cervantes seminar.

In his memorable liner notes to the Atlantic album, *The Art of John Coltrane,* the venerable jazz historian and commentator Martin Williams stated: " 'Giant Steps' is perhaps the full expression of Coltrane the harmonicist. An ingeniously constructed obstacle course of chord changes for the musician (and an almost perfect instruction piece for the student), it is also a gracefully exciting experience for the listener. Coltrane explained when it was recorded that 'the bass line is kind of a loping one. It goes from minor thirds to fourths, kind of a lopsided pattern in contrast to moving strictly in fourths and half steps.' Notice also the openness which Tommy Flanagan, a virtuoso pianist when he wants to be, wisely uses in his solo as a contrast to what Nat Hentoff called Coltrane's 'intensely crowded choruses.'"

Even though Trane's attractively laddered melody has become a jazz standard, recorded subsequently by the likes of Woody Herman, Rashaan Roland Kirk, Phineas Newborn, Joe Pass, Chaka Khan and Kenny Barron—to lightly skim the surface—my favorite version will always be the one my boy Michael used to do when he was two. While he enjoyed his nightly bath, laughing as he played with his tub toys—his rubber duckie and his boats and plastic people—Michael would gurgle the "Giant Steps" melody to the rhythm of water running or the sound of his own splashing.

"I like that one, Daddy," he told me more than once, his eyes afire, humming zealously the part of the melody that rises so beautifully as it moves backwards then forward in successively higher progressions—giant steps.

Of course I was struck by how a mere child could pick right up on something so intricate yet as fundamentally singable as this exquisite piece that for me runs all the way back to my teens. I can almost paint the never-decaying light of how it all glistened, bath bubbles and all, from memory.

In the lobby of the Michigan Union—upstairs where I'd buy Greyhound bus tickets to go visit all my homefolks in Detroit—I used to collapse in one of those big old cozy leather chairs and style or pose or wait and sometimes doze. To this day, I'm convinced those chairs were either guarded by Morpheus or some other deity, some minor god of naps. Once I'd plunked down for my round-trip bus ticket to the Motor City, I would settle back of, say, an early Friday evening and pretend I was a college boy: the real thing, like all those kids from Grosse Pointe, Bloomfield Hills, New York, Bucks County, Long Island, Silver Spring, Shaker Heights, and the city of Paris, France. Leaning back, resting my tired eyes just enough to keep peripheral, squinting vision of what was going on outside my head, I would dream about all those writers whose work I valued, where they'd gone or hadn't gone to school, and I would imagine myself as each of them.

But I would also dream of all the many musicians I wouldn't have minded being at the time, either. When the bus finally pulled up, I'd either be asleep or numb with fantasy. When the driver would ask my destination, I'd say, "Going home to Detroit." But actually I was never sure. Buzzing through my head were other questions: Where was home? Where was I really headed? Where had I been? Where was I now?

There's no way to get around having to take these giant steps; at least if we're lucky. My son keeps taking them; I can't keep up with him. My grandmother, who was born in 1892, told me one New Year's Day: "Just try and keep up with yourself, son. It's so easy to get ahead of yourself or behind yourself. The best thing to do is stay right with yourself. That's not easy to do, but can you understand what I'm saying?"

I think I understood.

This much is clear: There are steps and there are steps, but it's that slow, dumb moving through the world of shadow and act, emotion and stealth, hunches and hits, that propels every single one of us forward toward home—no matter how roundabout the path may be.

Passion Flower

Billy Strayhorn, composer

LISTENING to Duke Ellington's band deliver this Billy Strayhorn beauty, how can you not be taken back to the very childhood of spirit by Johnny Hodges's sound?

You know exactly where you are. You don't need no map, no compass, no geography lesson. The men moving around you now are, every last one of them, you. They're all dressed the way you thought, in the forties, you were going to have to look when you grew up, with one of those big-lidded detective hats on your pomaded head to top it all off. And the women are all you too: lovely, slightly perfumed and fanning themselves, their hair piled high, Lena Horne high, and sloe-eyed.

You know exactly where you are. You're in heaven. And the moon of your return to earth is as full as it'll ever be. Something sails past: a thought, a notion? The peace of mind that's coloring in the spaces on this blissful map of yours is so all-assuring that you can barely make out what it is. Surely it might be there in the breeze by itself;

in the magnetic wind of roses that keeps pulling and drawing the soreness from your lopsided sorrow like a kiss or a lyric or a lark.

You can talk about your skylarks and your nightingales and doves, but when it comes to sonic ecstasy, Johnny Hodges will beat a jolly, doleful songbird, wings down, every time.

Listen to the way Hodges plays with time; kneading the years like cookie dough, and making us laugh and weep that they be brought back, but only in the Johnny Hodges/Billy Strayhorn/Edward Ellington fashion. Flowering yet never flowered, and always fragrant with passion.

Improvisando Jazz

Tito Moya y su Conjunto, 1963

IT HAD BEEN 471 years since the Moors and their Jewish allies had been run out of Spain in the wake of the Inquisition, and I was stepping around Madrid on a rainy afternoon in early autumn. All of twenty-four years old, I was thin, thirsty, lonely, impetuous, almost broke and dream-ridden. I kept big and little notebooks and liked to read everything, especially signs and long complicated posters and announcements in Spanish. The bestseller you saw in all the bookstore windows that fall in Spain happened to have been a history of the Spanish Civil War by Generalíssimo Francisco Franco. It was getting smash reviews.

Actually I didn't know what Spain I was in. I would walk the main boulevard, José Antonio, El Gran Via they called it, nights and pretend I was back in Lorca's Spain, or sometimes I'd turn a corner and there I'd be in the backstreet world of Benito Pérez Galdós, or I would be sitting up in some park or public square in the working-class outskirts of town, wondering what Carmen

Laforet was really trying to tell us about life in postwar Spain in her sparse little novel, *Nada*.

But that afternoon I was enjoying the rain so much I wanted to get out of it for awhile so I could look out at it. Sometimes it's fun to dry off just so you can get yourself wet all over again. There was this little bar not far from my pension, El Galápagos in Calle Hortaleza, so I dropped in to have a beer and gaze back at the drizzle.

Some hometown stranger, a bright, young madrileño, a kid maybe thirteen or fourteen, but even poorer than most, was sitting at a table behind me. This young man—Mario, Enrique, Manuel, I forget—took me at once for an American, which I didn't at the time think I genuinely was. Watching while I sat and sipped my *cerveza* (thair-VAY-tha), he followed me to the jukebox and lingered while I dropped my pesetas in the slot, then paused to read all the complicated, punchable selections.

"Any suggestions?" I asked him in my most relaxed Mexico City Spanish, pointing out a title at random.

"*Ese no,*" he said, "*toca este.*" Nah, not that one, play this one here. He mashed the button, grinning as if he had just done me a big secret favor that I would never quite grasp. While I stood there, eager to hear what was going to come out of the machine, I couldn't stop thinking about how "to play," as in "to play music," and "to touch" share the same verb—*tocar*. And since poets don't know when to leave well enough alone, I even took it a little further. I thought about the letters themselves and saw *to car* as a possible English verb, as in "to transport someone or something." Oh, you have no idea how writers clutter up the insides of their heads, especially when they're just coming along, with such silliness.

But when the music came out, that is, when it started pouring and tumbling from the jukebox in great tides of Latin-like Afro-Cuban rhythm and the robust Dexter Gordon sound of the tenor player, whom I presumed to be Tito Moya himself, reached my homesick ears, I wanted to hug this kid. How could he have known that this was exactly what I needed to hear—a little hit of North American/South American salsa with some brooding bebop stirred in to bring a little heat to the beat?

"Le gusta," he said to me.

"Me gusta," I told him needlessly.

I bought him a grande de Coca-Cola and we sat there at the table and talked about the weather and did some solemn rain watching; then he told me he had to get going. I couldn't figure out what he had been doing in a bar in the first place, except he did seem to know the bartender, and could have been related. Such connections didn't trouble me in the least.

I dropped more coins into the jukebox and listened to some hot local vocals before punching up Tito Moya again.

Why the incident was of consequence at all, I still don't entirely comprehend. But our journeying on Earth leads us inevitably to such exotic yet all too familiar locations and subtle situations, where one heart reaches out to another to touch and play and listen and transport the feeling of the moment elsewhere.

Summer Sequence

Woody Herman, 1950

COOLED BY REFRIGERATION was how the old banners read that you'd see hung up outside movie houses, restaurants, department stores and other serious palaces of commerce. The ice-blue lettering would always be frosted over with brittle, snowy icicles, and you couldn't wait to get inside, out of that breezeless heat of high summer, in order to enjoy what some of the denizens of Houston, Texas still refer to as "a freeze."

Sometimes my shiftless buddies and I would hang around the entrances of such architectured iceboxes just to savor the vaporous, momentary chill that spilled out into the melting streets when anyone exited or rushed inside for cover. And that's where Woody Herman's fabulous *Summer Sequence* comes in, for this lilting piece of music covered this experience for me. But it was the soothing cool of autumn—celebrated on the record by the throaty whisper of tenor saxophonist Stan Getz—that to this day continues to surface in my mind as the way things actually were then, when I was fifteen

238

and sixteen and seventeen, rather than as musical conceit. And back there too, back there in the solar plexus of the Herman band, among all the others, was Bill Harris, keeping the whole sound toasty and profound with his balmy trombone sound, which, like the title of the ballad he wrote, went "Everywhere."

There was something about the way the air-conditioning in public places worked in those days that draws this lovely Ralph Burns suite back to heart so clearly. I'd slip the sapphire needle into that little jewel of a ten-inch Columbia LP—one of the truly early LPs; no pictures on the jacket, just black print on a blue and white background; a little like those uniformly designed editions of Penguin paperbacks I saved up to buy, the plays of George Bernard Shaw especially, for 35, 40 and 50 cents—then I'd post myself by the window in my attic room at the house on Edison Street in Detroit and watch summer parade past down there on the sidewalks of 12th Street. And once I'd gotten wise to earphones, that listening and watching the promenade would last long into the sticky, steaming night.

Yes, air-conditioning. There was something about the Herman band of that era that had Ellington stamped all over it. Perhaps it was Ralph Burns, whose arrangements and compositions they were, who'd fallen under Duke's spell. All I know is that, tonally, *Summer Sequence* took me all the way from the school's-out jubilance of June clean on down to the wistful fake-out of September; that is, from that part of the cycle where it took some doing to tell spring from summer to the interlude where early autumn catches fire as a smell in the leaves people would be burning all up and down the street and all over town, and sometimes there was Nat King Cole intoning: "La de da/de la de la/'tis autumn."

But it was summer and the promise of summer that always sent a thrill through the hearts of all the kids I knew then, just as it still does. *Summer Sequence* seemed to have the goods on everything that was going on around that time of year; Ralph Burns and the Herman band had gotten the whole draggy, bubbly dream of summer down pat, one delicious version of it anyway. Certainly it was easy for me to imagine, while I was raptly tuned in and under the music's sway, those next-to-naked nights in that industrial city where sheets stuck to me in July and August, when I was endlessly turning my pillow over and over, opting for the cooler or coolest side and knowing I'd never uncover it until dawn turned up.

In that hot house of ours, I longed for any kind of air-conditioning, even though I was partial to the real old-fashioned kind that wasn't muted or subtle or energy-saving the way air-conditioning later became. I dreamed of the kind that was virtually freezer-like, exaggerated in its glacialness like those fictitious Good Humor bars they used to feature on the sides of ice cream trucks: chunky ice cream bars, armored in chocolate. And there was always one toothy-sweet vanilla bite missing that you could taste and feel as it chilled your mouth and throat going down.

Summer Sequence still goes down, even now, at the close of the twentieth century, the way a whopping scoop of chocolate or vanilla fizzles in a glass of wild cherry soda or ginger ale, reinforcing my addiction to the seasons. When I play it for myself sometimes in January or March, it's to check to see if I can still remember that exotic time of year when the sudden thought of a snowball fight is a dream.

Black Magic Woman

Santana, 1970

"MERIKANAC?"

"Da."

At that point the driver pushed the Santana cassette of "Black Magic Woman" into the car stereo of his taxi.

"Where you from?" he asked in Serbian English.

"San Francisco."

"Ah, eez beeyootiful, veddy, veddy beeyootiful. You like Beograd?"

"I'm enjoyed myself, yes."

"You are . . . You are poet, da?"

"Yes."

"You are Al Yahng."

"Da."

"I know thees, becawz I see you on tele-veeshun." And, turning up the music while he whisked his head round for a glimpse of me, he said, "So, tell me, how eet eez going, theez long poem you are riding about moon?"

Recently I had been on Belgrade radio and television, and among the things I'd talked about were the Moon Poems I'd been composing as I traveled through that lovely, complicated country as guest of the Yugoslav Writers' Union. My acquaintances, Djórdge Ristič —an ex-jazz singer turned painter—and his schoolteacher wife Lubica, called it the Science Fiction Republic of Yugoslavia (jocularly reinterpreting the nation's initials of S.F.R.J., which actually stood for the Federal Socialist Republic of Jugoslavija).

What happened during the months I spent there in the mid-eighties would stack up quickly into a hefty novella, maybe even a novel, but for now we're talking anecdotes; we're talking "Black Magic Woman" in a Belgrade cab taking me home to the Street of the Unknown Soldiers out there where I was rooming with a widow named Vera Cvijivič and her two sons, Djórdge and Vuk, not far from where President Tito used to live.

It was midnight, raining, and I was leaving the Writers' Club Restaurant and a night of being so homesick that when Brano Prelevič, a poet of Montenegrin origins, had introduced me to a visiting student from Mexico City, a young woman named Cristina Barajas, who was as far from home and as disoriented as I was, I choked up with emotion and, forgetting how rusty my Spanish had become, spoke ardently with her about everything that came to mind all evening long. At one point, Ivana Milankhova, my Serbian translator and a poet herself, recognizing the state of mind I was in, had said to me across the after-dinner table in English: "I know what it is your are experiencing. When I am in Los Angeles, I meet a Polish man from Warsaw and I cannot stop the tears that pour from me like rainfall."

Anyway, it was raining and I was eager to get to Neznanog Junaka, my street across town, but the driver was bobbing his head and saying, "You like thees music, you like eet, yes?"

"Yes, I do." And I did. The sound of Santana in Belgrade was enough to turn anybody's wistfulness around. It turned me all the way back around to the summer of 1969 when I'd last vacationed in Mexico City and Pátzcuaro in the state of Michoacán. And, while the tape played, I thought too of my mother, who hadn't long passed away. I had last seen her alive during visits to Mexico, Baja California, where she'd gone for laetrile treatments. And I thought about my wife's cancer and my actor brother's recent suicide. There was lot of stuff going on in that taxi as it rolled me momentarily homeward.

Just as I was getting reacquainted with the snappy, salsa rock of Santana, the driver ejected the tape, then pushed in another; this one of Aretha Franklin singing "Chain of Fools." Whew! The driver's emotion-filled response to that number gave me new insights into the meaning of those lines in the song that go: "My doctor said:/'Take it easy . . . '/All of your lovin' is much too strong . . . /I'm talkin' to you. . . . "

"I love theez black singers from your country," the driver said suddenly with the purest of feeling. "They are reminding me of the music here, of our Serbian music. You are hearing what I am telling you, yes?"

"I hear you talking to me," I admitted, thinking secretly of "Hear Me Talkin' to Ya" and of Louis Armstrong who'd written that blues and Gertrude "Ma" Rainey's version of it.

"They have in their voice that cry," said the driver. "Ees the same as in our music. Ees sad, ees, how you say? . . . Ees from the heart for the heart. My English ees not so good, but you understand, da?

"I am loving too your B.B. King and Sam Cooke and all of thees women who sing bloos."

"Hvala," I told him in baby Serbo-Croatian, *"mnogo vam hvala."* Meaning "Thanks; thanks a lot."

It didn't make sense to be saying that, but why the hell not. I felt inexplicably happy and wanted to break out into song myself. When I did sing a line or two along with Aretha—"Chain, chain, chain/Chain, chain, chaaaiiinnn/Chain, chain, chaaii-yaiiinn-yainnn-yainnn-yainnnn/Chain of foo-oools"—the reality of what that song had been trying to tell us broke inside my head like thunder over the Danube. And I'll always believe from the driver's laugh that he must've heard it too. It was a chain reaction. We drove home that way, laughing.

Prelude to a Kiss

Duke Ellington, composer
Ben Webster, 1953

TAKE 1

In foreign streets, just beneath closed eyelids, horns squawk and traffic melodizes itself in Ben's gruff, glistening whisper, and there's no telling what always went on underneath that tight-fitting hat of his.

The Brute, as he was called, hardly ever went bareheaded. You'd see him in the Negro nights, eyelids fluttering as if in a dream. What is this thing called color? It's hard to imagine anyone but Ben Webster coming up with that sound, *that* "I Got It Bad and That Ain't Good," *that* "Sophisticated Lady," *this* "Prelude to a Kiss."

In the darkness of a five a.m. vision, you picture the very sound he's wrapped around the luminous layer of your being; the other body, visible only to seers, just as Ben's country glistens for listeners alone.

TAKE 2

Barely touched elegance. This is what jazz is, this. You grow up with your elbows sticking to jam left on a kitchen table set for peanut butter and jelly sandwiches kind of sound, and then somebody lets you taste something that makes you into a gourmand for the rest of your music-hungry life. Didn't your grandmother tell you where it said in the Bible that the eye isn't filled with seeing, nor the ear with hearing?

Finally you're seductively reduced to essences, and then to essence. Since Ben Webster's come to your drowsing ear more than once in a dream, the world is a lot more bearable.

You know Ben was a bear of a man, prone to violence, people who knew him will tell you; always looking for a fight after he'd gotten himself a snootful. But what does this smattering of information matter? All he plays is what he loved.

In foreign streets—Stockholm, Copenhagen, Amsterdam, Munich, Tokyo, Nice—just beneath closed eyelids, horns squawk and traffic melodizes itself. That kiss Ben's been helping you work up to is now becoming as unnecessary as a midnight splash in the sea.

You drift back to that movie house where Ben played piano in that silent movie house in Amarillo, Texas. Staring at that screen, you listen to the story he plays of how he'll go and be gone with the wind; working early with Dutch Campbell's band (Did he know he would settle decades later in Holland?), then it was W.H. Young (Lester's dad), Jap Allen, Blanche Calloway, Bennie Moten, Andy Kirk, Fletcher Henderson, Benny Carter, Duke Ellington, Jay McShann, Jazz at the Philharmonic. But it wasn't harmonious; Ben couldn't make a living, so he flew the coop and emigrated, sort of, and departed to foreign soil.

You enter this giant's castle a brute and come out tingling like a poet, in time to be flown back home for a giggly snooze and surrender all your crowns and your thorns. And the fluttering, which runs deeper than eyelid-level now, goes on and on and on.

Encore

Dust My Broom

Toward a Robert Leroy Johnson
Memorial Museum

THE FAMOUS PHOTOGRAPH is the first thing to catch my eye as I step inside my much-imagined Robert Leroy Johnson Memorial Museum in Greenwood, Mississippi. At a Saturday night dance in Three Forks, fifteen miles from Greenwood, in the summer of 1938, Robert Johnson, so stories go, got very sick after he drank from an unsealed half-pint of strychnine-laced whiskey the vengeful owner of a popular Delta juke joint had presumably earmarked for him. Johnson, a professional entertainer, obsessed with music, women, and wanderlust, had evidently been seeing the roadhouse owner's wife on the sly. But this particular weekend, Johnson—along with bluesmen Honeyboy Edwards and Sonny Boy Williamson II (Rice Miller)—had been performing at the juke at the owner's invitation. When Johnson became so ill that he could no longer play or sing, he was driven back to Greenwood, where he died that Tuesday, August 16.

To look at this nice-looking, small-boned man beaming so openly, warmly tinged with shyness, resplendent in his steam-pressed, pinstriped suit, I can only guess that there must've been a slew of women, married and unmarried, who wouldn't have minded taking their chances with such a visiting musician.

The picture is actually one of two shots Robert Johnson posed for in Memphis, when his nephew was leaving town to hitch up with the navy. They say that the companion picture shows Uncle Robert and the teenager posed side by side, but few have ever seen it. And, frankly, who needs it? What mere picture could ever be big enough to contain a world-sized fellow like Johnson? Or even match the aural snapshots, sketches and portraits he left us of himself?

Standing there at the entrance, overjoyed, I still can't believe that some semitangible form of tribute is finally being paid to this legendary blues genius, whose influence, more than fifty years after his death, continues to color and fuel the blues, as well as its off-color offspring, rock and roll.

While I'm suspended in that state, animated by imagination, wondering where I can get me a suit as sharp as Johnson's, a little brown-skinned gent in short sleeves and tie—the museum guide, I gather—sort of floats up to me. There's something special, almost spectral about him. Clearly accustomed to dealing with reverential Johnsonites, he takes good care not to pop my dream bubble.

"Ain't no fixed donation," he tells me in resonant Southern tones, "but we do appreciate whatever you can contribute."

"Oh, sure," I say and reach for my wallet. At the same time, I can't help staring at this wiry fellow. In white shirt and glasses, with the belt and suspenders he wears to keep up his well-worn but pressed seersucker britches, he makes me think of those straight-backed, hat-wearing Baptist men I grew up around; men who might raise natural hell on a Saturday night, then turn around and preach blood-boiling, fire-and-brimstone sermons in their Sunday-go-to-meeting gear.

Of course it isn't every day I get to hang out in such illustrious history. Even rarer is to run into another black person—African-American, if you will—concerned about blues preservation. After all, whenever I turn up at a blues festival in the U.S.—unless popular blues-and-soul artists are headlined: B.B. King, Koko Taylor, Bobby Blue Bland, Katie Webster, Etta James, Albert Collins, James Cotton, or Robert Cray—I can count on being just one of handfuls of nonwhites peppering the crowd. And don't let any of the old authentic or even halfway authentic country blues survivors take to the stage at a so-called blues festival today. An air of amused bewilderment, which is actually a kind of courteous resentment, will often fall over the audience.

"If you have any questions, feel free to ask 'em," the friendly man says, then takes the bill I hand him and tucks it into the slot of a collection box.

"Sir, is there a guidebook? Do you have a scheduled tour?"

"Why, yes—" He hands me a modestly printed booklet with the identical dapper Johnson on its cover. Eyeing it again, I think automatically of blues great Johnny Shines, who traveled extensively with Johnson between 1935 and 1937 throughout the South and on up into Chicago, Detroit, and Canada. It was Shines who said: "Robert could ride highways and things like that all day long and you'd look down at yourself and you'd be as filthy as a pig and Robert'd be clean—how, I don't know."

"That'll be two dollars, please," the museum keeper says. "Far as tours go, I just now got through showing a group of people from overseas around this place. Europeans mostly, but it was some Japanese mixed in with 'em." He gives his watch a worried look. "Fact of business, I was thinking 'bout going on my break. But maybe I could be inspired to walk you through the museum and give you a little rundown—if you got the time. We got a few pictures and a mural the Arts Council got some local artists and college kids to do. We even got a little listening room, where you can kick back and enjoy a taste of that good music of Robert's."

Even as I wonder how much "inspiration" a tour might end up costing me, I can't help liking the old guy.

Finally he holds out his hand and says, "I'm Luther Washington."

"Oh," I say, closing in for the handshake, "Al Young."

"You from round here?"

"Not really," I explain. "But I *was* born in Mississippi, the year after Johnson died."

"Where bout?"

"Ocean Springs—over there on the coast near Biloxi."

"Hmmph," he snorts and clucks his tongue knowingly. "That's Walter Anderson country. He was *some* painter, wasn't he?"

"Yeah," I say, "Anderson's art rules on the coast, but the Delta here is Robert Johnson country."

From the way he looks me up and down, I can tell Mr. Washington is as curious about me as I am about him. Taking an educated stab at what I might be up to, he says, "You some kinda critic or scholar or something?"

"No, Mr. Washington. I'm just a poet—and a Robert Johnson fan, of course."

"Is that a fact?" Luther Washington looks tickled. "Well, even though I am older than you, don't be scared to call me Luther. A poet, hunh? Now, to me, that's what Robert was—a poet."

Luther's words land bull's-eye smack in my heart. Way back when the sound of him first blew into my life, it was the poetry Robert Johnson stirred up, while he was dusting his musical broom, that had swept me off my feet.

It was in 1961, and Columbia had just brought out the first of its two *Robert Johnson, King of the Delta Blues Singers* albums. These, of course, were sides Johnson had cut in November of 1936 at San Antonio, Texas and in June of 1937 at Dallas for the American Record Company's Vocalion label. Everything connected with those recordings is now gilded with myth: H. C. Speir, the white music shop owner in Jackson who auditioned and made records of area talent in the back of his shop, the man Johnson came to see about getting himself recorded. Ernie Oertle, the regional scout for ARC, who got Johnson's name from Speir and was impressed enough when he heard Johnson to bring him over to San Antonio, where A & R man Don Law and recording director Art Satherly recorded him at the Gunter Hotel. In three working days Johnson cut sixteen sides.

It is from Law that we get the famous stories about how Johnson, asked to play for a group of Mexican musicians that ARC was also recording, absolutely refused to play while facing them. "Johnson turned his back to the wall," Law said. "Eventually he calmed down sufficiently to play, but he never faced his audience." And there is the companion story Law told of having to go Johnson's bail after he got himself locked up for vagrancy. Fearful of having the recording schedule blown, Law virtually locked Johnson up in a San Antonio hotel. Within hours, Law got a telephone call from Johnson. "I'm lonesome," Johnson told him. "You're lonesome?" Law asked. "What do you mean, you're lonesome?" Then Johnson is reported to have said, "I'm lonesome and there's a lady here. She wants fifty cents and I lacks a nickel."

Historic sessions they have, indeed, become. At the time, however, Johnson, like many a gifted dark horse musician, was being groomed strictly for the so-called race market; that is, for black record buyers. His "Terraplane Blues," which is still being analyzed, deconstructed, and oohed and ahhed over by blues cognoscenti, was actually a late thirties hit.

By the time Johnson went back to Texas—this time to Dallas— six months later, he was something of a star.

By 1961 I was singing and playing folk music in coffee houses and cabarets, and keeping company with so-called folkies, who relished being hip about the legends surrounding black country blues artists. But what blew me away about Johnson weren't apocryphal myths but, rather, the haunting, raw, beautiful music he made; it was Johnson's heart-stopping guitar work and that plangent, soul-priming catch in his voice; his cry.

To me, that cry told the whole history of human longing and hurt; it told Johnson's personal story too. The cry in Robert Johnson's music is the same one that always makes me heat up and shiver when I listen to great ethnic music. That cry, seemingly a kind of longing or yearning, is firmly fixed all over the globe in soulful musical idiom. Whether it be African-derived devotional music, gypsy flamenco or *cante jondo,* traditional Balkan and Slavic song, karnatic music of Southern India, Gregorian chant, Scots-Irish balladry, Japanese koto song, Indonesian, Hawaiian, or Middle Eastern music, or African song in its complex varieties—this cry sweetens and deepens them all.

Urgency is what I've always heard in Robert Johnson's cry. Totally devoted to music, as we now have learned, Johnson appears to be proof that latter-day anthropologists, in defining the human species, are wise to cite religiousness as one of our intrinsic attributes. Whether it be God or some manner of divine intelligence, nature, mankind, love, wealth, fame, glory or power in any of its infinite forms, including sheer sensual pleasure, we seem to have an indwelling need to believe in something grander or, in any case, bigger than ourselves, to which we're willing to sacrifice the little self; something immeasurable by which we might measure ourselves and the meaning of being alive. As mythologists such as the late Joseph Campbell elaborately point out, it is as though we are forever questing for something we need to complete ourselves; something that promises to dissolve the painful notion that we are born on earth to suffer time and loss, then die. Can there be any form of human expression more worldly than the blues? And yet Robert Johnston, the greatest of Delta blues artists, in his beautifully sad "Stones in My Passway," could cry to us:

> *I have a bird to whistle and I have a bird to sing;*
> *Have a bird to whistle and I have a bird to sing;*
> *I got a woman that I'm lovin', boy, but she don't mean a thing.*

For Johnson, that something seems to have been music, even though his obsession with women and with unrequited love might have run music a close second. The sonic urgency so evident in most of Johnson's recordings has about it an unutterable quality that is not unlike what speakers of Spanish call *duende*. In its goblinesque, demon-like aspect, as well as its aspect of charm or personal magnetism, the power of *duende* is spiritual.

Even today, decades after I first heard Johnson sing, "You better come on/in my kitchen, baby/it's goin' to be rainin' outdoors," I still think I know the exact kitchen he might've had up his sleeve. It was my grandmother's kitchen, with no electricity, no running water, in the town of Pachuta in Southeast Mississippi's Clarke Country, all farm and piney woods back then. The sound of Johnson's quivering voice was as ancient as rain to my ear; it whetted my poetry-starved appetite.

I could smell the dusty, sweet, rain-damp earth, barnyards, hickory nut shells, and big-leafed fig trees waving in the high, cooling breeze that always rose before a storm. And I could feel the warmth of the woodstove, even taste the leftover cornbread and turnip greens and scraps of blackeyed peas, the purple remains of black- berry cobbler; see and smell dishwater souring in a deep, round, enamel pan, and squint at the table draped with fading, checkered oilcloth. And the whole wicked while, the wick of a kerosene lamp would be burning down slow; a dry, heated, sniffable flame at the dark-dead end of day.

When Robert Johnson cried, "I got to keep movin'/I've got to keep movin'/blues fallin' down like hail/blues fallin' down like hail . . . And the days keeps on worryin' me/There's a hellhound on my trail/hellhound on my trail," I had no trouble picturing either the hellhound or the trail.

I could see the man slipping through the woods by stark moon- light, out there past the spring where Mama used to send me and other grandkids with capped glass jars and jugs to collect stream- fresh mineral water. And the hellhound? He would be night-black; wild, feral, and funky, huge and scraggly looking, with red-hot fire- place coals for eyes and yellowed-out, scissor-sharp teeth.

But what was Johnson running from? Where did he think he was headed? I sometimes wondered this in the space of the same few moments I might've taken time out to wonder about the lifetime flight of jazz ace Charlie "Bird" Parker (Johnson's junior by only eight years) or the poet Dylan Thomas's hellish inclinations. The generation of black entertainers born around the turn of the cen- tury up through the twenties, not all that long after Emancipation; so many of those great blues and jazz performers—and there were con artists and hustlers among them—led self-destructive lives.

While Ferdinand "Jelly Roll" Morton, for example, early jazz's premiere pianist and composer, might not qualify temporally, it can't be altogether dismissed that his original intention was to use his fabulous musical talents as a front for his pool shark ambitions. A legend in his own mind, Morton, the self-proclaimed inventor of jazz, figured that if he played things right, he'd be headed for bluer skies than he'd known in New Orleans, and greener pockets too.

Robert Johnson was headed, like me, or so I imagined then, in my lavishly romantic adolescence, straight into the heart of dark- ness. After all, that was the surest way to reach the light, wasn't it?

Over the last half century, Robert Johnson—who seems to have absorbed more blues influences than any other blues artist—has had a greater impact on the blues and, by extension, American popular music than any other single musician. His impassioned singing and astonishing guitar techniques—which go together like bees and flowers—have had a powerful influence on musicians the world over, from Jimi Hendrix, Ike Turner, Robert Lowry (who could win any Robert Johnson sound-alike contest), Taj Mahal and Robert Cray, all the way back to Elmore James, Muddy Waters, Howlin' Wolf, Robert Nighthawk, Eddie Taylor, Johnny Shines and Baby Boy Warren, to name a handful. This isn't to even begin to speak of Johnson's influential white, rock-embedded exponents like Eric Clapton, John Paul Hammond, Johnny Winter, Keith Richards and Bonnie Raitt.

It was Robert Johnson who brought to blues guitar-playing the so-called turnaround chord which ended on a dominant seventh instead of the tonic. And it was Johnson's refinement of his hero Charlie Patton's boogie-woogie walking bass line that paved the way for the electrified Chicago blues, and the rhythm and blues of the forties and fifties, which had a pronounced effect on late-century rock and roll. But mainly Robert Johnson brought to blues performance a personal commitment and emotional intensity at a level so high that artists working in the idiom today may still measure themselves or be measured by standards he set in the thirties.

So affecting was the sense of passionate intensity Johnson's bottleneck slide guitar and voice-cry emitted that one of his prime disciples, Muddy Waters (born McKinley Morganfield) is sometimes credited, rather simplistically, with having brought the electric guitar into blues playing, thereby preserving the passion and intensity of Delta blues while updating them for up-north, urban ears. Waters, who loved Johnson's music and regarded Johnson as his main influence, put the Mississippi Delta's Stovall plantation behind him—geographically, at least—when he moved to Chicago in 1943. A year later he bought his first electric guitar, mostly to make sure what he played would be heard when he worked Southside Chicago bars with a band that eventually included Jimmy Rogers, Little Walter Jacobs and "Baby Face" Leroy Foster. But, as Robert

Palmer points out in his lovingly penned *Deep Blues: A Musical and Cultural History of the Mississippi Delta:*

> *"Muddy and his associates can't claim to have invented electric blues, but they were the first important electric band, the first to use amplification to make their ensemble music rawer, more ferocious, more physical, instead of simply making it a little louder. And they spearheaded the transformation of Delta blues from a regional folk music into a truly popular music that developed first a large black following, then a European following, and finally a worldwide following of immense proportions."*

The proportions of any one musician's influence on music can never be satisfactorily calculated. It is safe to say, however, that Johnson not only set standards, he wrote a few too: "Sweet Home Chicago," "Dust My Broom," "Rambling on My Mind" and "Love in Vain" have all become classics, recorded and re-recorded by scores of blues, folk, pop, and rock artists—from Elmore James and His Broomdusters, Robert Jr. Lockwood (Johnson's stepson) and Otis Spann to Ike and Tina Turner, Taj Mahal and the Rolling Stones.

Stories stack up in the blues history books about Johnson, who played harmonica well as a boy; stories about how hopeless he sounded when he first took up guitar, which he loved. According to ear- and eyewitness accounts, Johnson's technical and emotional proficiency on guitar took a not-so-quiet quantum leap forward during his late teen years.

It wouldn't be until late 1963 that I'd meet Bukka White, the guitarist, pianist and harmonica player who was splitting the bill with me at the Jabberwock, a relatively elegant restaurant and cabaret on Berkeley's Telegraph Avenue. Folk music was in, and so were old-time, rediscovered blues musicians. Gifted guitarist John Fahey and his buddy Ed Denson had unearthed Bukka White at a Memphis rooming house and brought him out to the San Francisco Bay Area. During that period, White and I were also turning up on the bill, separately, at the Cabal, a funky, ultrabohemian Berkeley folk club down on San Pablo Avenue. It still thrills and intrigues me to ponder what I remember White saying about Robert Johnson, although, as I've come to realize, it was doubtless more hearsay than daresay; their paths as performers don't seem to have ever crossed.

"Robert couldn't play," I remember White saying. "He was piti-ful. He'd slip out the house and try to play with Son House and them, but he wouldn't be doing nothing. Then, a year and a half slip by, and here he jump up sounding like y'all heard him on that record. Now, you mean to tell me he ain't made some kinda deal with the Devil?"

The early sixties was the folk blues revival era. Enthusiastic and enterprising young Yankees were systematically journeying South, sojourning, and returning with valuable cargo—Furry Lewis, Mississippi John Hurt, Mississippi Fred McDowell, Sleepy John Estes, Hammie Nixon, Bukka White. It was possible to drop by Jon Lundberg's Guitar Shop on Berkeley's Shattuck Avenue of a slow afternoon and shake glad hands with Texas songster Mance Lipscomb, a marvelous discovery of Berkeley-based Arhoolie Records's Chris Strachwitz.

One night, in the Cabal dressing room, Lipscomb told me: "Frank Sinatra is all right with me. He's putting my new record out [Lipscomb had just signed with Sinatra's newly formed Reprise label], and give me enough money to get me a new pickup truck to ride my dogs around in back. Yeah, I'm doing all right." Old-timers like Lipscomb, White, Lightin' Hopkins, and Big Joe Williams— and numerous others I'd heard and learned about from relatively obscure sources—were being resurrected and booked into folk clubs, college concerts and festivals throughout the U.S., the U.K. and Western Europe. The revival biz was whizzing right along by 1963.

Two years later, 1965, in the pages of the folk music magazine *Sing Out,* Son House, companion to Willie Brown and perhaps one of Johnson's most important teachers, told folklorist Julius Lester: "Willie and I were playing again out at a little place east of Robinsonville called Banks, Mississippi. We were playing there one Saturday night, and all of a sudden somebody came in through the door. Who but him! He had a guitar swinging on his back. I said, 'Bill!' He said, 'Huh?' I said, 'Look who's coming in the door.' He looked at me and said 'Yeah, Little Robert.' I said, 'And he's got a guitar.' And Willie and I laughed about it. Robert finally wiggled through the crowd and got to where we were. He spoke, and I said, 'Well, boy, you still got a guitar, huh? What do you do with that thing? You can't do nothing with it.' He said, 'Well, I'll tell you what.' I said, 'What?' He said, 'Let me have your seat a minute.' So I said, 'All right, and you better do something with it, too,' and I winked my eye at Willie. So he sat down there and finally got started. And man! He was so good! When he finished, all our mouths were standing open. I said, 'Well, ain't that fast! He's gone now!' "

The dramatic possibility/idea that Johnson actually might have sold his soul to get so good at singing and playing blues guitar in such a short spell has been shoveled up and heaped so high and deep around the Johnson legend that it continues to fertilize world imagination. Who doesn't love a good story? As often happens, myth and hearsay are so firmly rooted in the planting of the Johnson legend that it has become difficult to tell the true flower from its hothouse look-alike.

The 1986 movie *Crossroads,* directed by Walter Hill, gave us a thoroughly Hollywoodized account of how this sort of devil's deal is cut. In the film, a young, contemporary Long Island white classical guitarist and Juilliard student named Eugene Martone (played by Ralph Macchio) takes a janitorial job in a nursing home in order to get next to a man he believes to be Willie Brown, Johnson's fabled early mentor and sidekick. At a dusty crossroads, shot in sepia-tone to dramatize Brown's disturbing flashback-memories of himself, we see Brown as a young man literally signing a written contract with Legba, a Southern U.S. version of the West African trickster-deity. In exchange for his soul, Legba will make Willie Brown a blues ace. Later, at another crossroads, shot in full color to represent more or less contemporary Mississippi, it's an aged Devil-as-trickster we meet. He snidely proposes a way for Willie Brown and Eugene "Lightnin' " Martone to "buy back" Willie's soul. For collateral—after Martone tells this folksy devil, "I don't believe in any of this shit anyway!"—the Devil wants nothing less than this simpering white boy's soul.

People all down the ages have never tired of stories thick with the Faust motif, in which someone makes a no-win pact with the Devil by exchanging or sacrificing priceless spiritual treasure for worldly wealth, knowledge or power. And since instruments of Satan will always have strings attached, banjo players, guitarists and fiddlers often play the central role in this ageless myth.

Like Niccolo Paganini, the great violinist and composer, Johnson was at times known to conceal his chords and fingerings from other musicians when he performed in public. What better way to either arouse or confirm public suspicion and rumor? Both geniuses were believed to have struck bargains with the Devil. The truth, though, is that Paganini's father drove his prodigy son mercilessly in his violin studies, so that by the time Paganini was thirteen, he was known as the "wonder child." And, like Robert Johnson, who openly encouraged rumors of his satanic bedazzlement, Paganini—whose cadaverous appearance enhanced his own sinister image—seems to have known quite well that such a reputation, if work were playing theater and concert gigs, sold tickets.

Was Robert Johnson himself selling wolf tickets? Considering the frequency with which he made musical reference to either Hell or the Devil, expressed his impending sense of personal damnation or infernal doom—and given Johnson's admiration for players like Peetie Wheatstraw, who bragged of being hell-connected—it wouldn't be hard to build a case for Johnson being a sly, far-seeing self-publicist who knew the value of a canny showbiz gimmick. Wherever he went, especially after his Vocalion singles came out, he never failed to draw crowds.

While developing his own electrifying playing and singing styles, Johnson borrowed licks, motifs, colorations and rhythms, specific phrases, lyrics and whole songs from numerous predecessors as well as from pop blues artists of his era, the twenties and thirties. His long-awaited recorded legacy of some forty-one known recorded sides, alternate takes included, was not made available until half a century after his death.

Being a lot more interested in music than school or sharecropping, Johnson took up the Jew's harp, then the mouth harp (or harmonica) before settling down with guitar in his late teens. It isn't difficult to see how anyone with any semblance of ambition would've schemed to break away from the various plantations where he grew up and, for the most part, lived his brief life.

For his earliest days—at a time when his mother was partnerless, an itinerant Delta labor camp and plantation worker, doing the best she could to provide and care for her daughters Bessie and Carrie and baby son Robert—Johnson had seen and known hard work. Once his mother found and married Dusty Willis, they raised Johnson to the brink of adulthood on the Abbay and Leatherman plantation in Robinsonville. Because of Johnson's contempt for picking cotton and any other kind of field labor, he and his hard-working stepfather didn't get along.

When Johnson first got married, he and his bride took up residence with his older half-sister Bessie and her husband on the Klein plantation near Robinsonville in Copiah County. Music must have been a powerfully attractive alternative to hard labor for someone like Johnson, who learned to play harmonica, tap-dance, sing and play guitar. By the time he and bluesman Johnny Shines met up in 1935 and hit the road together—sometimes hoboing and hopping freights with Shines's guitar-picking cousin Calvin Frazier, who had killed a man—the charismatic Johnson, always musically astute, had become quite the versatile crowd-pleaser.

"Robert could play anything," the eloquent Johnny Shines in interview told equally eloquent American music portraitist Peter Guralnick. "He could play in the style of Lonnie Johnson, Blind Blake, Blind Boy Fuller, Blind Willie McTell, all those guys. And the country singer—Jimmie Rodgers—me and Robert used to play a hell of a lot of his tunes, man. Ragtime, pop tunes, waltz numbers, polkas—shoot, a polka hound, man. Robert just picked up songs out of the air. You could have the radio on, and he'd be talking to you, and you'd have no idea that he'd be thinking about it because he'd go right on talking, but later he'd play that song note for note. Hillbilly, blues, and all the rest."

And there are stories about Johnson, just before his death, playing electric guitar in a drummer-backed band that sounds as if it might have been influenced by swing jazz and the just-emerging black urban style, grounded in shuffle rhythm and boogie accents, that came to be known as jump music. According to Stephen C. LaVere, the photographic archivist and Robert Johnson historian, "[Johnson] took St. Louis, Detroit and New York in easy stride. His musical approach was altered a bit—he began playing with a small combo. He used a pianist and a drummer in a Belzoni jook joint—the drummer had 'Robert Johnson' painted in black letters across his bass drum—before a large crowd of people, a good many of them musicians. And as he was able to play anything people wanted, he began to concentrate less and less on the blues. He may have gotten away from it almost entirely had it not been for some divine intervention."

LaVere, who holds copyrights to at least two existing photographs of Johnson (the famous Memphis studio shot of him all suited up, and another, taken in a dimestore booth, that shows him in shirtsleeves, suspendered, all sullen and sad-eyed, with guitar in tow and an unlit cigarette dangling from the left side of his lower lip), is one of three men who have devoted much of their lives to filling in the glittering, titillating holes and gaps that made Robert Johnson's life so enticing to admirers and musicologists. The others are blues sleuth Gayle Dean Wardlow, the first to track down Johnson's death certificate, and Houston folklorist Mack McCormick, whose *Biography of a Phantom,* snatches and fragments of which have turned up in journals and blues tracts over the years, is surely the most famous unpublished manuscript about the lubricious Johnson. The book shows every sign of being definitive.

If you discount the first things his older half-brother Charles Leroy (their mother loved the name Leroy) showed him on guitar, or the later, inescapable influence of Robinsonville's "Whiskey Red" Brown and Myles Robson, Johnson's earliest in-the-flesh musical influence was Willie Brown, another town resident, who sometimes worked local juke joints with the roving, rambunctious Charlie Patton, who, even then, was a legend: an extraordinary, smoke-and-whiskey-throated, white-looking blues veteran.

Plantation parties, barbecues (also known as get-backs), levee camps, logging camps and juke joints; fish fries, country dances, sandlot ball games, roadhouses—these were some of the lucrative venues accessible to the likes of these blues songsters throughout Mississippi between 1916 and 1934.

Aside from his living models, there were country and urban blues artists and stylists whose recordings fascinated Robert Johnson and from whom he borrowed during those formative years. They include pianist Leroy Carr and guitarist Scrapper Blackwell (their 1928 "How Long Blues" was one of Johnson's earliest "learning" tunes, and Blackwell's 1928 "Milk Cow Blues" begot Johnson's "Milkcow's Calf Blues"); singer and instrumentalist Lonnie Johnson (whose vibratoless, matter-of-fact vocalizing Robert Johnson imitates coolly on "Drunken Hearted Man" and "Malted Milk"); slide guitarist Kokomo Arnold (his "Sagefield Woman Blues" and "Old Original Kokomo Blues," a 1934 race record smash, directly and respectively inspired Johnson's best-known classics, "Dust My Broom" and "Sweet Home Chicago"); the professional bootlegger William Bunch, who sang under the name Peetie Wheatstraw, billing himself variously as the High Sheriff from Hell or the Devil's Son-in-Law, and whose sexual savvy—so his macho, braggadocio lyrics let on—was a direct result of his close "family" connections; Skip James, whose 1931 Paramount recording of the sadistic, even mean-spirited "22-20" became, in Johnson's deft hands, the "32-20 Blues" (James's "Devil Got My Woman" probably inspired Johnson's "Hellhound on My Trail"); and the Mississippi Sheiks (Johnson closely followed their best-selling "Sitting on Top of the World" to create his ruefully erotic "Come on in My Kitchen").

There were records by others (Henry Thomas, Johnnie Temple and Casey Bill Weldon, for example) that Johnson assimilated as well. *The Roots of Robert Johnson,* a valuable anthology released in 1988 by Yazoo Records, features tracks by several of these persuasive country blues stylists.

Robert Johnson's biggest singing inspiration, however, was Eddie "Son" House, a preacher and bluesman who served a year in Mississippi's infamous yet fabled correction facility, Parchman State Farm, but set up residence in Johnson's home base of Robinsonville. In House's emotional vocalizing, secular and sacred seem to fuse in a fury of locked horns and ruffled wings. Listening to him and to the Robert Johnson his vocal spirit begot, it's possible to experience almost directly the two-faced, flip-sided fervor of the blues and gospel idioms. Saturday night the term of endearment is Baby; Sunday it's Jesus—and both call for great rejoicing. One listen to Son House's "My Black Mama, Pt. 1" or "Preachin' the Blues, Pt. 1" is enough to convey the raw, emotionally uninsulated, high-voltage vocalizing of House's vocal style. So urgently dramatic, it must have set the intense, teenage Johnson's soul on fire when he first heard it.

To arrive at his "Walkin' Blues," Johnson slowed and steadied the tempo of "My Black Mama," shaped it into a twelve-bar blues, and allowed his guitar to "talk back" exquisitely to his lyrics, which contain one of the loveliest poetic descriptions of feminine physical magnetism in all of recorded blues:

She got, uh, Elgin movement from her head down to her toes
Break in on a dollar most anywhere goes. Ooo ooooooooo
To her head down to her toes. (Oh, honey,
Lord) She break in on a dollar most anywhere she goes.

Like practically everything else about him except his music, the details of Robert Johnson's childhood are as sketchy as any blues lyric; nothing about the man is easy to pin down, much less fill out.

He seems to have been born May 8, 1911, at Hazlehurst, Mississippi, to Julia Dodds and Noah Johnson. Robert's mother, however, wasn't legally married to Robert's father but, rather, to one Charles Dodds, an independent farmer and furniture maker. In 1907, under a cloud, and in the face of a lynch mob, Dodds had been forced to abandon Hazlehurst for Memphis, where he was going by the name of Spencer.

Although she had to accept the fact that besides their daughters Bessie and Carrie, Dodds/Spencer also had children by a live-in mistress, Julia was briefly reunited with Charles Spencer in his Memphis household. With her she had brought little Robert—the "outside" child whom Spencer resented—and Carrie, Robert's baby half-sister. But before long she'd moved back to Mississippi, without her children, to the cotton-farming town of Robinsonville. There she married Willie "Dusty" Willis, an exemplary, no-nonsense, dust-raising farm laborer, who didn't cotton much to the kind of foolishness music represented. Dusty Willis became Robert's new stepfather the year Robert turned nine, when he was sent from the Spencer home in Memphis back to the Delta to live Willis and Robert's mother. Robinsonville remained Johnson's home base until he was grown, at which time he seems to have beat a path back to Hazlehurst, his birthplace, to find Noah Johnson, his biological father.

Before leaving the Robinsonville area altogether, Johnson—who by then must have been somewhat "mannish" (i.e., sexually precocious)—fell in love with fifteen-year-old Virginia Travis, whom he married early in 1929 at Penton, Mississippi. The two moved in with Johnson's half-sister Bessie, officially Mrs. Granville Hines. That summer, during their stay with the Hineses on the Klein plantation near Robinsonville, Virginia got pregnant. Neither the baby nor Virginia, however, survived childbirth.

While you'd certainly have to had been in Robert Johnson's shoes to know exactly what he felt, it's still possible to imagine his desolation. "Crossroads Blues" could very well have described his feelings in the wake of that grave personal tragedy. So awesome is the sense of loss and the feeling of abject, prostrate desperation projected by Johnson's breaking voice and guitar in this key recording that it continues to give fiery credence to the notion, which Johnson the performer helped promote, that he had come by his musical powers occultly.

I went to the crossroad, fell down on my knees:
I went to the crossroad, fell down on my knees;
Asked the Lord above, "Have mercy now, save poor Bob, if you
*   please" . . .*
I went to the crossroad, mama, I looked east and west;
I went to the crossroad, baby, I looked east and west:
Lord, I didn't have no sweet woman, ooh, well, babe, in my
*   distress . . .*

Never much for either school or sharecropping, and now armed with a guitar, Robert Johnson started hitting the roadhouses and other gigs with Willie Brown and Son House. Under the sleepy-looking but watchful and teacherly eye of the older, Alabama-born blues guitarist Ike Zinnerman, Johnson would soon be working around the timber mills, the road gangs, and, of course, the ever-jumping jukes.

Two years later Robert Johnson married again, this time to Calletta "Callie" Craft, who, by all accounts, adored and served him faithfully. In the mounted photo enlargement of her that hangs in my mind-erected Robert Leroy Johnson Memorial Museum, Callie Craft, all got up in what was probably her Sunday best—white dress, white stockings, white cloche, and black pumps—looks a little vulnerable, yet strong and long-suffering; not quite like someone who enjoyed dancing or sitting on her husband's knee while he performed.

Was this originally a secret wedding picture to go with her secret marriage to Robert? Who snapped it? Finally it's the serious, "I'm-for-real" aspect of her; the overeasy melancholy that makes her eyelids droop, the bittersweet radiance of her face, so vulnerable that I can't help wondering if it was the worshipful Calletta (whom he abandoned to devote the rest of his life to playing music and serious rambling) on that quiet, reflective cut he called "When You Got a Good Friend":

Wonder could I dare apologize
or would she sympathize with me
Mmmmmm mmm mmm
would she sympathize with me
She's a brownskin woman
just as sweet as a girlfriend can be . . .

Irresistible, too, is the temptation to speculate further about Johnson's abandonment of Callie. Did it flavor the sentiments expressed in his devastating "Kindhearted Woman Blues"?

I got a kindhearted mama,
do anything in this world for me
I got a kindhearted mama
do anything in this world for me
But these evil-hearted women,
man, they will not let me be . . .
She's a kindhearted woman she studies evil all the time
She's a kindhearted woman she studies evil all the time
You well's to kill me as to have it on your mind . . .

Given all the women Johnson mentions by name in his music, it would be practically impossible to guess which fictitious or real-life lovers might have inspired which of his songs. In his ground-breaking work, *The Bluesmen: The Story and the Music of the Men Who Made the Blues,* Samuel Charters takes a slowed down look at Johnson's sweethearts and many flames.

"Many blues men spent a lot of time thinking about women," Charters writes, "but Son House remembers that Robert was driven by sexuality. The relationships at least left Robert with names to use in his songs. His 'girl friends'—the term he used in 'When You Got a Good Friend'—included Beatrice in 'Phonograph blues,' Bernice in 'Walking Blues,' Thelma in 'I Believe I'll Dust My Broom,' Ida Bell in 'Last Fair Deal Gone Down,' Betty Mae in 'Honeymoon Blues,' and Willie Mae in 'Love in Vain.' There is no way of knowing who they were, or if they were anything more to him than someone to spend a few nights with in a new town."

That Robert Johnson, in fashioning his thrilling song repertoire, seized upon and synthesized whatever he heard, saw, experienced, and felt is now as clear to me as the sound of that famous octave-slide with which he introduced "I Believe I'll Dust My Broom." What hasn't been so clear—and why should it?—is what went on in that same restless mind to turn Johnson into an absolutely obsessive rambler and rake.

While notions about what psychiatric therapists might have to say about Johnson's behavior roll around in my head *(He was looking for love and acceptance. He was away from his mother for too long and felt rejected, then his father rejected him, too—and so did his stepfathers! His first wife and baby died on him. There was no strong sense of family. He came from a twice-broken home. He was the outside child. His childhood was far too peripatetic to produce a healthy, stable adult.),* my ears pop open to what Luther Washington, the museum guide, is telling me that odd, factually-researched-but-situationally-hazy afternoon.

"The way it came down to me," Luther says, pausing to make sure he's got my attention, "is that Robert used to go looking for women he figured would be glad to even have him look at 'em. They wouldn't necessarily be the prettiest women, but they would be the kind that'd be flattered to be all up, under and around somebody like Robert—a sharp-dressing musician, kinda delicate and good-looking. Well, from what they say, Callie Craft was like that.

She taken good care of Robert. Like the song say, she picked the seeds outta his watermelon and put a pillow up under his head; kept him well-fed and dressed and didn't ask him where he was going or when was he coming back. Now, you just didn't hardly run up on that type of woman everyday, you know.

"So Robert," Luther continues, "he laid around Hazlehurst a coupla years, learnt everything he could from Ike Zinnerman, and practiced every minute he could. They say a lotta the East Coast-sounding blues that Robert put out might've come from Zinnerman. Ain't no way of telling, since Ike never made a record. What's amazing to me is all the stuff Robert picked up off records. He was the first one to come along, far as blues is concerned, and put all them country styles together, then turned around and put 'em in a trick."

"How do you mean," I ask Luther, " 'put 'em in a trick'?"

"Well," says Luther, "Robert Johnson put some type of spin on everything he shot for. After he got through popping 'em one, they not only stayed popped; they was headed someplace else, too. And he knew what he was doing, too. Didn't matter to him where he himself or anything else was headed, long as it was moving."

"Luther, I've always been crazy about the way Johnson closed 'Dust My Broom.' "

"Sing it for me," says Luther.

I'mo call up China,
see is my good girl over there:
I'm gon call up China,
see is my good girl over there.
If I can't find her on Philippine's Island,
she must be in Ethiopia somewhere.

"You got a nice voice," Luther tells me. "But what is it fascinates you about those words?"

"Luther, how could someone who threw around global references like that actually believe Chicago was in California?"

"Hard to say. But he sure as hell knew it wasn't down here in Mississippi, didn't he? One of the things we'd love to get our hands on for our collection is the little book Robert used to write his songs down in. Wouldn't that be something to have around here! I understand he had pretty handwriting too."

"Now, how would you know something like that?"

"His old running buddy Johnny Shines put that out. Aw, it's so much we'll never know about Robert Johnson, don't care how many bits and fragments they try to glue together."

"How long did he stay with Callie?" I ask Luther.

"Evidently not all that long. He walked out on her and their kids and left Copiah County for the Delta. Then he went back to Robinsonville; that's where he blew Son House and Willie Brown's minds with his singing and picking. He hit the Delta part of Arkansas—Helena and West Helena—and that's where it all started coming together. Robert started playing with everybody that came through there—and going off everyplace. Helena was a jumping little river town, wide-open; that's where Robert Johnson came to be Robert Jr. Lockwood's stepdaddy, I reckon you might say. Robert taken a liking to the boy's mother and moved in with her. Her name was Estella Coleman, but she answered to Stella. And, I'll tell you, Robert must've been a good teacher, too; that Robert Jr. Lockwood can go!"

"He sure can!"

"Can't he play the blues? Down here in Mississippi, we're just starting to appreciate a lot of the old blues and the people who played 'em. You might say that culture—blues and storytelling, literature—is one of our heaviest exports. We had to fight Greenville to get this little museum put up here in Greenwood, and it isn't all that much, but it's a beginning."

Already, way down the hall in the next room, I can see a portion of the mural Luther mentioned when I first walked in, and all I can make out are some Mexican-looking fellows in big sombreros, the kind worn by mariachi musicians. I can hardly wait to see what the mural is all about.

"Look here," says Luther, "I'm not trying to make out it's things I know about Robert Johnson that don't nobody else know. I got most of my information from the same sources you probably got yours—from other people's writings and interviews and all like that. But I am old enough to remember when records like 'Terraplane' first came out."

"Really? What was that like?"

"Well, I had to listen to it on the sly, you know. But I liked it. My daddy caught me at it one time, though. You know how it is being a preacher's kid; feel like you got to prove to everybody that you regular and OK. My folks didn't much allow me to be listening to no blues, not up in the house anyway. My daddy was a preacher and my mama taught school. They were kinda on the sanctified side. The blues represented everything they were trying to forget. But, I got to admit, I loved 'Terraplane Blues,' and I know it had something to do with my daddy owning one."

"But I thought you said your parents didn't approve of blues records."

Luther laughs. "Naw, I'm talking about the car, not the song! The Terraplane was a six-cylinder sedan that Hudson Motors put out. And sometime they'd let me drive it." A devilish gleam lights up Luther's eyes as he sings a verse of Johnson's "Terraplane Blues" lyric out loud:

Now you know the coils ain't even buzzin',
little generator won't get the spark;
Motor's in a bad condition,
you gotta have these batteries charged.
But I'm cryin' pleeease,
pleee-hease don't do me wrong;
Who been drivin' my Terraplane now for
you-hooo since I been gone? . . .

"What you think?" Luther asks, turning to me. "Think I coulda made a living singing the blues?"

"You might have to get a little help down at the crossroads," I say.

"Aww, man, don't come bringing that up! I'm so tired of this crossroads stuff I don't know what to do. All the people they talked with—friends, his women, all kinds of people—and they all say Robert played that guitar all the time; I mean, *all* the time. One woman I read about said she got up in the middle of the night one time and seen him standing by the window in the moonlight fingerin his guitar. Anybody with that kinda obsession is bound to get good in a hurry, don't you think?"

"But the crossroads myth *sounds* so good."

"Yeah, I know," says Luther as I follow him into the mural-walled room. "But, see, we have always had these hoodoo and conjure people all 'round down in here. It's plenty Negroes my age from the South know about John the Conquerer root, root doctors, silver dimes, rabbit and coon feet, mixing up hair with nails and needles and thimbles, mojo hands, goofer dust and all such as that. And you better believe Robert knew it too. But that don't mean he had to be on good personal terms with the Devil to play as outstanding as he did."

Luther looks around, as though to make sure we're still the only ones in the museum.

"Tell you," he says in a low voice, "sometimes it's weeks'll go by before anybody colored walks through that door. Plenty of white folks show up, though, especially white folks from overseas. And lately it's been a lotta Japanese too. You know, the Japanese be all down here in the Delta nowdays, with all kinds of business development projects and what have you. You can stand right there at the airport in Greenville and watch 'em fly in and out. They probably know more about the blues than I do. All I did was live 'em."

"Luther," I say. "The other day I was listening to Robert Cray. . . . "

"Sure," Luther interrupts, "I know him . . . young fellow, used to play with Albert Collins, put out that *Strong Persuader* album."

"Yeah, well, Cray was being interviewed on the radio, on Terry Gross's show, 'Fresh Air.' And he was saying that you don't find too many black people at blues festivals or patronizing the blues because the blues mostly represents things we'd just as soon forget."

"Sure, like bad luck and hard times and all like that. My folks thought like that. My daddy caught me listening to a Robert Johnson record one time and he took the record off the Victrola and broke it. Said, 'You listen at this, then next thing you know, you'll be drinking and gambling and laying around with these old donies'—that's the name they use to have for lowlife women—'and hanging around places where you get your head cut. After you leave my house, you can listen at whatever you want to. But as long as you under my roof, there won't be any blues.' "

"Do you think your father was right?"

With an undecipherable grin twitching around his lips, Luther looks at me and looks at me for the longest. Then he breaks out into a dark little laugh and says, "Yeah, I would have to say yes, Reverend Washington knew what he was talking about. But there's another side of the blues that sanctified people like my folks didn't realize."

"Which is . . . "

"You know how Robert Johnson sings, 'She's a kindhearted woman, she studies evil all the time'? Well, the Bible does say: All things worketh for good. It's a lotta holier-than-thou types that's got evil minds. By the same token, I know a gang of blues singers that spend a lotta their time thinking about God and trying to straighten up. The way I see it, you go far enough in any one direction, you gonna come out the other side and meet yourself going the other way. Now, let's go in here and look at this mural and listen to us some Robert Johnson."

"You're right," I tell Luther, reaching to shake his hand again. "If I'm feeling bad and listen to some good blues, sometimes it makes me feel better just knowing others suffer too."

When I extend my hand to touch Luther's, he suddenly breaks into song. Suddenly I'm shivering, my arm breaking out in goose-bumps. That's when it hits me how much he sounds like Johnson—*exactly* like Robert Johnson—and he's playing the sultry afternoon air like a guitar that sounds like Johnson's too. It's quite as though Luther Washington—if there ever was a Luther Washington in the first place—is lip-synching or miming Johnson's electrifying record of "Preaching Blues (Up Jumped the Devil)":

The bluu-uuu-uues
*   is a lowdown shakin' chill;*
Mmmmmm-mmmmm . . .
*   is a lowdown shakin' chill;*
You ain't never had 'em, I
*   hope you never will.*

When I blink hard and look again, there is no Luther. There's no Robert Leroy Johnson Museum; only the sound of this century's pioneer modern blues genius, crying in what I now think actually might have been the Greenwood, Mississippi night. The only thing I'm certain of is that the music is as real as it is haunting.